Local Partnerships and Social Exclusion in the European Union

This book explores local partnership-based initiatives to tackle European-wide problems of poverty and social exclusion. In both the UK and the EU, these are amongst the most pressing problems confronting politicians and policy makers today; and 'partnership' is widely identified as an essential element in any solution. From the UK government's National Strategy for Neighbourhood Renewal to the European Commission's strategy for managing social and economic disparity and issues such as immigration, partnerships are central to the policy response.

However, although partnership is a term now pivotal to the policy discourses and practices of the EU and some member states, it is still an anomaly in other places. Furthermore, partnership and exclusion are contested concepts – with a range of meanings and policy implications. *Local Partnerships and Social Exclusion in the European Union* traces the evolution of this complex and rapidly developing sphere of public policy, exploring its different contents and the ways they are being shaped by European, national and local influences.

This book is a major comparative study of the key contemporary theme of social exclusion, and looks at its causes, effects and at the ways it might be combated through both national and supra-national measures. Based on in depth, cross national research, it spans Scandinavian to Iberian countries; from Ireland to the UK to France and Germany. It provides a uniquely authoritative account of the complexities of policy development in the EU, and will be invaluable to researchers in European studies, politics, and economics as well as to professionals in public policy, social policy and urban and regional planning.

Mike Geddes is Principal Research Fellow and Research Manager in the Local Government Centre, University of Warwick. His previous publications include *Partnership against Social Exclusion? Local Regeneration Strategies and Excluded Communities*.

John Benington is Professor of Public Policy and Management at the University of Warwick, and Director of the Local Government Centre since its inception in 1988. He has published widely, including coediting *Restructuring the Local Economy*, and coauthoring *Changing Europe*, and *Urban Poverty, The Economy and Public Policy*. He has acted as adviser to government ministers, senior policy makers and managers in the UK, EU and Africa. He is currently leading the development of a new Institute of Governance and Public Management at the University of Warwick.

Routledge Studies in Governance and Public Policy

Local Partnerships and Social Exclusion in the European Union

New forms of local social governance?

Edited by Mike Geddes and John Benington

London and New York

First published 2001
by Routledge
11 New Fetter Lane, London EC4P 4EE

Simultaneously published in the USA and Canada
by Routledge
29 West 35th Street, New York, NY 10001

Routledge is an imprint of the Taylor & Francis Group

Typeset in Baskerville by BC Typesetting, Bristol
Printed and bound in Great Britain by MPG Books Ltd, Bodmin

British Library Cataloguing in Publication Data
A catalogue record for this book is available from the British Library

Library of Congress Cataloging in Publication Data
Local partnerships and social exclusion in the European Union:
new forms of local social governance?/edited by Mike Geddes
and John Benington.
       p.   cm. – (Routledge studies in governance and public policy; 5)
    Includes bibliographical references and index.
    1. Marginality, Social – European Union countries. 2. European Union
countries – Social policy. 3. Economic assistance, Domestic – European
Union countries. 4. Poverty – European Union countries. 5. Local
government – European Union countries. 6. Public-private sector
cooperation – European Union countries. I. Geddes, Mike, 1943–
II. Benington, John. III. Series.

HN380.Z9 L63 2001
305.5'6'094–dc21   00-062792

ISBN 0–415–23922-2

Contents

Notes on contributors

Karl Birkhölzer is Director of the Interdisciplinary Research Group, Local Economy, at the Technical University of Berlin. He is co-founder of the European Network for Economic Self-Help and Local Development.

Jordi Estivill is Director of the Gabinet d'Estudis Socials, a social research agency, and Professor at the University School of Social Work of Barcelona. He is author of numerous publications and research studies on European social policy and social economy.

Patrick Le Galès is CNRS senior research fellow at CEVIPOF (Sciences Po Paris). He is associate professor of politics and sociology at Sciences Po Paris. He has published *Politique urbaine et développement local*, Paris, L'Harmattan, 1993; *Les réseaux de politique publique*, Paris, L'Harmattan, 1995 (with M Thatcher); *Regions in Europe, the Paradox of Power*, Routledge, 1998 (with C Lequesne); *Cities in Contemporary Europe*, 2000, Cambridge University Press (with A Bagnasco); and *The Governance of Local Economies in Europe* (with C Crouch, C Trigilia and H Voeltzkow), Oxford University Press, 2001. He is the editor of the *International Journal of Urban and Regional Research*.

Matti Heikkilä is a Research Professor at the National Research and Development Centre for Welfare and Health (STAKES) in Helsinki, Finland. His principal research interests are poverty, deprivation and the welfare state.

Mikko Kautto is a Researcher at the National Research and Development Centre for Welfare and Health (STAKES) in Helsinki, Finland. His research interest is in comparative welfare state research. He recently authored a comparison of welfare state adaptation in Finland and Sweden during the 1990s. He is one of the editors of *Nordic Social Policy* (Routledge 1999) and *Nordic Welfare States in the European Context* (Routledge 2001).

Patricia Loncle-Moriceau, Political scientist, researcher at the National School of Public Health, Laboratory of Analysis of Social and Health

Policies. Main areas of research: youth policies, social policies at local level, policies of struggle against Aids and alcoholism.

Günther Lorenz is a researcher with the Interdisciplinary Research Group, Local Economy, at the Technical University of Berlin.

Fernanda Rodrigues holds a PhD in Social Work from the Pontifícia Universidade Católica (PUC) of São Paulo, Brazil. She is currently teaching at the Instituto Superior de Serviço Social of Oporto, Portugal, where she co-ordinates an MA programme in Social Policy and Social Work. She was evaluator of the European Combat Poverty 3 Programme.

Stephen R Stoer is Professor of Sociology of Education at the Faculdade de Psicologia e de Ciências da Educação of the University of Oporto where he is Director of the Centre of Research and Intervention in Education. He is also Director of the international journal *Educação, Sociedade & Culturas*.

Jim Walsh is research and policy analyst with the Combat Poverty Agency (Ireland), where he is responsible for the development and co-ordination of economic and social policies in relation to poverty. His research interests include child income support, local anti-poverty initiatives, indebtedness and access to financial services. He is co-editor of *Poor people, poor places*, a study of the geography of poverty and deprivation in Ireland (Oak Tree Press, 1999) and principal author of *Local Partnerships for Social Inclusion?* (Oak Tree Press, 1998) a study of local partnership interventions to tackle social exclusion in Ireland.

Acknowledgements

We would like to thank numerous individuals for the contributions they have made to this book.

In the first place, the book originated in a cross-national research project of the European Foundation for the Improvement of Living and Working Conditions, Dublin. This project, which was undertaken between 1994 and 1998, was managed for the Foundation by Wendy O'Conghaile and Robert Anderson, Senior Research Managers at the Foundation. We are grateful to the Foundation for permission to use material deriving from the research project, and to Wendy and Robert for their expert and incisive contributions to the research, and thus to the framework of ideas in this book, although of course the specific interpretations and conclusions here remain the responsibility of ourselves as editors and of the authors of the various chapters, not the Foundation.

Secondly, we wish to thank the contributors to the research project from different EU countries. Many of these are authors of chapters in the book: Matti Heikkilä and Mikko Kautto; Patrick Le Galès and Patricia Loncle-Moriceau; Jim Walsh; Jordi Estivill: Fernanda Rodrigues and Steve Stoer; Karl Birkhölzer and Günther Lorenz. Our thanks to them for the diverse perspectives which they have brought to the book, and their patience with us through its gestation. In particular, we are indebted to Patrick Le Galès for his contribution to the conceptual frameworks which we have used in the introductory and concluding chapters, and his encouragement to us at critical points. Others contributed national studies to the research which, although not directly represented here, helped to inform the wider project: Eva Kain and Ingrid Rosian from Austria and Ides Nicaise and Savas Robolis and their colleagues from Belgium and Greece respectively.

Finally, our thanks to our supportive editors at Routledge, Craig Fowlie, Milon Nagi and Lesley Felce, and Ruth Austin of Positive Images, who took over responsibility for our manuscript from Caroline Wintersgill of UCL Press and have helped us to bring the project to fruition.

Mike Geddes and John Benington
Warwick

1 Introduction

Social exclusion, partnership and local governance – new problems, new policy discourses in the European Union

John Benington and Mike Geddes

Local Partnerships and Social Exclusion in the European Union discusses the local partnership-based initiatives that have been set up to tackle European-wide problems of poverty and social exclusion. In both the United Kingdom and the European Union today, social exclusion is one of the most pressing problems facing citizens and one of the 'wicked' cross-cutting issues of governance confronting politicians and policy-makers, while 'partnership' between public, private, voluntary and community organisations and interests is widely identified as an essential element in any solution. In the United Kingdom, one of the first acts of the New Labour government when it entered office in 1997 was to set up a Social Exclusion Unit (SEU) in the Cabinet Office at the heart of government. The SEU is a concrete symbol of the new government's recognition of the severity of problems of poverty and social exclusion in the United Kingdom – in contrast to previous Conservative administrations, which reputedly banned the 'p' word from all government documents – and the adoption of the language of social exclusion, with its EU associations, seemed to signify Labour's wish to be at the heart of European policy in this area. The SEU's proposals for a National Strategy for Neighbourhood Renewal (NSNR), published in spring 2000 (Social Exclusion Unit 2000), have brought the problems of poor neighbourhoods and excluded communities into even sharper focus, and reinforced the commitment to partnership as a method of tackling them. Notably, strategic local partnerships are at the core of the policy package which the NSNR proposes.

In the EU, the period from 1995–9 saw issues of social exclusion slip down the policy agenda, after the British and German governments challenged the EU's competence in this sphere, and other pressing issues (from enlargement to the single currency and the crisis in the Balkans) dominated the attention of the European Parliament, the Council of Ministers and the European Commission. But these very issues have themselves served to emphasise the new problems of exclusion facing the EU, as enlargement is set to massively widen economic and social disparities, and as migrations triggered by the Balkan conflict expose the exclusive tendencies in European society (Young 1999). These are reflected most acutely in the rise of far-right parties such as the Freedom Party in Austria, but more generally by media and political attitudes to asylum seekers and others on the margins of society. However, the EU's Lisbon Summit in spring 2000 indicated that the logjam in EU policy on social exclusion may now be breaking up, with new proposals emerging from the Commission for the EU to co-ordinate and evaluate national and local policies to tackle exclusion, in a new policy partnership between the EU, member states, and regional and local actors.

This book is intended to contribute to both academic and policy debates around these developments by reviewing and evaluating recent experience in tackling poverty and social exclusion by local partnership-based initiatives across the EU. As the title suggests, the book revolves around four concepts, each of which is slippery, contested, and capable of a range of interpretations: partnership, social exclusion, 'the local', and governance. This book aims to contribute to a greater understanding of their complexities, interrelationships and policy implications.

Partnership

'Partnership' is a term which is now central to the policy discourses and practices of the EU and several member states, but which is still an 'exotic species' or foreign import in a number of other EU countries. One important aim of this book is to trace the evolution of this complex and rapidly developing concept and practice, to analyse its different meanings, and the ways in which they are shaped and translated by European, national, regional and more local histories and traditions.

'Partnership' has emerged as one of the homogenising concepts within the EU, supporting the notion of European integration by emphasising the possibilities for collaboration between a number of different stakeholders with potentially competing or conflicting interests. We identify the use of partnership as a concept to promote integration both vertically (between different tiers of government – European, national, regional, local and grass roots) and horizontally (between different spheres of society – public, private, voluntary and civil). We also argue, however, that the reality of partnership is a contradictory one in terms of the tension between forces for integration versus forces for disintegration within the EU. Local partnership may reflect the tendencies towards the fragmentation of the European policy arena as much as tendencies towards cohesion.

Partnership is not a phenomenon that can be wholly differentiated, conceptually or empirically, from other forms of policy collaboration and inter-organisational working. One way of conceptualising this is to think of partnership as one point on a continuum, with formally and tightly defined contractual relationships at one end, and looser and more fluid 'network' relationships at the other. The partnerships that are studied in this book share some characteristics with each of these other two related forms of organisation (contracts and networks), but also exhibit distinctive features. In the cross-national research project from which this book developed, we proposed a working definition of local partnership based on four key features:

- A formal organisational structure for policy-making and implementation
- The mobilisation of a coalition of interests and the commitment of a range of different partners
- A common agenda and multi-dimensional action programme
- A forum by which to combat unemployment, poverty and social exclusion, and promote social cohesion and inclusion.

Our intention was to differentiate these partnerships from the much wider field of joint working, inter-organisational collaboration and networking. However, one conclusion from the research is that, while more formal models of partnership are becoming increasingly prevalent, they do not reflect the full range of partnership-types or concepts emerging within the EU member states, and this book seeks to reflect this diversity. Nonetheless, the emergence of partnership does represent a distinctive development in the conceptual and operational frameworks for, and processes of, policy-making in the EU and in several of the member states. This new more pluralistic form of relationship between policy actors at different levels and in different sectors is clearly different from the formal corporatist relationships with the traditional 'social partners' (the peak organisations representing employers and trade unions), although the latter still have an important influence, in the Structural Funds for example.

The new partnerships reflect a growing recognition that traditional forms of governmental intervention are not capable of addressing the complex, cross-cutting problems facing citizens and communities in many parts of Europe (e.g. unemployment, poverty and social exclusion, crime and community safety), and which threaten the cohesion of the emerging European community. The new partnerships reflect a search for more flexible, participative forms of EU and governmental intervention, through the involvement ('mobilisation' in EU discourse) in the policy process of actors from three tiers (European, national and local) and three spheres (state, market and civil society) (Benington 1998).

One of the main areas in which partnership has been introduced as a new policy instrument is that of 'social exclusion'.

Social exclusion

The idea of 'social exclusion', and its alter ego, 'inclusion', have come to dominate debate over the last decade in relation to contemporary patterns and processes of poverty, deprivation, disparity, marginalisation, *fracture*, *précarité*, and so on. The conception of social exclusion within the EU policy context is, however, complex and contested. In a simple but potentially quite radical sense, social exclusion stands for the notion that poverty and marginalisation are (at least partially) caused by processes of exclusion from the mainstream economy, polity and society. This concept of exclusion therefore emphasises the fundamental structural processes that cause poverty, rather than the consequent symptoms or 'static state' of poverty. In much EU discourse however, social exclusion has come to be used in a much less pointed way, as a portmanteau word for a wide range of poverty-related phenomena, often associated with the concept of multi-dimensional disadvantage, or multiple deprivation, in which poverty is often associated with a range of interrelated disadvantages, in relation to housing, health, education, transport, leisure etc., and with limited participation in the decisions affecting life chances.

In Chapter 2 we review some of the debates surrounding social exclusion, and their implications for policy, and show that an important theme in the literature is concerned with how patterns and processes of exclusion differ from country to country and locality to locality. Such differences are further explored in the chapters on each country, both in terms of national patterns and processes, and those in the localities where the specific partnership initiatives are located. However, it is important to emphasise that the research on which the book is based did not include primary research on patterns and processes of inclusion and exclusion. Thus, while the nature of exclusion is a key context in which local partnership is located, our primary concern is less with social exclusion *per se*, than with partnership as a policy response to social exclusion.

The 'local'

While the ideology and practice of partnership is increasingly present in all spatial levels of policy, our focus is on partnership at the local level. A key concern of the book, therefore, is the role of 'the local' in an era of globalisation and complexity. We explore the extent to which partnership is associated with a 'localisation' (or glocalisation?) of social policy, in the context in which the nation state is seen by some commentators as too small to respond effectively to the macro-level issues (e.g. global warming, transnational corporations, international crime), but too big to respond flexibly to the micro-level concerns of citizens and communities (e.g. crime and safety, family pressures, job insecurity).

An important thread running through this book is the extent to which a localisation of policy implies a fragmentation of social policy and the welfare state, and an erosion of the principle of universalism in public services. Another is the complex relationship between the 'local' and other concepts with which it is commonly associated or counterposed, as for example in the phrase 'local community', and in the traditional distinction between local and national government (with local often implying 'lower' in the pecking order). Some of the national studies show that such associations may have rather different connotations in different member states (e.g. 'local' can range in meaning from the regional/provincial to the neighbourhood level).

However, while a key objective of this book is to reflect, and reflect on, such differences across the EU member states, we also emphasise the common features of local partnerships that are in place to combat social exclusion – that is, as an organisational framework or arena in which a plural coalition of diverse interests may be negotiated and mobilised around some notion of a common 'local' interest, in this case to combat poverty and social exclusion. The nature of this 'local' coalition, the ways in which conflicting interests are 'resolved' or accommodated under the umbrella of a local partnership framework, and the extent to which such a coalition may be mobilised and maintained by defining an effective action space at the local level, are key issues which are explored in the chapters on individual countries and again in the closing chapters.

Governance

The fourth key concept within our framework is that of governance. This is as equally imprecise a notion as the other three, with a range of different definitions and usages in different contexts and different countries. In the United Kingdom, the notion of corporate governance has emerged in the private sector to indicate a concern with the accountability of companies to social values and a range of stakeholder interests, in addition to those of shareholders. In a recent exploration of urban governance, Le Galès seeks to link the concept of governance to that of regulation, while maintaining a distance between the two, and similarly to make connections between the governance of firms and the governance of regional and local territories (Le Galès 1998). In UK public policy (and particularly in local government) the concept of governance has come to encompass four main features:

- A conception of governing as an active political process, distinct from government as a set of institutions
- A consequent shift of emphasis towards the task of leading and governing the community (with its pluralistic and diverse networks of public, private and voluntary organisations, informal associations and grass roots movements), in addition to managing and administering the public bureaucracy (with its committees, budgets, services and staff)
- A recognition that actively leading and governing the community is not a matter for elected governments on their own, but requires joint ventures, coalitions and partnerships between a range of public, private, voluntary and grass roots organisations
- A shift in the core paradigm and discourse of governance away from its traditional locus in the ideas and practices of the state, and towards both

'market' principles of competition and efficiency, and towards civil society
and the notion of citizen-centred government.

This is the language of 're-inventing' and 'modernising' governance, the
rhetoric of which at least has found expression on many public platforms,
and in many policy documents, in the USA, the United Kingdom and
increasingly in the EU and in several (but by no means all) of the member
states. More critical commentators interpret these developments in discourses and practices as a rationalisation for continued cutbacks in public
expenditure and services, and a shift of responsibility for tackling complex
problems away from the state and on to individuals, families, voluntary
organisations and informal associations, questioning both the capacity and
the transparency of key aspects of new governance systems, including
partnerships (see, for example, Healey 1998).

One of the key themes of this book, therefore, is that partnership is a
defining element in new patterns of local governance, which are emerging
as ways of regulating some of the tensions and contradictions within the
political economy of the EU as it grapples with the complex and contradictory forces of fragmentation as well as of integration. Partnership reflects
the shift in ideas and practices from 'government' to 'governance' through a
crossing of the institutionalised boundaries between different levels of the
state (local, regional, national, supranational), and between the state, the
private market (both employers and trade unions), the voluntary sector and
civil society. We discuss the ways in which these new models of partnership
and of multi-level, multi-nodal local governance are emerging across the
EU and within its institutions. One conclusion from this however, is to stress
the provisional and unstable nature of current arrangements. In particular,
we draw on theories of policy and welfare regimes to explore the ways in
which the emergence of new forms of governance at the local level are related
to the evolution of different regimes, and to the specific forms of convergence
taking place within the EU under the hegemony of economic neo-liberalism
and social democracy.

Drawing together our four concerns – partnership, social exclusion, the
local and governance – we can say that any assessment of the capacity of
partnership as a form of local governance needs to analyse three dimensions.
First, the local capacity of *partnerships* as quasi-institutions (their cohesion,
resources, structures and processes etc. as vehicles for effective governance);
second, the capacity of the *local* level of governance in the context of the
power of other tiers and spheres of political and economic decision-making;
and third, the capacity of *social policy* as a potentially progressive force
within a capitalist economy.

The evidence of this book is that the impact and outcomes of this new mode
of local governance are extremely variable in terms of the 'success' claimed
and achieved by the local initiatives that are discussed. Partnerships can
improve collaboration and trust, and promote policy innovation and

resource synergy, but they also frequently marginalise the excluded themselves, who remain largely the objects of policy, and may weaken the accountability of the policy processes, in terms of traditional representative democracy. The degree to which localised policy embodies greater responsiveness to diverse patterns of need or merely masks a withdrawal from 'nationalised' or universalised state policy, provision and responsibility, depends on the terms of engagement between local actors and the policy process. Social policy objectives may be strengthened by multidimensional local action which attempts to bridge the gulf between the economic and the social domains, but key economic decisions inevitably remain outside the control of local partnerships. We conclude, therefore, that the new model of local social governance *reformulates* rather than resolves the problem of a socially just path to European integration.

The research evidence

The contribution of this book to such questions is derived in large part from a major transnational research programme, which reviewed and evaluated the role of local partnerships in tackling social exclusion across the EU.[1] The programme reflected an awareness that more needed to be known about the impact and outcomes of local partnerships, both in contributing to solutions to problems of unemployment, poverty and social exclusion, and in contributing to new policy approaches on the part of government, public authorities and other actors. To what extent have partnerships realised the expectations and objectives of the various organisations and interests involved? What kind of time horizons are needed for partnerships to be established and achieve results? How far have partnerships been able to develop and implement more effective multidimensional strategies by drawing together the contributions of different partners? How effectively have the activities undertaken by partnerships, and their outcomes, been evaluated? Many of the programmes that have supported local partnerships have been either experimental in nature or limited in timescale, scope and/or resources. There are important questions, therefore, about how the experiences gained in pilot and experimental programmes can be transferred to mainstream policy and action. How can the experiences of individual local partnerships be shared more effectively so that good practice is disseminated not only at the grass roots, but is also evaluated, applied and integrated into wider policy networks and programmes?

---

1 The research, for the European Foundation for the Improvement of Living and Working Conditions, involved research studies in ten member states (Austria, Belgium, France, Finland, Germany, Greece, Ireland, Portugal, Spain, United Kingdom) with supplementary research on the other five. Up to ten local partnerships were initially identified in each country, giving a sample of 86 local partnerships across the EU. Thirty detailed case studies were then undertaken (three in each of the above ten member states) of the process and impact of partnership working, involving a series of semi-structured interviews with key actors.

A further dimension is added to such questions by the important differences between member states. In some countries (the United Kingdom and Ireland, for example) the practice of local partnership is widely understood because of the impact of national government programmes. In other countries (Spain and Portugal, for example) the usage is much less widespread, and is still quite closely associated with EU programmes rather than national policies. In others (Germany, for example), the term partnership is primarily associated with corporatist-type collaboration between government and the social partners, rather than between local actors and interests. In some countries, there are different terms conveying important parts of the concept, for example distinguishing between formal institutional partnership and informal 'community' partnership.

The central concern of our research was to explore questions such as these, and to identify the specific contribution which partnership can make to policies to combat poverty and exclusion. The methodology for the research programme was developed in order to both analyse and understand the different circumstances bearing on the development of local partnerships in each member state, but also to gain an overview of wider trends across the EU. This implied a need to survey a considerable number of local partnerships, in order to reflect different approaches, experiences and outcomes.

To meet these objectives, the research included several interrelated elements. First, an initial review of existing literature and practice was undertaken, and discussed with a panel of experts, to identify key themes and issues (Geddes 1995). Ten national research studies were then commissioned. These ten national studies, ranging from Finland to Portugal and Ireland to Greece, and including the United Kingdom, France and Germany, and undertaken by experts in the country concerned, ensured that the diversity of contexts and experience across the EU were reflected in the research. Each national research study included three elements:

- A review of the history and origins of the partnership approach in each country; the current national policy context for local partnerships; and the views of leading policy-makers and actors about the partnership approach in the country concerned.
- Each national review also described a number of partnerships (6–8), which illustrated important issues and trends in the country concerned. Together with supplementary research on the countries not covered by major research studies, this meant that the research identified 86 local partnerships spread across the EU.
- Detailed case studies of three local partnerships were then undertaken in each country. These were chosen to illustrate recent national experience, including apparently successful outcomes but also the problems that had been encountered. These case studies were carefully selected to provide detailed analyses of the operation of local partnerships in different spatial and socio-economic contexts (e.g. inner city, peripheral housing estates,

rural areas; supported by a wide range of EU and national programmes) to illustrate a range of partnership structures and relationships involving public agencies, employers, trade unions and the voluntary and community sector, and to ensure coverage of important issues, such as gender and equal opportunity perspectives.

Each case study included extensive interviews (using a semi-structured questionnaire developed by the transnational research team to ensure cross-national compatibility of findings) with those involved in local partnerships, as 'partners', employees or stakeholders. The framework established for the case studies, while permitting national and local specificities to emerge, focused on a number of issues. These included the representation of interests in partnerships, and the relative power and influence of different partners; processes of negotiation and conflict within the partnership in developing and implementing local strategies and projects; and the resources, skills and working methods deployed by different partnerships. The case studies were concerned to evaluate the strengths and weaknesses of processes of partnership working, both as a method of policy formulation and delivery at the local level and in terms of the wider impact on the policy process. Finally, the case studies tried to identify policy outcomes, and in particular to identify the extent to which outcomes were associated (either positively or negatively) with the partnership framework.

Each national research study concluded by identifying key issues for policy-makers at European, national and local levels and for those directly involved in local partnerships. The final stage of the research programme involved a review of the national research studies on a transnational basis within the research team, leading to a European research report (Geddes 1998).

The structure and methodology of the research programme embodied a number of significant strengths, but also certain limitations which should be acknowledged. The research team itself, comprised of national experts, brought together a number of relevant disciplines (social policy, urban and regional studies, public administration, local development) and both academic and policy-related expertise. Different elements of the methodology permitted both a wide-ranging overview of policy developments at European level and in member states, and an in-depth qualitative analysis of partnership at the local level. While the research cannot claim to be comprehensive or representative in the strict sense, considerable pains were taken to ensure that the diversity of European experience was reflected as fully as possible. Among the limitations of the research evidence, the most important issues concern the problems of evaluating the specific outcomes of partnership working (Monnier 1997).

No claim is made to offer large-scale, quantitative evidence of the outcomes of local, partnership-based initiatives to combat poverty and social exclusion – and, indeed, the research programme tended to confirm both the limited amount of quantitative information on partnership outcomes available, and its frequently questionable reliability. On the other hand, through the combination of expert reviews of national experience and in-depth qualitative case studies with key actors, the research can justifiably claim to offer both wide-ranging and authoritative perspectives on local practice across the EU.

The structure of the book

The book essentially falls into three parts. In Chapter 2 Mike Geddes and John Benington provide an overview of the growth of poverty and social exclusion in Europe, and a review of some of the main debates and explanations for the nature and causes of exclusion, and of the policies concerned with it. This chapter also reviews the way in which the concept and practice of local partnership has taken hold within the EU and the European Commission. Geddes and Benington identify three distinct stages in the development of the concept and practice of local partnership as one of the EU's favoured policy instruments for tackling problems of poverty, unemployment and social exclusion.

Chapters 3 through 9 then examine the emergence of local partnerships to combat social exclusion in a wide range of European countries – from Finland in the north through Germany, France, the United Kingdom and Ireland, to Spain and Portugal in the south. Taken together, these chapters enable us to present and explore the diversity of the context and experience of partnership across the EU, including as they do both longer-term and more recent EU member states, in some of which EU policies and funding have had a major impact on policies concerned with social exclusion (Ireland, Portugal, Spain) and others where national policy regimes and programmes have tended to be more important than EU programmes (the United Kingdom, Germany). In addition to situating each country in its European context, each chapter emphasises and illuminates specific themes and issues important in the country in question.

In Chapter 3 Mikko Kautto and Matti Heikkilä discuss the Nordic experience and look for explanations for the low profile of partnership strategies in Finland. They explain this in terms of the institutional and state-centric characteristics of the Finnish welfare system, which crowds out other actors from the handling of social problems. Although there are signs of both economic and ideological change in Finland, with some weakening in welfare goals of full employment and equality, only time will tell whether partnerships will emerge as part of an alternative approach.

In Chapter 4 Patrick Le Galès and Patricia Loncle-Moriceau debate the dilemmas surrounding the concept of partnership in France. They present partnership as alien to the tradition of dirigiste state control, and to the legal distinctions and divisions which separate the public and the private. They analyse a number of French policies and initiatives that are now

presented in terms of partnership, but argue that these remain largely dominated by public and quasi-public bodies and values. They also analyse some
of the strengths and weaknesses of the partnership form – the potential for
highlighting problems which are too often hidden, for mobilising new actors
from the voluntary sector, for stimulating innovation and experiment; but
also the risks of domination by a new breed of partnership professional, with
an addiction to networking but with little accountability, the reluctance of
private sector organisations to join in partnerships, and the dangers of
bureaucratisation. They conclude that partnership has potential for introducing greater flexibility and innovation, but that the advantages and results
are not yet proven to a point at which they would justify a retreat by the
state from its role in funding and providing for social issues.

In Chapter 5 Karl Birkhölzer and Günther Lorenz take a different
perspective on partnerships in Germany. Their focus is on grass roots
community-based partnerships, rather than more formal public-private
partnerships. Part of their argument is that poverty and social exclusion are
spatially concentrated in areas of multiple deprivation, and that this requires
area-based, community-led approaches. Partnership approaches in these
situations need to be as inclusive as possible of all population groups (e.g.
social assistance claimants, women and migrants) to avoid stigmatisation or
exclusion of some of the poor at the expense of others. They also conclude
that to be effective in combating poverty, partnerships need to address the
economic problems of the poor, as well as the social or the cultural. Their
arguments constitute an important counterbalance to some of the dominant
models of partnership in the EU and in countries such as the United
Kingdom.

In clear contrast to both the French and German experience, in Chapter 6
Jim Walsh documents a major process of public policy reform in Ireland,
where local partnership has been a major catalyst for change. The Irish
government, with support from the EU, has stimulated the creation of over
100 local partnerships, in multi-agency structures that bring together state
agencies, businesses, trade unions and community groups, to promote local,
socio-economic development in disadvantaged rural and urban areas.
One of the distinctive features of the Irish experience is the high level of
national government support for local partnerships through public funding,
ministerial leadership, and inter-departmental policy co-ordination. Walsh
claims some impressive achievements for these local development programmes in terms of the number of unemployed people placed in employment, the number of children on preventive educational projects, and so on.
However, he argues that their greatest significance lies in instituting a new
model of local governance, with the potential to revolutionise social policy
from the bottom up. But in order to be effective in combating poverty, local
partnerships need to be linked in more closely to a national anti-poverty
strategy, and to the democratic processes of local government.

Fernanda Rodrigues and Stephen Stoer remind us in Chapter 7 of the battle in Portugal between dictatorship and democracy, and between authoritarian corporatism and populist syndicalism, which has characterised recent Portuguese history, and which sets the context for partnership working. They also make a crucial distinction between 'partenariado' (a formal partnership between organisations at national or EU levels) and 'parceria' (an informal partnership between people with shared objectives and interests). The latter approach is associated with a community development approach in which local leaders ('forces vives') are identified to act as catalysts for change. They argue that since Portugal's accession to the EU, partnership as 'parceria' has been overtaken by more formal partnership as 'partenariado', partly in order to gain EU funding and legitimation. However, they conclude that partnerships will not be effective in tackling poverty unless they harness the formal planning processes associated with 'partenariado' to the informal participation processes associated with 'parceria'.

Jordi Estivill, in Chapter 8, starts his review of the Spanish experience of partnership by looking at the root meanings and usages of the concept in Greek, Latin, 14th-century English and the French revolution! He goes on to try to identify the economic, social and political conditions that either favour or hamper the progress of partnership. He also highlights the contributions that the Spanish situation and experiences can provide – discussing the economic context of partnership; the changing structure of the state, its role in social welfare and relations between the three spheres of state, market and civil society; local power relations; and the character and distribution of poverty and social exclusion. In Spain, the 'unravelling' of the centralist, authoritarian state, the expansion of the not-for-profit sector, and a relaxation of the rigid postures of the social partners, are combining to promote partnership. At the local level, however, the emergence of horizontal partnership between different actors depends on the structures of local power and the way in which it is exercised.

Estivill concludes by emphasising the continuing influence of socio-cultural identities and informal social networks, and the need for more formal partnerships to connect with these if they are to be broadly based and sustainable. In Spain, the history of partnership is relatively young. However, from its initial importation as an exotic term from 'Europe', it has achieved considerable national currency in the context of local development, and as a result of decentralising tendencies within the state, and a new fluidity in the social policy roles of the public, private, and voluntary and community sectors. Partnership can be linked, problematically, to traditions of 'caciquismo' (clientilism), but also more positively to the contribution of informal social networks to social solidarity and inclusion in the face of unemployment and the multi-faceted urban and rural crisis that affected many parts of Spain in the 1990s.

In Chapter 9 Mike Geddes reviews local partnerships and social exclusion in the United Kingdom. The chapter starts by noting that the United Kingdom has experienced a more rapid increase in social inequality and poverty than most other EU member states, as a result of exclusion from employment and growing differentials in income from paid employment. At the same time, partnership has become one of the vogue words of the 1990s in the UK policy community, with central and local government, private business, and the voluntary and community sectors increasingly genuflecting to the values and virtues of partnership working. However, although partnership is more deeply embedded in the ideology and practice of the United Kingdom than in nearly any other EU country, it remains caught up in considerable debate and ambiguity. Chapter 9 locates the emergence of partnership in the United Kingdom in its historical context, with the restructuring of Fordist patterns of production and ownership of industry, the collapse of the post-war consensus in support of the Keynesian welfare state, and the emergence of a new poverty affecting far larger swathes of the population. Geddes argues that partnership began to emerge as a means by which other actors than the state might be induced to share responsibility for, and find new solutions to, problems of urban regeneration including social exclusion and poverty, alongside an increasingly constrained public sector. After looking at three case studies, Geddes concludes by interpreting partnerships as part of a new pattern of local governance in the United Kingdom. He sees this as a shift of emphasis away from local government as an arena in which conflicting party political agendas are shaped and worked out, to one which brings to the fore a consensual relationship between the local authority and a citizen body presumed to share a common interest. He concludes with a critical assessment of partnerships as the banner under which society is invited to join in the neo-liberal project as stakeholders in its outcomes. Local partnerships offer the excluded a stake in the market – but as is the case for small stakeholders generally, this may not be a stake that carries much clout.

The two concluding chapters then build on the earlier arguments to draw out some more general conclusions. In Chapter 10 John Benington offers an interpretation of partnerships as a specific form of a more general phenomenon – the emergence of new patterns of networked governance. Developing an analysis which links key aspects of socio-economic and technological change to a network paradigm, and linking together findings from the chapters on specific countries, Benington analyses some of the ways in which networks and partnerships may help nation states and the nascent European state to respond to dilemmas they face in relation to four key challenges: political legitimation, economic innovation, social problem-solving, and organisational complexity. In Chapter 11 Geddes and Le Galès draw on the national studies to relate the phenomenon of local partnership to current debates, including those about the hollowing out of the nation state, the restructuring of welfare regimes and the emergence of a 'new localism' in public policy. They draw a number of conclusions. In the first place, this transnational review of the experience of local partnership initiatives to combat social exclusion demonstrates the continuing diversity of national experience. The distinctive socio-economic patterns, practices and cultures formed and maintained within national boundaries, and the considerable differences in the nature, structure and impact of national state policies, are central to a sophisticated explanation of the development of local partnership across the EU. But important as national specificity continues to be, the trend towards local partnership cannot be understood solely in national terms (as too many policy-makers in the United Kingdom at least continue to do). On the one hand, they show that by drawing on the debate on the restructuring of European welfare regimes we can better understand both the manner in which, and the extent to which, local partnership has emerged in different countries.

At the same time, the research evidence presented in this book can contribute to a better understanding of the specifically local dimensions of different welfare regimes. Local partnerships, they argue, are one indication of a growing element of territorialisation/localisation of European social policies. The rise of local partnership denotes, partly, a 'bottom up' policy logic, reflecting local mobilisation to combat poverty and social exclusion. Geddes and Le Galès stress, though, the ambiguity of this 'new localism' in social policy: its potential in some circumstances to act as a vehicle for the implementation of cuts to social expenditure and the erosion of redistributive social objectives rather than the creation of more democratically rooted, inclusive, integrated and effective local social welfare systems. Local partnership is, they conclude, a contested and contestable arena of local social governance, open to capture by different interests within the EU, in nation states, and locally and at the grass roots.

References

Benington J (1998) Risk, reciprocity and civil society, in Coulson A (ed.) *Trust in the public domain*, Bristol: Policy Press, 227–41.

Geddes M (1995) *The role of partnerships in promoting social cohesion: A discussion paper.* Dublin: European Foundation for the Improvement of Living and Working Conditions, WP/95/38/EN.

Geddes M (1998) *Local partnerships: A successful strategy for social cohesion?* Luxembourg: Office for Official Publications of the European Communities.

Healey P (1998) Institutionalist theory, social exclusion and governance, in Madanipour A, Cars G and Allen J. *Social exclusion in European cities*, London: Jessica Kingsley.

Le Galès P (1998) Regulations and governance in European cities, *International Journal of Urban and Regional Research*, 22, 3, 482–506.

Monnier E (1997) 'Vertical' partnerships: The opportunities and constraints which they pose for high quality evaluation. *Evaluation*, 3, 1, 110–18.

Social Exclusion Unit (2000) *National Strategy for Neighbourhood Renewal: A framework for consultation.* London: Social Exclusion Unit, Cabinet Office.

Young J (1999) *The Exclusive Society*. London: Sage.

2 Social exclusion and partnership in the European Union

Mike Geddes and John Benington

Introduction

This chapter has two main objectives. First, it discusses contemporary problems of poverty and social exclusion in the European Union, and offers an overview of the main debates concerning the nature and causes of exclusion, and the policies that are in place to promote greater social inclusion and cohesion. Second, it describes the increasing prominence of the concept and practice of local partnership in the policies and programmes of the EU and its member states. The chapter concludes by raising a number of questions about local partnerships as institutional arenas within which a plurality of interests are brought together to address issues of poverty and social exclusion and to promote local development and regeneration.

Unemployment, poverty and deprivation in Europe

The recent process of European economic integration, propelled by the creation of the Single Market, is intended to provide a new impetus to economic growth, but is also intimately associated with the emergence of new patterns of unemployment, poverty and social exclusion, as economic and other changes impact in different ways on regions, localities and neighbourhoods. Social exclusion and poverty – unemployment and marginalisation in the labour market, homelessness, delinquency, crime – have become more entrenched across the EU (Abrahamson and Hansen 1996; Room 1995). It is against this background, with its implications for social cohesion and inclusion, that the concept of partnership is increasingly being introduced into the policies and programmes of the EU and its member states.

The economic and social challenges facing the Union may be seen to stem from three broad groups of linked processes (Mingione 1996; 1997): industrial restructuring and the intensified pressures of competitiveness; the crisis of welfare and public services; and the reshaping of patterns of political representation and citizenship. Over the last ten or fifteen years, European capital has encountered new challenges to its competitiveness in a more globalised world economy, while at the same time suffering the impact of successive recessions, with fragile intervening periods of economic growth. The collapse of the Fordist regime of accumulation (Harvey 1990; Dunford and Perrons 1994) has been associated with a major economic shift from manufacturing to services; the introduction of new less labour-intensive production methods; and an increase in low-paid, part-time, temporary, casual and insecure work. Trends such as these have produced higher and longer-lasting unemployment, and mean that poverty and economic insecurity is experienced by a significant number of those in work as well as those without jobs, posing fundamental problems for social cohesion within the EU (Amin and Tomaney 1995). The problems engendered by industrial restructuring and the crisis of the welfare state have impacted unevenly across the EU. A notable feature of recent change is the way in which poverty and exclusion have now become concentrated and entrenched in certain localities, from inner city neighbourhoods to peripheral housing estates and some rural areas. There is not only a 'new poverty', but a new 'geography of poverty' (Moulaert 1994).

At the same time, demographic and social changes (partly caused by the rise and retreat of Fordism), including the weakening of the nuclear family and extended family networks; the increasing numbers of lone parent families, especially young single jobless parents; increasing homelessness; and the ageing of the population, mean that there are new social groups experiencing poverty and social exclusion, and thus putting greater pressure on welfare systems (Benington and Taylor 1994). The collapse of stable economic growth, high levels of unemployment, and neo-liberal fiscal regimes, linked in many countries to monetary union, have simultaneously undermined the tax base of post-war welfare regimes (Liebfried and Pierson 1992; 1995), while the private sector has seized on the new profit opportunities to be had from the privatisation of those public services organised into substantial markets by the Fordist extension of collective consumption. These pressures have stretched public agencies to, and sometimes beyond, the limits of their ability to meet changing and expanding patterns of need. In some places, the inability of the welfare system to cope has been reflected in community breakdown, expressed in outbreaks of crime, riot and disorder (Campbell 1994; Power 1997).

This economic and social restructuring of Fordist patterns of accumulation and social reproduction has undermined party political systems based around the class interests of mass production, while challenges to traditional patterns and processes of political representation and policy formulation have reflected a widespread disillusionment with established political parties, with the limitations of representative democratic mechanisms, and a growing interest in and more demand for the more direct involvement of citizens and 'communities' – of place, of identity and of interest – in the political and policy process (Hirst 1994; Fraser 1996). In some countries, established patterns of consultation between the social partners have been weakened or found inadequate in coping with new problems. Within a context of global-isation, many commentators identify a shift of political and policy activity away from the nation state, both upwards to European and other supra-national institutions and downwards to the local or regional level (Held 1995; Jessop 1993).

These problems have forced the EU to develop new strategies for economic growth, competitiveness and employment (Commission of the European Communities 1993b; 1995b), including a new emphasis on the contribution of local development initiatives (Commission of the European Communities 1994b; 1995a), and to explore new directions for social policy (Commission of the European Communities 1993a; 1994a) for social welfare and social protection (Cousins M 1997) and public services (Deakin, Davis and Thomas 1995). In general, these new policy directions have paralleled the growing conversion to neo-liberalism among member states. Primacy is given to global economic competitiveness through competition, monetary union and deregulation policies, while social policy is restructured in the light of perceived public expenditure constraints and a closer alignment with competitiveness, for example through so-called 'active' labour market policies (Cousins M 1997). These policy priorities reflect the dominance of financial and business interests within the neo-corporatist framework of EU policy-making, while the failure of the EU to move towards an integrated social policy is associated with the relative weakness of organised labour and social democratic parties (Leibfried and Pierson 1995; Streek 1995). Along-side, but subordinate to the dominant neo-liberal thrust, is the policy objec-tive of social cohesion, pursued most notably through the Structural Funds and associated policy initiatives (Adshead and Quinn 1998), which have emerged as a major means of managing the formidable spatial inequalities that neo-liberalism has generated.

While the relatively privileged position of the EU within the global econ-omy means that many of Europe's citizens have benefited from increased incomes and improved living conditions, a significant and growing minority have suffered poverty, unemployment and various other forms of social and economic disadvantage. They have been variously termed 'the excluded', 'the marginalised', or an underclass that possesses one or more disadvantages that restrict their ability to cope with change.

During the majority of the 1990s the number of people employed in the EU declined, with unemployment remaining stubbornly high, at 10 per cent in mid-1998 (Commission of the European Communities 1999). Youth un-employment at over 20 per cent is nearly twice as high as that for adults, and long-term unemployment, the most intractable element of the European unemployment problem, stands at about 50 per cent of the total. The 1980s and early 1990s saw a greater involvement of women in paid work, with a positive correlation between women's participation and economic growth. However, regional variations are again considerable, with complex relation-ships between activity and unemployment rates and full and part-time work

(Perrons 1998). In addition, the rate of unemployment for women remains considerably higher than that for men, at 12.5 per cent compared with 9.5 per cent. The incidence of unemployment is also very uneven across the Union. In mid-1998, unemployment was below the level of 1994 (the previous peak) in all but four member states (Germany, Greece, Italy and Austria, where it was about 1 per cent higher), but only in Denmark, Ireland, Italy and the United Kingdom was it lower than at the beginning of the decade (Commission of the European Communities 1998). There are, therefore, distinctively national patterns of unemployment and labour market exclusion. However, rates of unemployment vary much more markedly between regions and localities than between countries. By 1995, the dispersion of regional unemployment rates across the Union was three times the level that it had been in the late 1970s, although regional rank-order remained remarkably similar, pointing to the growing entrenchment of unemployment in disadvantaged areas (Martin 1998). In 1997, un-employment exceeded 35 per cent in southern parts of Spain, over 25 per cent in many regions of southern Italy, and was around 20 per cent in much of the new Länder of Germany, as well as in parts of Finland. By contrast, unemployment was under 5 per cent in many areas of Denmark, southern Germany, northern Italy, the Netherlands, Austria and the southeast of the United Kingdom (Commission of the European Communities 1998).

High rates of unemployment and particularly long-term unemployment are the dominant factors associated with poverty. Poverty, defined as a lack of sufficient resources, is widespread in the EU, affecting maybe one in seven of all citizens, with Table 2.1 showing more than 57 million people living below the poverty line (Abrahamson and Hansen 1996; EAPN 1998). Poverty increased in the 1990s, leading to a growing polarisation of European societies. Within the EU, national differentials in poverty levels are, in general, remarkably longstanding and resilient (see Atkinson 1998). However, recent trends are also important: the United Kingdom stands out with a sharp rise in the 1980s, with more modest rises in West Germany and Sweden from the late 1970s to the mid-1980s, but little overall upward trend in countries such as Finland and France (Atkinson 1998; Van den Bosch 1998).

As with unemployment, poverty is unevenly distributed according to socio-economic characteristics, such as age, gender and household composition, and also according to place. High *rates* of poverty are found in regions of Europe with a large share of the population still employed in agriculture. Socio-economic groups likely to experience poverty include the self-employed, low skilled workers, women and immigrants/ethnic minorities. Transfer payments from the welfare system may be minimal for groups such as young unemployed people, single parents, and the elderly. The largest *numbers* of the poor (more than two-thirds) are to be found within more industrialised countries, where economic restructuring and de-industrialisation have caused unemployment, poverty and social exclusion in large cities and

Table 2.1 Poverty in the EU (thousands)

Country	Late 1980s	1993
Luxembourg	42	60
Denmark	220	318
Ireland	687	759
Belgium	928	1,289
Netherlands	706	1,919
Greece	2,048	2,255
Portugal	2,594	2,537
France	9,243	7,591
Spain	6,856	7,631
Germany	7,287	9,000
Italy	12,628	10,895
United Kingdom	8,721	12,805
EU 12	*51,960*	*57,162*
Finland		235
Sweden		485
EU 14		*57,882*

Source: European Anti-Poverty Network, 1998, using data for the late 1980s prepared for the European Commission, defining poverty in relation to per capita expenditure, and Eurostat data for 1993 (published in 1997) in which the poverty line is set by reference to household income.

old industrial areas particularly. The most vulnerable are those with low or outdated skill levels, including high proportions of women and older workers and ethnic groups.

Social exclusion

Unemployment and poverty are now widespread across the EU, posing a serious structural threat to social cohesion and the integration project (Organisation for Economic Cooperation and Development 1994; Vranken 1995).[1] While there are important national and regional differences, such problems are found across the territory of the Union: in formerly prosperous as well as traditionally depressed regions; in the urban periphery as well as the inner city; and in small and medium-sized towns as well as old industrial areas and large cities. In such areas, it has become commonplace in both policy and academic discourses to recognise that there is an accumulation and combination of several types of deprivation which go beyond poverty to *social exclusion*. Social exclusion is a contested concept – or, in Mingione's phrase, an 'intuitive short cut' to a different understanding of deprivation

---

1 Even more serious problems exist to the east, including in those countries soon to be acceding to the Union (Duffy 1998).

(Mingione 1996: xv). It is open to a range of interpretations and implications for action.

One set of interpretations of social exclusion starts from the notion of 'multidimensionality': social exclusion refers to the combined impact of factors such as lack of adequate education, deteriorating health conditions, homelessness, loss of family support, non-participation in the mainstream of society, and lack of job opportunities. Each type of deprivation has an impact on the others. The result is a vicious circle (Commission of the European Communities 1997b). An important issue for a 'multidimensional' approach to exclusion is whether social exclusion is broadly or narrowly defined: does it refer to specific groups suffering extreme deprivation (the homeless, residents of decaying public housing estates) or to a much broader conception, related to that of the 'new poverty', of a 'bottom 30 per cent' (or similar proportion) of society who are poor, marginalised and insecure? This issue is linked in turn to the relationship between a multidimensional conception of social exclusion and 'underclass' and 'dependency' theses. These are powerful particularly, but by no means exclusively, in the Anglo-Saxon context, in which dominant factors in the creation and perpetuation of exclusion are seen to be a combination of the barriers that public welfare erects against labour market participation and the entrenched behaviours and attitudes of excluded groups and communities themselves. The under-class analysis 'conflates economic disadvantage, institutional isolation, lack of employment opportunities, ethnic origins, cultural characteristics, forms of deviant behaviour and spatial concentration' (Mingione 1996: xvii), either without identifying causation, as is too often the case with the more naive versions of social exclusion, or attributing causation to behaviour and cultural deviance (Gans 1996; Fainstein 1996).[2]

For some, the importance of the concept of social exclusion is that it moves the poverty debate forward beyond (but not away from) the material dimensions of deprivation (Berghman 1992; Room 1994). Thus, Rodgers, for example (writing from the perspective of African and Asian as well as European experience), suggests that we need to recognise a number of dimensions of exclusion: from consumption of goods and services; from (or within) the labour market; from land and other resources, including credit; from security; from human rights; and from participation in political and policy processes (Rodgers 1995). We need to recognise not only the material deprivation of the poor, but also their inability to fully exercise their social, economic and political rights as citizens (Leibfried 1993). Exclusion occurs in the spheres of work and consumption, of welfare and social protection, and of political representation and participation. These perspectives have obvious implications for the mechanisms that create exclusion (and therefore

---

2 A further, more interesting strand of analysis seeks to root exclusion in social anthropological and psychoanalytical distinctions between the self and the 'other', of normality and deviance, and to associated notions of purity and defilement, of boundaries, and of power (Sibley 1995).

the arenas in which to do something about it). Gore (1995) identifies 'three exclusion mechanisms': the market, the state, and discrimination within civil society. These three dimensions may be given differing prominence. Levitas (1996), for example, criticises what she sees as the dominant focus of EU policies on labour market integration.

A further set of analyses are of interest for their attempts to differentiate between national discourses and practices. One influential perspective in this context is that of Silver (1994; 1995; 1996), who identifies four major 'traditions', which she labels as solidarist, specialisation, monopolist and organicist. In the solidarist perspective, associated primarily with the French republican tradition of an essentially cohesive society and the fundamental equality of citizens,[3] social exclusion represents the rupture of the social bond between individuals or groups of individuals and society. In the 'specialisation' perspective, exclusion is associated with barriers to individual freedom. Social differentiation, the economic division of labour, and the separation of spheres should not produce exclusion if individuals are free to move across boundaries and spheres are kept separate. The monopolistic interpretation associates social exclusion with the actions and interplay of powerful interests – multinational firms, government bureaucracies (and, one might add, patriarchal and other entrenched interests and practices within civil society). Finally, the organicist tradition is distinguished by a conservative conception of social order based on the recognition of different interest groups within society: exclusion is suffered by those (such as migrants or ethnic minorities) who do not belong within this organicist framework.

In a similar vein, Paugam (1998) proposes three 'ideal types' of poverty in the European context. 'Integrated poverty' exists where large sections of the population are poor, and consequently there is a low level of stigmatisation of poverty. 'Marginal poverty' denotes situations where deprivation is much more restricted, leading to the stigmatisation of the poor as 'special social cases'. 'Disabling poverty', by contrast, characterises those situations where growing numbers in diverse social contexts are becoming poor or excluded. Paugam tends to reserve the concept of social exclusion for the last of these types. Both Silver and Paugam develop a degree of association between specific countries and each 'tradition' or type (in Paugam's case, at particular historical periods). Thus, Silver associates the republican tradition with France, the monopolist tradition with Sweden, specialisation discourse with Anglo-American liberalism, and organicist traditions with Germany and Iberia. Paugam associates 'integrated poverty' with southern European countries; 'marginal poverty' with the European 'golden age' and still with Germany and some of the Scandinavian countries; and 'disabling poverty' with contemporary France and the United Kingdom. Such classifications

3 Levitas argues that this neglects the inequalities within paid work; between paid and unpaid work (and thence between women and men); and – centrally for her – between owners and non-owners of property.

and associations are thought-provoking but also problematic. Christine Cousins (1997) draws attention to the differences between 'neo-organicism' in Spain and Germany, while also linking divergences in patterns of social exclusion within the EU to the debate on welfare regimes, a question to which we will return in the final chapter of this book.

While Paugam introduces a temporal dimension in relation to his ideal types, another strand in the literature is more centrally concerned to develop a historical analysis of current patterns of social exclusion. Thus Mingione, for example, associates social exclusion (in western Europe) with the break-down of Fordist patterns of economic growth and the consequent failure of the Fordist welfare model. Here, social exclusion denotes the new fissures opening up in welfare capitalism, as increasing numbers of the population are exposed to, rather than shielded from, insecurity, and cannot rely on the extension of a stable employment base and high rates of economic growth (Mingione 1996: 13). Lea (1997) ascribes social polarisation and the emergence of 'permanent unemployment' to the assault by capital on the Fordist working class and the welfare state, an attack permitted by the 'discovery' of the potential for profitability to be obtained from a low wage, flexible workforce (see also Taylor-Gooby 1997). Byrne also seeks to understand social exclusion in terms of the recomposition of class relations, developing the conception of the 'social proletariat' to encompass all those groups excluded from, or within, the changing forms of the wage relationship (Byrne 1997). These analyses contrast post-war policy goals of full employment and the social wage with the post-Fordist neo-liberal orthodoxy of tight fiscal and monetary policy and the promotion of economic competitiveness within what is seen as an increasingly globalised economy. Strategies for social inclusion are seen to be contingent on global competitiveness, although critics argue that inclusion is incompatible with the globalised market.

The location of the main causes of exclusion in the dynamics of a post-Fordist or globalised capitalism is challenged by those who emphasise the deficiencies of government and welfare systems.[4] Thus, a powerful contemporary argument, advanced not only by those on the more traditional right, is that dependency induced among the recipients of state welfare is a dominant factor in creating exclusion from the mainstream, in reinforcing cultures of exclusion, and in inhibiting 'enterprise', in the broader social as well as the narrower economic sense (Giddens 1998). Relatedly, government may be seen more as part of the problem than as part of the answer. State services and welfare are criticised as producer- rather than user-focused; as offering fragmented rather than holistic solutions; as being remote from communities; and as focusing on post-hoc palliatives rather than prevention (Perri 6, 1997). The recent tendency (promoted, ironically, by governments sharing

4 It is, of course, possible to locate institutional factors alongside economic restructuring, as two aspects of the crisis of Fordism (Mingione 1997).

much of the above analysis) to impose business methods and narrow performance targets on state agencies may have exacerbated many of these problems.

Postmodernist approaches have stimulated new perspectives on poverty and social exclusion which share some of the foregoing arguments, but reposition them within a distinctive set of perspectives. Bauman (1998), for example, argues that contemporary poverty and exclusion can only be understood by reference to a consumerist capitalism which is undermining not only the productivism of many analyses but also the work ethic itself and welfare systems predicated on work, in a world where capital no longer needs the work-disciplined reserve army of the past. For Bauman, contemporary exclusion is exclusion from commodity consumption, as much as from work. Leonard (1997) offers a critique of the exclusionary and dominatory character of 'modernist' welfare and the hierarchy and rigidity of 'modern' organisations. Challenging the dependency of the poor on either the state or the market, he defends a discourse of collectivism against individualism while, crucially, seeking to recognise diversity. Social movements of the excluded, he argues, are more open to the discourse of community than that of universalism, and with organisational principles of networks rather than hierarchies. These analyses, while by no means in full agreement with each other, reflect the postmodernist identification of the impact of post-Fordist or late capitalism in weakening and 'churning up' traditional class distinctions and allegiances, and promoting the growth of segmented identities and social divisions on ethnic, sexual or local lines, in an as yet unstable class structure in which 'those above have the coherence of privilege, while those below lack unity and solidarity' (Anderson 1998; Jameson 1991). The rejection by some, though not all, postmodernists of 'meta' discourses brings us back to 'multidimensional' conceptions of social exclusion in which no causative processes are privileged; and in this sense social exclusion can, perhaps, be recognised as a distinctively postmodern theorisation of poverty and inequality.

Our understanding of the causes of social exclusion is of course linked to the ways in which we may formulate approaches to action against exclusion. Gore (1995) suggests that, despite differences in nation-state policies, there have been several key dimensions of western European experience in this respect:

- policies for income support tied to social and professional insertion
- education and training
- multidimensional local initiatives
- support for micro-enterprises and community work.

Within this broad approach, however, there are a number of important debates. One of these concerns the extent to which 'solutions' to the problem of exclusion are seen to depend on the wage or on the social wage, on integration into the labour market and action concerning the terms of labour market integration, or on social and welfare support, and on income support to supplement the wage.[5] A second revolves around the extent to which tackling exclusion is regarded as a question of rethinking policies *for* the excluded, or of looking to the excluded themselves for solutions. The latter may itself involve, on the one hand, notions of solidarity with, and support for, excluded communities by other actors (Beresford and Turner 1997), or a (communitarian) emphasis on the responsibilities (as well as rights) of communities, which may well become coupled with a retreat by the state and other actors from previous commitments.

Finally, an active debate, which is central to this book, concerns the roles of actors and institutions at different spatial scales, from the local to the supra- and transnational in combating poverty and social exclusion. In western Europe, pressures on the social policy capacity of nation states has led to an increasing interest in the contribution of local initiatives to the achievement of social inclusion. This is reflected in the numerous policy initiatives of both the EU and some member states, which resource local projects to promote local development and counter social exclusion, reflecting widespread evidence of the recent intensification of poverty and exclusion in local areas or neighbourhoods (Power 1997; Madanipour, Cars and Allen 1998). These may be seen in a positive light as experimental projects which in due course will need to be 'mainstreamed', but also – more critically and problemati- cally – as a fragmentation or localisation of policy against social exclusion, related to the 'hollowing out' of the nation state (Jessop 1993). Local action may be viewed as a laudable recognition of grass roots capacity and compe- tence – 'think global, act local', as the saying went – or as 'local dumping' of issues that the nation state cannot resolve. Moreover, the spatialised analysis of 'global-local' is itself contested by the argument that we need to think in terms of 'networked governance' transcending spatial hierarchies and levels (Benington and Harvey 1999; Benington, Chapter 10).

Increased interest in the local dimensions of policy reflects the 'spatiality' of social exclusion (Madanipour 1998). Spatial patterns of social exclusion occur not only between the North, including the EU, and the South within the global economy, and between nation states within the EU, but much more locally; and such patterns reflect the interpenetration of forces working at these different levels. Thus, for example, shifts in the global economy lead to migration between North and South, with different impacts in different countries and regions of the EU, with some southern European countries becoming net recipients of migration rather than, as in the past, places of emigration. These migratory movements coalesce with those caused by the changing geography of economic opportunity within the EU, leading to complex patterns of ethnic/migrant populations in major cities, in Germany

5 See, for example, the opposing positions taken on this issue by Robinson and Gregg in the recent edited volume by Oppenheim (1998).

for example, or in the capital of the EU itself, Brussels (Kesteloot 1995). Women in southern European countries, Vaiou (1995) suggests, are marginalised both because they cannot move in search of work as men can and because the European 'social partnership' model tends to have little concern for their forms and experience of work. The experience of integration or exclusion of such immigrant populations is influenced by differences in national and local state policies, in terms of citizenship, welfare, social housing and so forth. It is both correct and relevant to argue that the 'local' dimensions of social exclusion are part and parcel of wider, shifting spatial patterns, and that social and economic, political and socio-cultural elements of marginality should not be separated analytically (Hadjimichalis and Sadler 1995; Madanipour 1998), not least to combat the tendency among policy-makers to reduce exclusion to the status of a localised phenomenon. This, however, should not prevent us from recognising the fact that certain spatial dimensions of social exclusion were particularly prominent in the 1990s. These include those concentrations of the poor in large public (Fordist) housing estates, sometimes in peripheral locations where physical barriers exacerbate exclusion (Bartley 1998), but also in other urban locations frequently cheek by jowl with affluence, including neighbourhoods with large migrant and/or ethnic populations or 'racial ghettos' (Wacquant 1993; Peach 1998; Zukin 1998) and remoter rural regions (Pugliese 1995; Oska 1995). The local case studies discussed in this book reflect such contemporary patterns of localised concentrations of exclusion. At the same time, it must be remembered that social exclusion is not confined to such localities – indeed, the experience of exclusion may be exacerbated where, for example, marginalisation within work is an integral dimension of a 'growth region' such as south east England (Allen, Massey and Cochrane 1998).

Local partnership in the EU

It is within this context of a recognition of the 'localisation' of social exclusion that partnerships between public, private, voluntary and community interests and organisations have been offered as a policy response to the growth and intractability of poverty and social exclusion in the EU and in many member states. Partnership is of course not new: it builds on a history of inter-agency collaboration and participation by local communities in the implementation of programmes and the delivery of services in many countries. Nonetheless, the current focus of policy debate around partnership reflects a widespread view within the policy community that traditional social policies, of either a sectoral nature (e.g. housing, health, education) or targeted on specific social categories (e.g. women, the elderly, the young, those with disabilities, ethnic groups and migrants) must be supplemented by a more integrated, multidimensional and geographically targeted approach, reflecting the complex causes of social exclusion.

An important driving force behind this trend has been the EU itself. Partnership, especially at the local level, has become an increasingly important reference in major social and economic policy statements emanating from the Commission, such as the White Paper on European Social Policy and the Medium-Term Social Action Programme. In its second report for 1992, the European Community's Observatory on National Policies to Combat Social Exclusion commented that 'the debates about social exclusion are, as much as anything, debates about the new partnerships which must be forged within our European societies' (Robbins 1992). Partnership has become an important element in the way in which the EU is grappling with the profound and wide-ranging changes in the political, economic, social and technological structure of Europe, and the challenge to formulate a new European model of development. We argue that the development of the idea and practice of partnership in the EU has taken place in three main phases.

The traditional model of partnership

In the first phase, which lasted well into the 1980s, 'partnership' in the European Community was conceived in fairly formal terms, as constitutional or institutional relationships between formal representative bodies, primarily at supra-national level. This was prevalent from early in the history of the Community and its institutions, such as the Economic and Social Committee (ECOSOC), which provides a formalised channel for the views of the social partners and other key social actors. This type of 'partnership' at European level was a reflection and expression of the pacts between capital, labour and the state, which had been negotiated within the member states as part of the post-war settlement. This corporatist concept has persisted (and been expanded in the post-Maastricht Social Dialogue) at European level, even though it has increasingly been overlain by a neo-liberal, 'free market' philosophy which has supplanted corporatist arrangements in some of the member states.

The broadening and deepening of partnership

In the second phase, partnership-type approaches were progressively both broadened and deepened within the EU, to the extent that during the 1990s a partnership approach has become a key feature of the EU's mainstream policies and programmes over a very wide field. It was enshrined as a principle within the 1988 Reform of the Structural Funds, and confirmed at the following Lisbon Council. It was reinforced by the Maastricht Treaty commitment to strengthening the role of the social partners, and establishing the Committee of the Regions as a consultative body. The European Parliament recorded its support for a partnership approach to local development, for example with reference to the Commission's proposals for territorial employment pacts, where 'broad local alliances between public authorities, private organisations, the social partners and the population seem particularly well suited' (European Parliament 1997).

This new emphasis on partnership appears to have been supported by many of the key stakeholders in EU policy. The Economic and Social Committee (ECOSOC) was prominent in advocating a stronger involvement of the social partners and the local authorities in Structural Fund partnerships, and also suggesting that the practice of partnership needed to be extended beyond the economic and social partners, and the other socio-economic agencies and professions, to include direct participation of citizens and their representatives. ECOSOC expressed its commitment to proactive, pluralistic partnership in its Opinions on Social Exclusion (October 1993) and on the Medium-Term Action Programme to Combat Exclusion and Promote Solidarity (December 1993), arguing that the EU can add value to member states' initiatives by, among other things, 'creating and supporting networks...mobilising the relevant players...identifying and promoting good practice, knowledge and expertise...incorporating the fight against social exclusion into the Community's general policies...preventing rather than remedying unemployment and social exclusion'.[6] A little later, in its Opinion on the First Cohesion report, ECOSOC drew attention to member states such as Ireland and Sweden where the social partners and local authorities are actively involved in Monitoring Committees, and expressed the view that vertical and horizontal partnership could be deepened further and made more effective through the greater involvement of local levels and the economic and social partners, helping to bridge the gap between Community structural assistance and citizens at the grass roots. The further development of partnership was, according to ECOSOC, 'of far reaching importance for the development of Union citizenship and of democracy and solidarity' (European Communities, Economic and Social Committee 1997).

The trade unions supported the principles of partnership both in the Structural Funds and in relation to anti-poverty policy. The European Trade Union Congress (ETUC) committed itself to 'un partenariat engagé' and the formation of a European trade union network of struggle against exclusion (Fonteneau, undated). Although the position taken at European level was not always mirrored by practice on the ground, there were numerous examples of trade union activity in local partnership contexts to combat labour market exclusion and marginalisation, in combination with

6 A distinctive feature of ECOSOC's Opinion was the criticism that the issue of discrimination was not properly addressed: 'Negative discrimination, and allied phenomena, such as prejudice, intolerance, extremism and segregation, are structures common to the exclusion faced in many dimensions of social and economic life, by many groups. ECOSOC particularly highlights the needs of women, black and ethnic minority people, disabled people, people with mental illnesses, and religious minorities (European Communities, Economic and Social Committee, 1993a and b).

employers and public and voluntary agencies (Nicaise and Henriques 1995; LASAIRE 1995). The ETUC argued for the 'close consultations' with the social partners 'to be defined in more concrete terms' in the application of the Structural Funds (European Trade Union Institute 1993), as partnership in the Structural Funds was not living up to their expectations, and looked towards the proposed new Employment Chapter, and territorial employment pacts, as important new contexts for partnership in the employment field.

While the enthusiasm of business was a good deal more limited than that of the trade unions, the European Declaration of Businesses against Exclusion and the European Business Network for Social Cohesion represented a significant initiative by a number of prominent employers to combat exclusion. The Guidelines for Action attached to the Declaration detail specific proposals for businesses to join with other organisations in counteracting exclusion by promoting the labour market integration of excluded groups; helping to improve vocational training; avoiding exclusion within the business; minimising redundancies or providing for appropriate measures where they are inevitable; promoting the creation of new jobs and businesses; and contributing to social integration in particularly deprived areas and of particularly marginalised groups, including the development of 'priority partnerships with players from associations, co-operatives and mutual societies, who can offer particularly marginalised persons special assistance with a view to ensuring they can satisfy basic needs...and have access to a job or other activity giving them resources, a regular lifestyle and social recognition' (CEEP 1994; Griffiths 1995; European Business Network for Social Cohesion 1996). The Union of Industrial and Employers Confederations of Europe (UNICE) has also indicated cautious support for partnership, for example in a joint contribution by the social partners in the framework of the European Confidence Pact for Employment. In its position paper on the First Cohesion Report, UNICE argued that the social partners should be involved more closely at all stages of structural policy, from design through to monitoring and evaluation, and supports innovation in the future use of the Structural Funds, in order 'to carry out integrated actions targeting economic and social development on the ground' (UNICE 1997).

Regional and local authorities supported the concept of partnership as a means of promoting cohesion but wanted earlier and more active involvement in the processes both of policy formulation and implementation. The establishment of the Committee of the Regions (COR) provided a formal vehicle for regional and local authorities to be consulted and to offer opinions, but their response to the White Paper on European Social Policy suggested that they wanted partnership to go further than this, emphasising the importance of strengthening the involvement of local and regional authorities in the European Social Fund monitoring committees.[7]

As part of its search for more broadly based partnership, the European Commission has actively cultivated a working relationship with the voluntary sector and non-governmental organisations. In relation to social exclusion, it has given financial and administrative support to the European Anti-Poverty Network (EAPN), a federal organisation made up from national networks of (largely) voluntary and community organisations in the different member states. The Commission has drawn EAPN into a close consultative relationship on social policy issues, together with other European level organisations such as The Confederation of Family Organisations in the European Community (COFACE), the ETUC and UNICE. Thus, in March 1996 the European Social Policy Forum brought together NGOs and the social partners with the European Commission and representatives of other institutions. All participants in the Forum recognised the importance of a wide partnership in the struggle against unemployment and exclusion, and NGOs demanded more permanent involvement as partners in programmes to combat unemployment and aid the most disadvantaged groups, with their position in decision-making consolidated through more structured partnership with Community institutions and the social partners (M Cousins 1997). EAPN has continued to play an active role in dialogue with the Commission on social exclusion and social policy more generally.

By the mid-1990s the principle of partnership had thus been extended beyond the traditional consultation with the social partners, not only to embrace other tiers of government, and to include the national, regional and local authorities in new forms of co-operation, but also to include a wider range of bodies outside government, from the public, private, voluntary and grass roots sectors. This extension of partnership-type relationships has been driven by financial, operational and developmental factors. Many of the Commission's main programmes depend upon co-financing by the member states or regional and local authorities, and partnership is also one way of recognising the different stakeholders within the monitoring and control arrangements for the implementation of EU policies on the ground. Partnership can produce added value from the European Commission's point of view by enabling local projects and actors from the public, private, voluntary and community sectors to collaborate in innovatory projects and learning networks, and transmitting knowledge and experience rapidly between the different 'partners'.

7 During the European Cohesion Forum in April 1997 numerous local and regional authorities and their national organisations developed this view. For example, the UK Local Government International Bureau stated its support for partnership as one of the four main principles governing the operation of the Structural Funds, and called for regional partnerships to have a stronger role alongside governments and the European Commission. The Federation of Swedish County Councils argued that 'locally and regionally based partnerships lead to both greater efficiency and the exercise of democratic influence over the Structural Fund system' (Commission of the European Communities 1997c).

Partnership became prominent in this phase in the mainstream Structural Funds, in the Community Initiatives, and in Social Action Programmes such as the Poverty 3 programme (1989–94). In the Structural Funds, the principle of partnership was closely linked to that of subsidiarity and a recognition of the advantages of decentralisation, involving the relevant authorities at all levels, and the social partners, in the pursuit of agreed objectives and the sharing of responsibilities for decision-making, including the involvement of those at the grass roots nearest to the problems for which solutions were being sought (Commission of the European Communities 1997a). In the mainstream Structural Funds, the main arena for a partnership approach were the Monitoring Committees, which bring together European Commission, national government and regional and local officials and representatives of the social partners in a 'vertical' form of partnership relationship, although the situation differed considerably between different member states, and the Commission commented on the need for better 'information on the functioning of partnerships in practice...to identify best practices and their transferability' (Commission of the European Communities 1997a: 121).

In the Community Initiatives and Social Action Programmes the Commission was in a position to promote wider 'horizontal' partnerships among local actors. A wide range of programmes and initiatives, such as Poverty 3, LEDA, LEADER, URBAN, INTERREG, NOW, Youthstart, HORIZON and INTEGRA, have promoted both a local partnership framework and transnational networks of local partnerships. URBAN, for example, offers financial support for development programmes for geographically defined and limited parts of cities, which are intended to address economic, social and environmental problems in a more comprehensive way, through integrated programmes based on local partnership.

In general, the Commission has taken a favourable view of the development of partnership in the Community Initiatives, regarding the fostering of co-operation and the formation of new partnerships, the generation of a spirit of experimentation and innovation, the encouragement of a grass roots 'bottom up' approach, and the dissemination of good practice as their strengths. However, it has also recognised that experience has been varied, with some initiatives – INTERREG, LEADER and URBAN, for example – having more success than others in adding value to Community cohesion policies (Commission of the European Communities 1997a: 111–12).

The European Poverty Programmes

The three successive Poverty programmes were of particular importance in developing the European Commission's thinking and policy on the role of partnership in tackling social exclusion over a period of two decades. In 1974, in the wake of the oil crisis, the European Council recognised the need to address the growing problem of poverty. A year later the Commission launched its first programme of pilot studies to combat poverty (1975–80). In practice, these were not so much 'studies' (research was brought in very late and could only be retrospective) as small-scale grass roots community action projects to tackle the immediate welfare needs of the most disadvantaged, such as the homeless (Commission of the European Communities 1989). Learning from this initial experience, the second European Programme to Combat Poverty (1984–8) adopted a more structural and categorical definition of 'new poverty' (e.g. long-term unemployment, rural poverty, ageing and elderly people), and involved agencies with some capacity to take action to resolve problems, not simply to voice them (e.g. national government agencies, local authorities, and voluntary organisations as well as grass roots community groups).

The concept of new poverty which prevailed in the second European Programme was, however, progressively supplanted in the early 1990s by notions of exclusion and integration, and the title of the Third European Programme (1989–94), 'a medium-term programme to foster the economic and social integration of the least privileged groups', reflected this. The approach of Poverty 3 crystallised around three core principles of multi-dimensionality, partnership and participation. In Poverty 3, partnership was a requirement in terms of the composition and structure of the formal management committee (Partnership Board) for each of the local 'Model Action' projects, bringing together a number of organisations and interests (local authorities, central or regional government officials, educational institutions, charities, churches, and other voluntary and community organisations) in a formal partnership board or committee, to share overall responsibility for steering the project, for managing the finances and hiring staff. Within the Poverty 3 programme, partnership was seen to have a number of benefits as part of local anti-poverty strategies. These included, first, better co-ordination of policies, programmes and activities between different actors and agencies, overcoming the compartmentalisation of policy issues between separate agencies and services, with the potential for the pooling of skills, resources and budgets between different organisations. Second, partnership promised a more pluralist and flexible approach to problems, encouraging cross-fertilisation of creative ideas and innovation, and also sharing of the risks in experimental/pilot projects in a changing and unpredictable policy environment (including an emphasis on lateral, local, inter-organisational and inter-personal networks as the basis for policy innovation). Third, partnership was seen as a basis for leverage of additional resources from external bodies (especially national governments) and bringing political clout in lobbying central governments and mainstream bodies.

Experience within the Poverty 3 programme also progressively highlighted a number of requirements for effective local partnership, as the attempt was made to put principles into practice in local projects. The initial tasks of developing a shared vision and values between all the partners and the careful negotiation of a joint strategy and programme of action were made easier where there was leadership (either by an individual or a team), which was trusted and respected both inside and beyond the partnership body. Implementation of the action programme required good working relations between the partnership committee or board and appointed staff. There needed to be a clear division of risks and sharing of any benefits arising from the partnership, in terms of finance, development opportunities, or publicity and public recognition (Vranken 1995).

In practice, however, the theory of partnership proved rather neater than the reality. A series of documents published by the Poverty 3 central and local teams (Conroy 1994; Bruto da Costa 1994; Estivill et al 1994) also high-lighted some of the costs, dilemmas, barriers and problems encountered by the Poverty 3 local partnerships. These included the danger of getting trapped in legal tangles and wrangles over the constitution for partnership bodies, and the diversity of values, interests and styles among different bodies represented in the partnership. Problems arising from the disparities in power, knowledge, expertise and resources available to the different stake-holders in the partnership were paralleled by needs for training, development and technical advice to enable partners from the voluntary and community sectors to play their full part.[8]

It also became increasingly clear that while the European Commission required an integrated partnership approach by regional and local actors and agencies, neither the Commission nor national governments practised the same level of partnership as they preached. The relative weakness of 'vertical' partnership has meant that, while Poverty 3 demonstrated the value of a partnership approach to tackling problems at the local level, and a few member states (most notably perhaps Ireland and Portugal) have built on the experience of the programme, more generally there has been only limited progress in disseminating and applying the lessons of Poverty 3 within and between the member states.

Towards partnership governance in the European Union?

Despite such difficulties in creating effective partnership on the ground, by the middle of the 1990s it appeared to be possible to identify a further, third stage in the development of partnership in the EU – a stage in which partner-ship would become more than a means to an end, and emerge as a key part of a new vision of European governance. Certainly, during the era of Jacques

---

8 Evaluation undertaken of the recent LEDA programme (Humphreys 1996), which supported innovative local economic development actions, similarly identified a number of advantages of partnership, arguing that partnership provides a forum for consensus, strategy building and co-ordinated action; access to different skills; enhanced outcomes for partners; promotion of innovation, and promoting local identity and community and competitiveness. But, as with Poverty 3, the evaluation also identifies several more problematic issues, ranging from the depth of the contributions made by key partners to the difficulties of evaluating the out-comes and impacts of partnerships and problems in sustaining them over the long term.

Delors' presidency, the EU was seeking to move into a more active set of partnerships with other bodies to accelerate the rapid development of a more extensive, interventionist and innovative European social policy and employment strategy. The Commission's proposals, adopted in April 1995, for a Medium-Term Social Action Programme for the period 1995–7, implied a more catalytic role for the Commission in the promotion of an integrated strategy for economic and social development in Europe, and in giving more active leadership within its partnerships with other public, private, voluntary and grass roots bodies. One of the new roles envisaged for the European Union was that of 'structuring the dialogue between the various key players':

> This implies the development of an additional type of response at European level to complement and reinforce the legislative activity which has formed the backbone of the social dimension in the past. It means the development of the role to be played at Community level in terms of promoting joint discussion, exchange of experience, and concerted action on a transnational basis in responding to common problems.
>
> (CEC 1995d: 9)

The Commission was proposing here to move beyond the kind of targeted measures for specific groups with specific needs which had previously characterised much of its social policy, towards a more broadly based strategy capable of addressing the larger policy issues such as unemployment, ageing of the population, social protection systems and the overall quality of life. In addition, the Commission initiated a number of actions in partnership with a wide range of other actors:

- The European Forum on Social Policy, which first met in March 1996, to pave the way for a possible revision and strengthening of the Social Charter to cover citizens' rights and responsibilities with Europe (CEC 1995d: 23).
- Support for the Declaration of European Businesses against Exclusion, and the subsequent 1998 Copenhagen Conference on Business and Social Cohesion.
- Encouraging the active participation of the social partners in European Social Fund (ESF) operations as an essential feature of the partnerships needed to maximise the impact of the Fund.
- A new interest, following the Essen Council, in local development and employment initiatives and partnership arrangements to promote them.
- The development of local and territorial Employment Pacts, which in some countries and areas have proved to be interesting new arenas for partnership between public bodies, the social partners, and, to an extent, community interests (Vignon 1996; Meadows 1996).

- The new arrangements for the Structural Funds post-2000 place increased emphasis on partnership.

Taken together, and at face value, such developments seemed to amount to a major development in the EU's conception of partnership. This involved not only a continued strengthening of the notion of partnership to include a much wider range of actors and agencies, in a more action-oriented programme orchestrated by the EC, but also the raising of the role of partnership from the implementation of programmes largely designed by the Commission, in formal consultative bodies, to a higher level of input into the process of strategy-making and policy formulation. In addition, there was a new emphasis on the importance of transnational partnerships and networks as flexible methods for exchanging experience, piloting innovation, policy borrowing and policy transfer, and for cross-national learning during a period of rapid social change.

However, with the waning of the Delors vision in recent years, there has been a retreat from the conception of a 'social Europe' in which regional and local interests have a more privileged role in governance. Other issues – the single currency, enlargement and the budget, not to mention the crisis over probity and accountability – took over the agenda. The Commission's proposals for a substantial anti-poverty programme to follow Poverty 3 were blocked in the Council of Ministers.

The precise future of partnership in the EU – especially partnership against social exclusion – is thus unclear. Nonetheless, poverty and social exclusion remain policy priorities for the Commission and are seen to require integrated action between many different agencies and actors, especially at the local level. For the Commission itself, partnership is a key principle in the attempt to counterbalance tendencies towards fragmentation with principles of cohesion and integration within the Union. Partnership, both vertically with other tiers of government and horizontally with other spheres and sectors, is a philosophy that has now entered the mainstream of EU thinking and practice. While there is a degree of rhetoric in this, partnership is being introduced not only into the language but into the structures, practices and processes of EU policy-making.

At the same time, and partly, though by no means exclusively, influenced by EU programmes, a number of national governments have also introduced policy programmes founded on local partnership principles. In the United Kingdom, in acknowledgment of the deficiencies of earlier initiatives which gave a leading role to the private sector in local regeneration, successive programmes such as City Challenge and the Single Regeneration Budget Challenge Fund allocated funding to localities able to demonstrate a framework of partnership between the public, private, voluntary and community sectors. Similar programmes apply the same principles to rural areas. In Ireland, where the influence of EU thinking and funding is significant, a range of government programmes funded local regeneration partnerships, including the Area Programme for Integrated Rural Development, the ABR Programme (Area-Based Response to Long-Term Unemployment), the Programme for Integrated Development, and the Local Enterprise Programme. In France, major programmes such as that for the Developpement Social des Quartiers (DSQ) and the more recent Contrat de Ville operated through a local partnership framework. The Social Renewal programme in the Netherlands and the Social Development Fund in Denmark are further examples. In this climate, local partnerships also began to emerge as a result of more local initiative, either from local agencies, or from grass roots social movements and associations.

The representation of interests in local partnerships in the EU

The institutional and social composition of local partnerships varies from country to country, and depending on the objectives and requirements of funding programmes (Geddes 1998). This diversity of partnership initiatives demonstrates how local partnership is now perceived as a highly adaptable policy, feasible in a wide range of socio-economic contexts, a vehicle for projects ranging from large-scale, multi-million, government and EU-funded regeneration programmes to small-scale self-help initiatives, in locations stretching from old industrial regions and inner cities to the rural periphery. However, despite this diversity, an essential feature of local partnership is of course the involvement of a wide range of interests and actors. Table 2.2 shows the interests represented as partners in the local partnerships studied in our research,[9] distinguishing between five categories:

- The public sector, including local and regional authorities (represented by both officials and/or local councillors), other public sector or quasi-public agencies, and national government departments.
- Employers, including both individual firms (either local employers or firms with an interest in the regeneration process, such as housing and construction businesses) and employer organisations, either local or more broadly based.
- Trade unions, including local labour and unemployed associations.
- The voluntary sector, including both local voluntary associations and nationally organised voluntary and not-for-profit organisations. These can be organisations providing local services, or churches and charities.
- The community sector, including local community organisations, community enterprises, and individual community representatives and activists.

9 The data for this table refers to the full sample of 86 local partnerships.

Table 2.2 Partners in local partnerships

Public sector: local	93
Public sector: regional/national	65
Employers	45
Trade unions	31
Voluntary sector	53
Community	51

The table shows the percentage of all partnerships in which each category of partner was represented.

Public sector involvement in partnership is often a corollary of the constraints on the public sector's resources and its more limited capacity for unilateral action. However, in most local partnerships, public sector agencies continue to play a leading or dominant role, however much their agendas may be influenced by other interests. In many Poverty 3 local partnerships, local, regional or national government agencies both initiated and led the projects. Even in programmes such as City Challenge in the United Kingdom, where private sector leadership was promoted by a neo-liberal government, the reality has often been somewhat different.

In some local partnerships a key dimension is the 'vertical partnership' between local, regional and national levels of administration. In France, urban policy has involved successive partnership initiatives in depressed neighbourhoods. The Developpement Social des Quartiers partnerships of the 1970s and 1980s were paralleled by a number of additional localised initiatives: the Zones d'Education Prioritaires (ZEPs), Operations ete-jeunes (OPEs), Conseils Communales de la Prevention de la Delinquance (CCPDs). In the early 1990s these initiatives were superseded by the Contrat du Plan framework, which aimed to overcome the fragmentation of initiatives and marked a shift from a neighbourhood focus to the wider urban/metropolitan area. In all these initiatives a main focus of partnership has been between national, regional and local state agencies, while private and voluntary sector participation has been relatively limited. In Spain and Ireland the 'vertical' dimension of partnership is similarly important. Local partnerships also frequently include a range of non-elected state and quasi-state agencies alongside 'democratic' local government. In England, these range from the Training and Enterprise Councils (TECs) to the police and health authorities. In countries such as Austria, Belgium, Portugal and Finland, for example, they include non-elected health and employment agencies.

Private sector/employer participation in local partnerships has been strongly promoted both by the EU's commitment to the neo-corporatist role of the 'social partners', and by member states such as Ireland and the United Kingdom (although according to rather different rationales), but far less actively in many other member states. There was business/employer representation in less than half the partnerships identified in the research, and in some of these cases the involvement was formal rather than substantive. Business involvement may take the form of participation by either individual employers or wider employer organisations. In some partnerships, such as those supported by national government programmes in the United Kingdom and Ireland, business membership of partnership bodies takes place on the basis of a clearly defined number of 'seats' for the business 'constituency', but elsewhere things are much more *ad hoc*. The nature and commitment of private sector interests can range from large-scale commercial and development interests for whom the financial stakes are considerable, to smaller and more locally-based firms. Some private sector partners will be looking to partnerships for the profit opportunities in large-scale regeneration schemes, or for the benefits from training and labour market schemes, whereas others may regard participation as a way of influencing the local policy agenda while at the same time being seen to be 'giving something back to the community' in terms of public relations and local goodwill, especially perhaps by involvement in partnership projects dealing with high-profile social issues such as youth crime or drug abuse. However, in some deprived areas the absence of significant private sector activity in the local economy may make it difficult for partnerships to find private sector partners.

Trade union involvement was a feature of only about one-third of the partnerships in the research, despite the EU's commitment to the involvement of both of the social partners. Trade unions were actively involved in a number of local partnerships, especially in countries where EU influence is strong such as Greece and Ireland, and in partnerships where the emphasis is on unemployment and the regeneration of the local economy, for example in some LEDA partnerships and other local partnership companies in Ireland, where trade union representation is derived from a formula established by national agreement (Walsh, Craig and McCafferty 1997). Trade union involvement is often in the form of activity by individual trade unionists, although there are also some examples of more formal organisational participation, as in local initiatives supported by the Fonds pour l'Emploi programme in Belgium, where an agreement between employers and trade unions to devote a small proportion of the wage bill to projects for excluded groups supports a number of locally-based initiatives (Carton, Delogne, Nicaise and Stengele 1996). In Germany and Austria trade unions have played an active role in a number of partnership-type initiatives concerned with issues such as employment and training. The Labour Foundation Programme in Carinthia, and the Women's Foundation in Steyr, both in Austria, both involve partnership between the social partners and public authorities at regional and local levels to provide new employment in areas of industrial restructuring (Kain and Rosian 1996).

Voluntary sector agencies and organisations were represented in over half the local partnerships identified in the research. This representation includes both major national and transnational charities – such as Barnardos or Caritas – and smaller, often local, voluntary and charitable organisations. Voluntary organisations were involved particularly in those partnerships focused on social issues, but also in many of the broader local regeneration or anti-poverty partnerships. This involvement reflects the emergence of a 'mixed market' in the provision of social services, with a greater role for not-for-profit providers in some (northern European) countries where public provision was previously dominant. In some other member states, especially in southern Europe, welfare has traditionally depended heavily on the non-governmental sector. In a number of cases, voluntary organisations acted as influential 'brokers' in partnerships between public agencies and local communities and excluded groups.

Community sector organisations and interests[10] were represented in about half the local partnerships analysed. This can happen in a number of ways – via community organisations, such as tenants and residents groups, or those representing communities of interest, such as women; or by the election or nomination of 'community' representatives on to partnership bodies (Chanan 1997). However, the direct representation of community interests was by no means a feature of all local partnerships. In some, 'community' interests were represented (or deemed to be represented) by local politicians or officials from local public agencies. In others, local communities or excluded groups were consulted or represented in specific projects but not in the main partnership structure.

Conclusion

Partnerships therefore represent local institutional arenas in which a plurality of local interests – the 'key players' in policy jargon – are brought together to address issues of economic and social regeneration. In partnerships, the conventions of pluralist 'interest' representation impose a framework within which class interests (of capital and labour, from the three spheres of the state, the market and civil society)[11] are mediated in a neo-corporatist or neo-pluralist arena, predicated upon the feasibility of a consensual politics and policy-making, engaging and managing conflicting needs and interests and differences in power. In the ensuing chapters, we will explore some of the issues that partnership raises and that are suggested by this initial overview. To an important extent, these issues differ, or emerge in a different form, from country to country, and part of the purpose of the book is to present and understand such differences. Nonetheless, a number of common themes can be identified.

10 The dividing line between 'voluntary' and 'community' interests and organisations is indistinct, both empirically and theoretically, although the distinction between NGOs and social movement is a relevant one.
11 And to a lesser extent those of gender and race.

Partnership is predicated on the possibility of consensus or coalition. To be effective, local partnership requires the identification by all those concerned of mutual interests, the negotiation of a common strategy and agenda of action, and the commitment of mutual resources (Mackintosh 1992). To do so will mean overcoming or managing a number of potential conflicts of interest or ideology, but there is considerable evidence of the difficulties of achieving this (Hastings 1996), at any rate to a more than very limited extent (Bassett 1996). The ability of partnerships to negotiate and manage such conflicts is a particularly acute issue when the 'stake' of partnership is poverty and social exclusion, and the objective is the distribution of power and resources towards less favoured areas and social groups (Estivill 1994; Geddes 1997; Harding 1997). While partnership may assume a shared commitment to the norms and ways of working of partnership activity, partners will bring different values and cultures into the partnership, and these differences will assume particular importance at times of conflict.

The current emphasis on partnership involves a good deal of rhetoric, and it is often not clear what commitments 'membership' of a partnership actually implies. There has been considerable doubt cast, for example, on the degree of real input of many businesses to partnerships to which they are formally 'signed up' (Imrie and Thomas 1993; Peck and Tickell 1995). Equally, for many public sector bodies, involvement in partnerships is seen as peripheral to their main responsibilities, and little political or technical support is given to representatives on partnership bodies. Moreover, many local partnerships have been either experimental in nature or limited in scope, timescale and/or resources, raising questions as to whether they possess the organisational capacity necessary to function as an important element in new structures of local governance (Healey 1998). There are further issues about whether and how the experiences gained in local partnerships that form part of experimental pilot programmes can be transferred to mainstream policy and action. How can the experiences of individual local partnerships be shared more effectively so that good practice is disseminated at the grass roots, and how can those local experiences be integrated into wider policy networks and programmes?

Some of these questions would be easier to answer if more were known about the impact and outcomes of local partnerships, but there is relatively limited hard evidence about the outcomes of partnership-based action against social exclusion. This reflects, partly, general difficulties in evaluating the impact of policy, and specifically the 'added value' of a partnership approach (Monnier 1997). In this book, the contributions from different countries offer important insights into the extent to which local partnerships 'work' as effective frameworks through which to tackle the problems of social exclusion. However, the fact that the current enthusiasm of governments for partnership is not underpinned by much empirical evidence of performance itself needs to be explained, and our concern will be as much to understand the conditions and contexts in which local partnership is, or is not, perceived as an important part of the 'answer' to social exclusion, as with the question of 'what works'.

References

6, Perri (1997a) *Escaping Poverty: From Safety Nets to Networks of Opportunity*. London: Demos.

6, Perri (1997b) Social exclusion: Time to be optimistic. *Demos Collection* 12, 3–9.

Abrahamson P and Hansen F K (1996) *Poverty in the European Union*. European Parliament.

Adshead M and Quinn B (1998) The move from government to governance: Irish development policy's paradigm shift. *Policy and Politics* 26, 2, 209–25.

Allen J (1998) Europe of the neighbourhoods: Class, citizenship and welfare regimes, in Madanipour, Cars and Allen (eds.), op cit, 25–51.

Allen J, Massey D and Cochrane A (1998) *Rethinking the Region*. London: Routledge.

Amin A and Tomaney J (eds.) (1995) *Behind the Myth of European Union: Prospects for Cohesion*. London: Routledge.

Anderson P (1998) *The Origins of Postmodernity*, London: Verso.

Atkinson A B (1998) *Poverty in Europe*, Oxford: Blackwell.

Bartley B (1998) Exclusion, invisibility and the neighbourhood in West Dublin, in Madanipour, Cars and Allen (eds.), op cit, 131–56.

Bassett K (1996) Partnerships, business elites and urban politics: New forms of governance in an English city. *Urban Studies* 33, 3, 539–55.

Bauman Z (1998) *Work, Consumerism and the New Poor*. Buckingham: Open University Press.

Benington J and Harvey J (1999) Networking in Europe, in Stoker G (ed.) *The New Management of Local Governance*. Basingstoke: Macmillan.

Benington J and Taylor M (1994) Changes and Challenges Facing the UK Welfare State in the Europe of the 1990s, in J Ferris and R Page (eds.) *Social Policy in Transition*, Avebury.

Beresford P and Turner M (1997) *It's Our Welfare: Report of the Citizens' Commission on the Welfare State*. London: National Institute for Social Work.

Berghman J (1992) A Multi-Method Approach to Monitor the Evaluation of Poverty. *Journal of European Social Policy* 2, 3, 193–213.

Bruto da Costa A (1994) *The Contribution of Poverty 3 to the Understanding of Poverty, Exclusion and Integration*, Lille: EEIG Animation et Recherche.

Byrne D (1997) Social exclusion and capitalism:the reserve army across space and time, *Critical Social Policy* 17, 27–51.

Campbell B (1994) *Goliath: Britain's Dangerous Places*. London: Methuen.

Carton B, Delogne R, Nicaise I and Stengele A (1996) *The Role of Partnerships in Promoting Social Cohesion: Research Report for Belgium*. Dublin: European Foundation for the Improvement of Living and Working Conditions.

CEEP (1994) *European Declaration of Businesses against Exclusion*. Brussels: European Centre of Enterprises with Public Participation.

Chanan G (1997) *Active Citizenship: Getting to the Roots*. Dublin: European Foundation for the Improvement of Living and Working Conditions.

Commission of the European Communities (1989) *Medium-Term Community Action Programme to Foster the Economic and Social Integration of the Least Privileged Groups*. Brussels: Bulletin of the European Communities, Supplement 4/89.

Commission of the European Communities (1993a) *European Social Policy: Options for the Union*, European Commission, DGV, COM (93) 551.

Commission of the European Communities (1993b) *Growth, Competitiveness, Employment. The Challenges and Ways Forward into the 21st Century*. White Paper, Bulletin, Supplement 6/93.

Commission of the European Communities (1994a) *European Social Policy – The Way Forward for the Union (White Paper)*. COM (94) 333.

Commission of the European Communities (1994b) *Local Development Strategies in Economically Disintegrated Areas: A Pro-Active Strategy Against Poverty in the European Community*. Brussels: European Commission Social Papers 5.

Commission of the European Communities (1994c) *Guide to Community Initiatives 1994–9*. Brussels.

Commission of the European Communities (1995a) *European Strategy for Encouraging Local Development and Employment Strategies*, Brussels: COM (95) 273 final.

Commission of the European Communities (1995b) *Medium-Term Social Action Programme 1995–97*, Brussels: Social Europe 1/95, DGV.

Commission of the European Communities (1996b) *Employment in Europe 1996*. Luxembourg: Office for Official Publications.

Commission of the European Communities (1997a) *First Report on Economic and Social Cohesion 1996*. Luxembourg: Office for Official Publications.

Commission of the European Communities (1997b) *Employment in Europe 1997*. Luxembourg: Office for Official Publications.

Commission of the European Communities (1997c) *European Cohesion Forum, Working Documents, Workshop 1 (Partnership)*. Brussels: European Cohesion Forum.

Commission of the European Communities (1998) *Employment in Europe 1997*. Luxembourg: Office for Official Publications.

Commission of the European Communities (1999) *Employment in Europe 1998*. Luxembourg: Office for Official Publications.

Conroy P (1994) Evaluation of the Achievements of Poverty 3: Synthesis. *Social Europe*, Vol 2. Brussels, European Commission DGV.

Cousins M (1997) *New Directions in Social Welfare: Report of a Conference of the Irish Presidency of the European Union*. Dublin: European Foundation for the Improvement of Living and Working Conditions.

Cousins C (1997) Social exclusion in Europe: Paradigms of social disadvantage in Germany, Spain, Sweden and the United Kingdom. *Policy and Politics* 26, 2, 127–46.

Deakin N, Davis A and Thomas N (1995) *Public Welfare Services and Social Exclusion: The Development of Consumer-Oriented Initiatives in the European Union*. Dublin: European Foundation for the Improvement of Living and Working Conditions.

Duffy K (1998) *Review of the International Dimensions of the Thematic Priority on Social Integration and Exclusion: a Report to the Economic and Social Research Council*. Leicester: de Montfort University.

Dunford M and Perrons D (1994) Regional inequality, regimes of accumulation and economic development in contemporary Europe, *Transactions of the Institute of British Geographers* 19, 163–82.

Estivill J et al (1994) *Partnership and the Fight against Exclusion*, Poverty 3 Programme. Lille: EEIG Animation et Recherche.

European Anti-poverty Network (1998) *Poverty in Europe*. Brussels: EAPN.

European Business Network for Social Cohesion (1996) *Corporate Initiatives: Putting Into Practice the European Declaration of Businesses Against Exclusion*. Brussels: King Baudouin Foundation.

European Communities, Economic and Social Committee (1993a) *Social Exclusion – Opinion*. Brussels.

European Communities, Economic and Social Committee (1993b) *Medium-Term Action Programme to Foster the Integration of the Most Disadvantaged Social Groups – Opinion*. Brussels.

European Communities, Economic and Social Committee (1997) *Opinion on the First Cohesion Report*. Brussels.

European Parliament (1997) *Assessment of the EU's Structural Expenditure, Part II: Social Policy Expenditure*. Luxembourg: European Parliament, Directorate General for Research.

European Trade Union Institute (ETUI) (1993) *The European Structural Funds in the Regions: Experiences of Trade Union Participation*. Brussels: ETUI.

Fainstein N (1996) A note on interpreting urban poverty, in Mingione E (ed.), *Urban Poverty and the Underclass: A Reader*. Oxford: Blackwell, 153–9.

Fonteneau G (undated) *Les Syndicats Face a L'Exclusion et aux Précarités Sociales*. Brussels: Bilan des Actions de la Confederation Europeenne des Syndicats et ses Organisations.

Fraser N (1996) The value of locality, in King D and Stoker G (eds.) *Rethinking Local Democracy*. Basingstoke: Macmillan.

Gans H J (1996) From 'underclass' to 'undercaste': Some observations about the future of the post-industrial economy and its major victims, in Mingione (ed.) (1996), 141–52.

Geddes M (1997) Poverty, excluded communities and local democracy, in McGregor S and Jewson N (eds.), *Transforming Cities: Contested Governance and New Spatial Divisions*. London: Routledge.

Geddes M (1998) *Local Partnership: A Successful Strategy for Social Cohesion?* Dublin: European Foundation for the Improvement of Living and Working Conditions.

Giddens A (1998) *The Third Way: The Renewal of Social Democracy*. Cambridge: Polity Press.

Gore C with Figueiredo J B and Rodgers G (1995) Introduction: markets, citizenship and social exclusion, in Rodgers, Gore and Figueiredo (eds.), op cit.

Griffiths J (1995) *Business and Social Exclusion: A Guide to Good Practice*. London: British Telecom.

Hadjimichalis C and Sadler D (eds.) (1995) *Europe at the Margins: New Mosaics of Inequality*. Chichester: John Wiley.

Hadjimichalis C and Sadler D (1995) Integration, Marginality and the New Europe, in Hadjimichalis and Sadler (eds.), op cit, 3–14.

Harding A (1997) Urban regimes in a Europe of the cities? *European Urban and Regional Studies* 4, 4, 291–314.

Harvey D (1990) *The Condition of Postmodernity*. Oxford: Blackwell.

Hastings A (1996) Unravelling the process of 'partnership' in urban regeneration policy. *Urban Studies* 33, 2, 253–68.

Hastings A, MacArthur A and McGregor A (1996) *Less Than Equal? Community Organisations and Estate Regeneration Partnerships*. Bristol: Policy Press.

Healey P (1998) Institutionalist theory, social exclusion and governance, in Madanipour, Cars and Allen (eds.), op cit, 53–73.

Held D (1995) *Democracy and the Global Order: From the Modern State to Cosmopolitan Governance*. Cambridge: Polity Press.

Hirst P (1994) *Associative Democracy*. Cambridge: Polity Press.

Humphreys E (1996) *LEDA Pilot Actions: Synthesis Report*. Brussels: European Commission, DGV.

Imrie R and Thomas H (1993) The limits of property-led regeneration, *Environment and Planning C: Government and Policy* 11, 87–102.

Jameson F (1991) *Postmodernism, or the Cultural Logic of Late Capitalism*. Durham: Duke University Press.

Jessop B (1993) Towards a Schumpeterian workfare state? Preliminary remarks on postFordist political economy, *Studies in Political Economy* 40, 7–39.

Kain E and Rosian I (1996) *The Role of Partnerships in Promoting Social Cohesion: Research Report for Austria*. Dublin: European Foundation for the Improvement of Living and Working Conditions.

Kesteloot C (1995) The creation of socio-spatial marginalisation in Brussels: A tale of flexibility, geographical competition and guestworker neighbourhoods, in Hadjimichalis and Sadler (eds.), op cit, 69–86.

LASAIRE (1995) *Combating Social Exclusion in Europe: Creating Integrated Labour Market Entry Schemes*. Lille: Proceedings of LASAIRE Seminar.

Lawless P, Martin R and Hardy S (1998) *Unemployment and Social Exclusion: Landscapes of Labour Inequality*. London: Jessica Kingsley.

Lea J (1997) Postfordism and criminality, in McGregor and Jewson (eds.), op cit, 42–55.

Leibfried S (1993) Towards a European welfare state? On integrating poverty regimes into the European Community, in Jones C (ed.) *New Perspectives on the Welfare State in Europe*. London: Routledge.

Leibfried S and Pierson P (1992) Prospects for social Europe, *Politics and Society* 20, 3, 333–66.

Leibfried S and Pierson P (eds.) (1995) *European Social Policy: Between Fragmentation and Integration*. Washington DC: Brookings Institute.

Leonard P (1997) *Postmodern Welfare: Reconstructing an Emancipatory Project*. London: Sage.

Levitas R (1996) The concept of social exclusion and the new Durkheimian hegemony, *Critical Social Policy* 16, 1, 5–20.

Mackintosh M (1992) Partnership: Issues of policy and negotiation. *Local Economy* 7, 3, 210–24.

Madanipour A (1998) Social exclusion and space, in Madanipour, Cars and Allen (eds.), op cit, 75–89.

Madanipour A, Cars G and Allen J (1998) *Social Exclusion in European Cities*. London: Jessica Kingsley.

Martin R (1998) *Regional Dimensions of Europe's Unemployment Crisis*, in Lawless, Martin and Hardy (eds.), op cit, 11–48.

McGregor S and Jewson N (1997) *Transforming Cities: Contested Governance and New Spatial Divisions*. London: Routledge.

Meadows G (1996) Territorial and local employment pacts, structural funds and European initiatives, in Cousins M (ed.) *Local Development: The Irish Experience in European Context*. Dublin: Department of the Taoiseach, 96–103.

Mingione E (ed.) (1996) *Urban Poverty and the Underclass: A Reader*. Oxford: Blackwell.

Mingione E (1997) Enterprise and exclusion, *Demos Collection* 12, 10–12.

Monnier E (1997) 'Vertical' partnerships: The opportunities and constraints which they pose for high quality evaluation, *Evaluation* 3, 1, 110–18.

Moulaert F (1994) *Restructuration économique urbaine: Polarisation sociale et réponses locales*. Paper to international conference on Cities, Enterprises and Society at the Eve of the XXIst Century. Lille: IFRESI, University of Lille.

Nicaise I and Henriques J-M (eds.) (1995) *Trade Unions, Unemployment and Social Exclusion*. Leuven: Hoger Instituut voor der Arbeit, K U Universitat.

Oppenheim C (1998) *An Inclusive Society: Strategies for Tackling Poverty*. London: IPPR.

Organisation for Economic Cooperation and Development, Environment Directorate (1994) *The Multi-sectoral Approach to Urban Regeneration: Towards a New Strategy for Social Integration, Housing Affordability and Livable Environments*. Final Report of the Project Group on Housing, Social Integration and Livable Environments in Cities, OECD, Paris, ENV/UA/H(94)1.

Oska J (1995) Remote rural areas: Villages on the northern margin, in Hadjimichalis and Sadler (eds.), op cit, 107–22.

Paugam S (1998) Poverty and social exclusion: A sociological view, in Rhodes and Meny (eds.), op cit, 41–62.

Peach C (1998) Loic Wacquant's 'Three Pernicious Premises in the Study of the American Ghetto', *International Journal of Urban and Regional Research* 22, 3, 507–10.

Peck J A and Tickell A (1995) Business goes local: dissecting the 'business agenda' in Manchester. *International Journal of Urban and Regional Research* 19, 1, 55–78.

Perrons D (1998) Gender as a form of social exclusion: Gender inequality in the regions of Europe, in Lawless, Martin and Hardy (eds.), op cit, 154–81.

Power A (1997) *Estates on the Edge*. London: Macmillan.

Pugliese E (1995) New international migrations and the 'European fortress', in Hadjimichalis and Sadler (eds.), op cit, 51–68.

Rhodes M and Meny Y (eds.) (1998) *The Future of European Welfare: A New Social Contract?* London: Macmillan.

Robbins D (ed.) (1992) *Observatory on National Policies to Combat Social Exclusion, Second Annual Report*. Lille: EEIG.

Rodgers G (1995) What is special about a social exclusion approach?, in Rodgers, Gore and Figueiredo (eds.), op cit, 43–56.

Rodgers G, Gore C and Figueiredo JB (1995) *Social Exclusion: Rhetoric, Reality, Responses*. Geneva: ILO.

Room G (ed.) (1995) *Beyond the Threshold: The Measurement and Analysis of Social Exclusion*. Bristol: Policy Press.

Room G (1994) *Poverty Studies in the European Union: Retrospect and Prospect*. Paper to conference on Understanding Social Exclusion: Lessons from Transnational Research Studies. London: PSI.

Sibley D (1995) *Geographies of Exclusion: Society and Difference in the West*. London and New York: Routledge.

Silver H (1994) Social exclusion and social solidarity: Three paradigms, *International Labour Review* 133 (5–6) 531–78.

Silver H (1996) Culture, politics and national discourses of the new urban underclass, in Mingione (ed.) (1996), op. cit, 105–37.

Silver H (1995) Reconceptualising social disadvantage: Three paradigms of social exclusion, in Rodgers, Gore and Figueiredo (eds.) op. cit, 57–80.

Streek W (1995) From market making to state building? Reflections on the political economy of European social policy. In Leibfried and Pierson (eds.) (1995), op. cit.

Taylor-Gooby P (1997) In defence of second best theory: State, class and capital in social policy, *Journal of Social Policy* 26, 2, 171–92.

UNICE (1997) *Position Paper on the First Report on Economic and Social Cohesion in the European Union*. Brussels: European Commission, European Cohesion Forum.

Vaiou D (1995) Women of the South after, like before, Maastricht, in Hadjimichalis and Sadler (eds.) op cit, 35–49.

Van den Bosch K (1998) The evolution of financial poverty in western Europe, in Rhodes and Meny (eds.), op cit, 97–124.

Vignon J (1996) European political framework: From local initiatives to local and territorial pacts. In Cousins M (ed.) *Local Development: The Irish Experience in European Context*. Dublin: Department of the Taoiseach, 65–69.

Vranken J (1995) *La dimension urbaine de l'exclusion sociale*. Conference, Territoires Urbains et Cohesion Sociale en Europe: Paris.

Wacquant L (1993) Urban outcasts: stigma and division in the black American ghetto and the French urban periphery, *International Journal of Urban and Regional Research* 17, 3, 366–83.

Walsh J, Craig S and McCafferty D (1997) *The Role of Partnerships in Promoting Social Cohesion: Research Report for Ireland*. Dublin: European Foundation for the Improvement of Living and Working Conditions.

Zukin S (1998) How bad is it? Institutions and intentions in the study of the American Ghetto, *International Journal of Urban and Regional Research* 22, 3, 511–20.

3 Partnerships against exclusion in a Nordic welfare state

A difficult mix?

Mikko Kautto and Matti Heikkilä

Introduction

In contrast to the experience of some other European countries, Finland appears as a country where partnerships have not risen to the level of political conciousness and where interest in them has so far appeared mild.[1] Only a few years ago even the notion 'partnership' was unfamiliar and not in common use. Thus not surprisingly, at the time of our study on partnerships in 1996 (Heikkilä and Kautto 1997), Finland had not introduced any national policy programmes that would promote partnership-type responses to exclusion, as had been done for instance in the UK and Ireland. In short, partnerships were neither recognised nor promoted at the national level. Yet there were local initiatives – although not referred to as 'partnerships' by their initiators and actors involved – that could well be distinguished as partnerships, if understood broadly as organised cooperation uniting local forces around a common agenda. However, these weak signs of local activity were not suggesting a breakthrough in the spread of partnerships, and so the key conclusion of the study was that partnerships were a marginal phenomenon in Finland.

In this chapter we look for explanations as to why partnerships in Finland, unlike in some other European countries, have not developed into significant tools in promoting social cohesion. The macro-perspective adopted in this article does not intend to imply that detailed studies of local partnerships would not reveal important insights and impediments to their progress in the local context. Our approach is actually motivated by our experience of those types of questions. As in the report on Local Partnerships and Social Cohesion in Finland (Heikkilä and Kautto 1997) our focus was precisely to

---

1 We examined the roles of partnerships in promoting social cohesion in Finland (Heikkilä and Kautto 1997) as part of the research project co-ordinated by the European Foundation for the Improvement of Living and Working Conditions.

study partnerships at work. Case studies revealed information about the use of resources, the views of key actors, the schemes in operation, how partnerships work in practice etc., but the additional insight gained in the course of the study was that there seemed to be something more than organisational characteristics to explain the diffusion of partnerships in Finland. In this article we attempt to go one step forward from the case studies to try to relate the diffusion and importance of partnerships to the characteristics of the Finnish (or more broadly, Nordic) welfare state.

In the first part of the article, we present some key characteristics of partnerships against exclusion in Finland. Partnership has not had a high profile as a solution to current problems, and when there have been attempts to establish partnerships they have faced some difficulty. Partnerships are rare and highly dependent on public sector actors. To a great extent this is due to the institutional characteristics of the Finnish welfare state, which have left neither room nor demand for alternative solutions in handling social problems. The leading proposition of the article is that in Finland not only have there been organisational and other micro-level impediments to flourishing partnerships, but also constraints created by the institutional logic of the Finnish welfare state. The article ends by pointing to a number of recent developments that could pave the way for the spread of partnerships in the future.

Partnerships in Finland: rare and dependent

In Finland, the notion of partnership is not widely used, partnerships have no place on the political agenda, and nor do they have any kind of legal status. Looking at forms of cooperation that could be termed as partnerships, a typical picture emerges of fairly heterogeneous operations, in which the dominant themes are young people's workshops, training and education schemes for the long-term unemployed and projects concerned with taking control of one's life. As a result of growing unemployment, training and rehabilitation centres and workshops can nowadays be found in nearly every region. They are clearly local initiatives based on a willingness to cooperate rather than a response to national or European level manifestos. Besides, most existing cooperation between different social actors cannot be characterised as 'real' partnerships in the sense of the UK for example, but as forms of cooperation such as employment projects, action centres, planning and development projects.

Thus, Finland cannot boast of a 'typically Finnish' approach to the principle of partnership. However, if we examine cooperation that fulfills the operational definition of partnership (see Chapter 1), a number of common features can be discerned. We shall now concentrate on three issues that we think important for understanding partnerships in the context of the Finnish welfare state: actors in partnerships, their aims, and financing issues.

Actors in partnerships

Taking a little closer look at key actors in the partnerships in Finland it becomes evident the major actors are the *local authorities*[2] and *voluntary organisations*. This overall pattern is broken by variation in what could be termed 'assisting' partners. The Church, local business, boards of trade, different societies and associations add to local variation, but there is very little involvement on the part of the social partners. The employers' associations and workers' organisations have not indicated any great desire to work at local levels, at least not along these lines. In addition to local authorities and voluntary organisations a third important actor should be stressed: the role of the state administration in the guise of its *ministries* is visible in the financing of projects. A common feature for most of the partnerships seems to be that funding comes from the ministries and/or municipality, and the key actors are the local authorities and voluntary organisations. Thus, if partnerships have a vertical dimension, it originates from one of the ministries dealing with welfare (especially the Ministries of Social Affairs and Health, Labour, Education and Environment).

A few words are needed to explain the relationships between these three central actors and partnership composition. In the Nordic countries the state and local authorities have had a paradoxical relationship (Baldersheim and Ståhlberg 1999). On the one hand, the country has been centrally led, yet there is a surprisingly high degree of local autonomy visible in taxation rights and forms of local democracy. Vertical governing relations have been efficient; over the years the local authorities have developed a portfolio of services to meet the legislation enacted at national level. The state has used ear-marked subsidies as a carrot to influence the local authorities' decisions and help the poorest ones to carry out the suggested reforms. The municipalities in turn have not questioned the mandate of the central government to guide and assist local development. It is not an overstatement to say that the 450 municipalities – covering every square metre of land area and incorporating every inhabitant – have been the tool for realising central government policies.

Turning from vertical relations to horizontal relations the relationship between the local authorities and the voluntary organisations in Finland is also special. There is no clear boundary between the public sector and civil society. Particularly over the last 20 years there has been a certain degree of coexistence at the local level: the municipalities have had a far-reaching responsibility for citizens' welfare, while voluntary organisations have retained a type of quality testing or product development role, or have been responsible for purchased services for target groups in some municipalities. It is important to note that they have not cast doubt on the municipalities'

2 Instead of the municipality as an entity, it would be more accurate to speak of different administrative sectors, which are very well adapted to independent cooperation.

role as key service providers. The relationship between municipality and voluntary organisations has thus been complementary rather than competitive (Matthies 1991).

One can argue that the close relations between the state and local authorities on the one hand and the local authorities and voluntary organisations on the other have contributed to Finland becoming a 'public service state' (Kohl 1981; Castles 1998). As a Nordic country, Finland is a public service state when it comes to social policy, with only little room for voluntary organisations (Kuhnle and Selle 1992; Ervasti 1996: 25). On the other hand, no society exists where the state (in a broad sense) is in sole charge of all welfare provision. The unofficial and private sectors have at least to some degree acted alongside the public sector in all welfare states. It is also noteworthy that in all the ideologies, theories and manifestos concerning the welfare state, an element of responsibility has remained with unofficial actors or the private sector (Ervasti 1996: 23).

In Finland, the activities of voluntary organisations in social policy have mainly been integrated into the operations of the public sector. Finnish organisations providing services are relatively wealthy and influential, but at the same time they tend to be paper tigers in relation to the public sector actors. Their close integration into the state is attributable to the financial arrangements but also to the mutual administrative interlockings between organisations and government. However, the close connections with government have not rendered voluntary operations altogether impossible (Anttonen and Sipilä 1992).

It is estimated that Finland has 155 nationwide organisations working in the welfare and health domain. They in turn have some 6,000 local associations or branch offices. Of these 155 organisations, 113 belong to the Association of Voluntary Health, Social and Welfare Organisations. Another source of information about the scope of voluntary organisations is provided by the Finnish Slot Machine Association.[3] In 1997, the Association gave assistance to over 900 organisations, the majority of which operated locally. The final accounts or turnovers of these 900 social and health organisations totalled 6.1 billion Finnish marks in 1997, and their balance sheets showed a grand total of almost 10 billion marks. The number of personnel in the 900 organisations subsidised by the Slot Machine Association amounted to 19,300.

When these figures are put into perspective with the public sector, one starting point is the public social expenditure, which in 1997 was some 195 billion Finnish marks. The staff employed in the social and health services numbered 220,000. Thus, the turnover of the organisations

---

3 The Finnish Slot Machine Association represents the interests of both the state (Ministry of Social Affairs and Health) and voluntary organisations (in the social and health sphere). It is a monopoly collecting the profits from slot machine gambling to be distributed for voluntary organisations' investments and operation costs.

supported by the Slot Machine Association corresponds to 3 per cent of public social expenditure. The personnel of the organisations corresponds to less than 9 per cent of the public sector staff.

Local parishes employed approximately 1000 deacons working in the social field in 1997. At the same time 3,200 people were employed in social work in municipalities or federations of municipalities. Thus, the personnel resources in parishes correspond to 33 per cent of municipal social work human resources. Judged by size, deacons are a group of social welfare professionals second only to municipal social services.

The most important potential of voluntary work is in the ideological and political capacity of the organisations. At their best, voluntary organisations can accomplish much more than the state or enterprises. On the other hand, voluntary sector social service provision involves certain problems, the most central of which is perhaps the particular nature of the activities: services are available to some people and in some places, but not for all those in need (Anttonen and Sipilä 1992: 447). This has been one important justification for the central government to allocate responsibility for services to munici-palities rather than to organisations belonging to civil society.

Aims of partnerships

Thus, public authorities are clearly dominant actors and they are pursuing mainly social goals. Accordingly, partnerships cannot be said to challenge the public sector. On the contrary, to some extent one could think of partner-ships as extensions to, or experiments within, the public sector. Based on our earlier study, partnerships could be interpreted as tools to mend holes in the welfare state machinery. Two interconnected reasons appeared to explain the activity of partnerships in Finland: addressing diverse forms of exclusion and rethinking sector-based boundaries of public administration.

Partnership activity has addressed diverse concerns but most often the target group is the part of the population in danger of social exclusion, i.e. mainly the unemployed and those for other reasons not adequately reached by existing policy. The dominant themes for local activity are young people's workshops, training and education schemes for the long-term unemployed and projects concerned with taking control of one's life. The majority of the projects are directly or indirectly the result of unemployment, which is generally seen as the prime cause of wider social exclusion.

From a realisation of the multidimensional nature of exclusion there thus emerged a far more general *raison d'être* for partnership schemes. The argu-ment for them is found in the inability of sectoral and social group-based policy to deal with social exclusion, which spreads across the sector/group borders. It should be stressed that there are few who call into question the necessity of existing organisational systems. Direct or indirect criticism of them flows instead in reaction to the inadequacy of either voluntary schemes or to the failure of social policy to address the needs of certain problem groups. Major justifications for partnerships in Finland thus appeared to be that:

1 they can tackle the problem of exclusion better than current organisations; and/or
2 they can, in some cases, deal with the socially excluded who are beyond
   the reach of the official support system.

In addition to benefiting their target groups, partnerships in Finland have often had another important agenda. One major goal was to improve the level of cooperation between organisations that were seen to be working along separate lines. Especially where public authorities had a leading position there was a search for new intersectoral working methods and cost-saving practices. Here the structural aspects of partnership were vitally important. The right selection of participant partners affected the extent to which the partnership had authority, and avoided conflict. The choice of partners also influenced the amount of disposable resources.

Funding

The international literature often refers to how partnerships may be good at attracting funding from different sources. Against this, the lack of non-public funding in Finland is striking. All the partnerships we examined worked mainly with the support of public money. Private funding was practically non-existent. The sources of funding for partnerships are the municipality, the Slot Machine Association or a ministry. So far, private business has not shown any interest in financing these kinds of local projects, and neither, apparently, have they been asked for help of this sort. The labour organisations still see their role as that of monitoring their members' welfare at the national level. Voluntary organisations do not have many resources for themselves, let alone enough to circulate more widely. Residents and target groups do not have any channels of funding to motivate them to participate.

It might also be wondered whether there are enough preconditions for partnerships based on principles of equality in Finland as long as their existence is made possible only with public financing. An important issue for the sustainability of partnerships is that public funding is always linked to political decisions and timescales. Partnerships need to justify their position by achieving better results or by achieving the same results more cheaply and efficiently. The procurement of resources and the assurance of continued support are thus basically uncertain, especially during times of economic instability, when the idea of long-term budgetary commitment is not entertained. This uncertainty of continued support is at odds with the long-term endeavour of preventing social exclusion.

Summing up the nature and scope of existing partnerships in Finland, it is necessary to refer both to partner-coalition, where the public actors usually play the leading roles, and to financing, as the lifespan of partnerships relies almost entirely on public funding. Thus, if the public actors think about withdrawal from a partnership, either as funders or as actors, this most likely also means the end of the partnership. Partnerships in Finland are both rare and, when they do exist, heavily dependent on the public sector.

The crucial role of public authorities and the social aims of partnerships lead to a perspective on partnerships as extension of the public sector rather than as independent challengers to the present system. From the public sector's perspective the question of how reasonable it is for the public sector to fund partnerships is a key consideration. Financing bodies must know why it is worth their while to support *ad hoc* partnerships rather than to channel money for the upkeep and development of the existing public social system. So far the answer has been to rely on traditional methods and we will examine reasons for this.

Partnerships have difficulty fitting in a Nordic welfare state

We believe that to understand the phenomenon of partnership in Finland, it is necessary to examine it in the context of the Finnish welfare state. From this perspective partnerships have so far not been an option for three important reasons. First, public policies have been all-encompassing, not leaving much room for other actors and alternative non-public solutions. Second, the normative principles of the Finnish welfare state are in opposition to some of the partnership principles. Third, policies have been efficient in the sense that poverty and exclusion haven't become widespread, thus creating little demand for other options to deal with these problems. In short, there has been lack of space, lack of legitimacy and lack of demand. We shall consider these three points next.

There is not much room for other than public policies

When Finland achieved independence in 1917, it was by European standards a poor country. An undeveloped social security system focused on the most obvious problems in society. Self-help schemes, employers' welfare schemes and voluntary organisations had an important role up to the start of the Second World War. Employers were, under the Poor Relief Act, obliged to take care of their employees and their spouses and minors and ensure that they did not become a burden on poor relief. Local authorities, for their part, were responsible for poor relief in their particular area in accordance with the provisions of the Poor Relief Act. The role of voluntary organisations was to attend to those needs that fell outside the protection afforded by work contracts and the Poor Relief Act. These organisations concentrated their efforts on various sectors of welfare. There were national organisations for different target groups such as children, the sick, the elderly and the disabled. The local authorities, parishes and voluntary organisations co-operated in the solution of local problems, while the means of cooperation depended on the issue to be solved. Any social activity on the part of a private company was generally confined to the welfare of its own staff. Similarly, workers' own associations and their mutual funds focused on improving the welfare of their members (Jaakkola, Pulma, Satka and Urponen 1994; Hellsten 1993).

Finnish society experienced rapid structural change from the 1950s (Alestalo and Uusitalo 1986), and the shift from what was mainly an agrarian society into an industrialised one meant the start of a period of socio-political reforms and increasing state involvement. Public policies went through a period of reassessment. In social policy, social insurance schemes now began to broaden in scale. Reforms in national insurance schemes were followed by the introduction of public health and social services in the 1970s and 1980s. Social expenditure rose on average 8 per cent a year and in the latter half of the 1980s Finland's began to match that of other European countries when measured as a proportion of the GNP. Assessed on a number of criteria, it could be established that by the 1980s Finland had become part of the Nordic social policy model (Kangas 1993).

Evidence from comparative studies has shown that Nordic countries usually cluster together (e.g. Esping-Andersen 1990, Castles 1993), hence the justification of talk of a separate Nordic model (Eriksson, Hansen, Ringen and Uusitalo 1987). Despite much research on the peculiarities of Nordic social policy, there is no agreed list of characteristics defining a Nordic welfare state. In comparative welfare state research, the Nordic notion, or Scandinavian model in its broadest sense, has been used to refer to countries that have been able to combine economic growth and good overall economic performance with high levels of social protection and social rights. At the beginning of the 1990s the Nordic countries Denmark, Finland, Norway and Sweden all had GNP/capita above the OECD average (OECD 1997). At the same time their poverty rates were among the lowest to be found in the world (Atkinson, Rainwater and Smeeding 1995). Politicians could boast how economic success – thanks to carefully designed redistribution policies – was contributing to the wellbeing of the whole population. In narrower terms, the Nordic model has been characterised by high employ-ment rates, a broad sphere of public policy, public services, and the principle of universalism in access both to income transfers and services, be they education, social or health services. Above all and summing up these traits, the Nordic countries have been famous for the breadth of the public sector.

In spending terms, the broad scope of the public sector is clearly visible. In international comparisons, the Nordic countries have the biggest shares of total government spending/GNP, social spending/GNP etc. The broad public sector is also visible in comparisons of taxation. In relation to tax as a proportion of GNP, income taxes as a percentage of earnings etc., the Nordic countries maintain the feared position as the countries of highest taxation. High spending and high taxation of course possess another face. Part of the tax income is redistributed from the well-off to the not-so-well-off as cash transfers and/or by means of a wide range of public services.

In social policy the high social spending figure can be taken to mean welfare effort (Wilensky 1975). Cash benefits cover the whole population and for those with earnings there is also a high compensation rate. Social spending is also used for services. Child care is arranged in public daycare centres, and in the Nordic countries the attendance of children at public day-care is the highest in Europe (European Observatory on National Family Policies 1995). Elderly care is to a great extent publicly arranged, both from the social service and health care side (Vaarama and Kautto 1998; Lehto, Moss and Rostgaard 1999). Primary health care is arranged through public provision (Alban and Christensen 1995). The scope of public activity is wide in other spheres also. Education is in public educational institutions from pre-school to higher education levels and is financed by taxation. Employment services are public and active labour market measures are financed by tax revenues. To give a full account of public sector performance is of course beyond the scope of this text, the point is to guide the reader's attention to the fact that the private (for-profit or not-for-profit) activity in the social, health and education (broadly understood as welfare) spheres is very limited indeed.

One prime and legitimate goal for central government has been to guarantee equal social rights and opportunities to all residents regardless of geographical, economic or other conditions. To reach this goal politicians and authorities have aimed to incorporate various types of responses to social problems as part of the normal state-controlled welfare policy. In the process the public sector has evolved sufficiently to crowd out other actors, leaving little room for other than public actors and public solutions.

Partnerships may call into question some of the normative principles of the Finnish welfare state

Why then has Finland developed such a broad spectrum of public activity? There is of course more than one reason for this. Here we attempt to concentrate on normative aspects of the Finnish welfare state and relate these to our knowledge of partnerships. We present a number of ideal-typical principles that have been used to describe the Finnish welfare state at least until the beginning of the 1990s. The argument put forward here is that space for partnerships appears limited not only due to the extent of the public sector but also due to the normative principles that legitimise the policies of the Finnish welfare state.

Welfare states have often been characterised as national projects, contributing to the building of the nation state. The link between social policy development and nation building may be most evident in the Swedish idea of creating a 'Folkhemmet' ('People's home'), but similarly also in Finland the building of social policies has contributed to the wellbeing of an ethnically homogenous population within national boundaries, also serving goals of a unified nation state. Partnerships, being by nature area-based initiatives that are tailor-made to meet local needs and pursue locally defined targets, can be seen as threats to uniformity, and even to development and equality. From this perspective it may not seem surprising that partnerships have not yet attracted the sympathies of policy-makers in Finland. In the interviews we carried out in 1996 among key national actors, we encountered a degree of suspicion and caution towards partnerships, especially from the side of key policy-makers.

In serving the wellbeing of a nation, a number of principles have been given priority over others, and heuristically it may be fruitful to contrast how partnership as a *modus operandi* seems to differ from the normative principles of the Finnish welfare state. Table 3.1 sums up in an exaggerated way the contrast between these two approaches in handling social problems and serves to highlight why partnerships may have legitimacy problems.

Highly institutionalised and public by its very nature, the Nordic model explicitly aims at a high level of social integration and equality. Uniform development in the country has been the goal. Locally differing solutions have been acceptable if they have served the goal of evening out disparities. Finnish social policy up to the late 1980s was very centralised in its decision-making and the implementation of those decisions always came from above. Decisions were made at national level on the organisation, staffing and resourcing of local authority health and social services. Needs have been presumed to be equal and thus it has been possible to respond to them with national legislation. 'Welfare for all' has been the government's guiding

Table 3.1 Differences between normative principles of the Finnish welfare state and characteristics of partnerships

	Normative principles of the Finnish Welfare State	*Characteristics of partnerships*
Aim	Uniform development in the country, equality and homogeneity	Local/regional development, difference
Nature of problems	Uniform problems	Differing problems
Way of solving problems	Central solutions	Local solutions
Methods	Structural policies, national legislation, universal solutions	Programmes, tailor-made solutions
Perspective	Preventive (also curative)	Reactive

principle and resources have accordingly been channelled into a structural social policy in which the role of the public sector has been supremely important with regard to providing social security and services. The provision of public services and state-level planning have been the tools for the realisation of these goals. Universal solutions have been the norm: for instance, in the income-related parts of cash benefits there are no occupationally differentiated schemes. In many policy reforms residence has been a more important criterion for eligibility than merit. As a normative principle policies have stressed prevention as an important goal.

With these features the welfare state system has favoured neither cooperation between social actors nor selective programmes or projects. From this perspective area-based initiatives answering locally differing needs and problems through tailor-made solutions could be interpreted as creating diversity, dissimilarity and inequality. Furthermore, the mere existence of partnership schemes could be interpreted as a vote of no confidence in public policies that have failed in prevention.

Contrasted with the normative principles of the Finnish welfare state, local decision-making – that is, necessarily resulting in varying solutions – can be seen as a threat to the goal of equality between citizens and different regions. We believe that the institutional nature of wide-ranging social policy and the normative principles behind it are essential factors in trying to understand the relatively small significance of the programme- and problem-centred approach.

Social exclusion in Finland does not call for area-based, local initiatives

Lack of demand is yet a third reason to explain why partnerships have failed to become more popular in Finland. Partnerships are created not for the fun of it, but to respond to certain problems. It can be argued there has been no demand for new solutions and models partly because exclusion in Finland has not become such a serious problem as to legitimise the implementation of a new approach. The homogenous Finnish population, an equal income distribution guaranteed by a progressive taxation system and income transfers have kept the level of poverty so low that the issue of exclusion has neither entered the rhetoric of politicians nor been the subject of public debate. To demonstrate the efficiency of the Nordic model, the usual reference is made to such achievements as low unemployment rates, low poverty levels, even income distribution, good health status, high education levels, equality between the regions and gender equality. Despite favourable international comparisons, Nordic countries actually also have their own poor and excluded. The argument put forward here is not to deny that social problems and disadvantage exist, but to refer to research findings that demonstrate that the proportion of the population below the poverty level is lower than elsewhere, and therefore demand for reactive schemes has been modest.

In Finland exclusion is understood as a process that leads to poverty, other types of deprivation and a marginal status in society generally. Deprivation can be examined in various problem areas and as an accumulation of various need factors. In Finland the whole problem area has been approached in various ways, such as evaluating financial deprivation, social deprivation, exclusion from power and participation, health-related deprivation, exclusion from the labour market and the housing market, and education-related deprivation (Rauhala 1991).

At an objectively measurable level it appears that the accumulation of the problems of unemployment, illness and poverty for the same individuals is not general at the level of the population as a whole (Heikkilä 1990). Nevertheless, it seems that where these problems do accumulate is among those groups approaching pension age in traditionally blue-collar occupations (Tuomikoski 1989). According to one study surveying local problems, things were clearly worse among those living alone than those in families (Ritakallio and Salavuo 1989). To generalise, in Finland the most severely excluded may be found among men without work and without family. Homelessness has always been a problem in Finland and this has been a major factor in social deprivation. The poor suffer more from ill health than average, their labour market position is unstable and their housing conditions are below standard. The use of intoxicants, mainly alcohol, has played its part in exclusion among Finnish men. Surveys show that, due to the individual nature of exclusion, the excluded lack the resources to pursue their own interests, and thus are politically passive. Therefore, although social policy is well developed, poverty and deprivation are not insignificant problems in Finnish society. Poverty has not been eradicated.

One major aim of the welfare state, and a measure of its success, is held to be the alleviation of poverty and exclusion. In international comparisons Finland and the other Nordic countries fare well. The number of people below the relative poverty line[4] in Finland was found to be 3–4 per cent of the population in the period 1990–94. A few years ago Finland seemed to be the country with the most equal income distribution and lowest poverty rates (Ritakallio 1995). Poverty can also be measured subjectively, or by the number of those on income support, by the number of those in extreme debt (overindebtness), or by the number of those with difficulty in paying bills (Kangas and Ritakallio 1996). With different methods the picture of poverty emerges in dissimilar ways, but it nonetheless appears that only a minority of those deprived in their living conditions are actually poor. Studies show that there is no accumulation of deprivation in Finland, which can be taken to indicate how successful the structural social policy has been. Furthermore, studies about urban segregation and geographical distribution of poverty suggest that there are no significant spatial poverty pockets in

---

4 Determined as receiving income below 50 per cent of the average.

the country, and little segregation among different residential areas. When segregation exists, it can be found inside blocks of flats (Vaattovaara 1998).

For the purposes of this chapter, the important question is whether partnerships are viable solutions to answer the problems related to social exclusion. Research results reporting low levels of poverty and exclusion, lack of accumulated deprivation, insignificant urban segregation and lack of spatial poverty pockets indicate the success of policies, but could also be used to warrant the claim that there has been not much demand for area-based solutions such as partnerships to tackle unemployment and unemployment-related problems.

Reasons to expect the spread of partnerships

Everything mentioned previously implies that there would not seem to be a place for partnerships as a means of combating exclusion in the Finnish welfare state. However, mention must now be made of some recent features of social development in Finland, which we feel suggest a possible increase in the number of partnership schemes in the future. To begin with, the public economy during the recession in the early 1990s ran swiftly into debt. High levels of unemployment were an important cause of the growing imbalance in state expenditure and income. Balancing the economy has required cuts in social spending. A number of the cuts have been targeted at state subsidies granted to local authorities, which in turn has had its effect on services provided by the municipalities, such as social and health services. The role of local authorities in providing a welfare service is in a state of flux, owing to reforms in the state subsidy system, cuts in state assistance and an intention to decentralise administration. The unacceptably high unemployment rate has led to increased exclusion, and although a large majority still support the role of the public sector in social security, support for alternative sources of security provision has increased slightly during the recession. The difficulties facing the public economy which have persisted throughout the 1990s and the structural changes that have taken place in production and working life with its attendant unemployment have cast a shadow on a social policy that still adheres to the 'old model'.

In short, the reshaping of welfare state arrangements resulting from economic problems and political reassessments, accompanied by unemployment and the resultant dangers of exclusion, suggest that there could be room and more demand for new initiatives such as partnerships to take root in addressing social questions.

The public sector is withdrawing, leaving more room for partnerships

Thus the sketchy, and admittedly even rosy, state-of-the-art picture of the Finnish welfare state presented above, if it ever existed, may now be confined to history. The dominant position of the public sector in the 1990s is, if not vanishing, at least eroding. Primarily, this is the result of financial pressures, although other arguments have also been advanced.

In 1990 the Finnish economy plunged into unparalleled recession. Notwithstanding differing opinions about the reasons for crisis, it is incontestable that their combined impact caused Finland to experience, in terms of economic indicators, the industrial countries' severest recession since the 1930s. GNP fell by 12 per cent in the three years from 1991 to 1993. Unemployment rose at the same time from 3 per cent to almost 18 per cent. Public and social spending as a proportion of the GNP increased rapidly, mainly as a result of the overall fall in the GNP itself. Social spending as a proportion of GNP reached a peak in 1993 at 37.9 per cent (Social Affairs and Health 1995). Unemployment and the financial crisis caused the national economy to weaken rapidly, and foreign borrowing increased exponentially. Not surprisingly, the economic situation forced the government to cut spending – including social spending.

Criticism of the welfare state, although not at all consistent either in scope or content, is adding to the financial problems. Some critics think the time of the centralised welfare state is over. Change, flexibility and efficiency are the key words these days in the private sector, and the same principles have to be applied to the excessive and over-rigid public sector. There have been voices heard, too, in favour of 'the spontaneous society' and 'welfare without the state'. Behind these slogans are claims that the welfare state destroys individual responsibility and the community's natural ability to care for those in need of help. By and large, however, few have given voice to these criticisms, and they have not managed to attract much political support. A general consensus regarding the basis and structure of the Finnish welfare state has prevailed within the different parties, even during the recession and in the population at large (Forma 1997; 1999a).

However, as a consequence of the need for savings in public expenditure and demands for less bureaucratisation and more citizen participation, in some areas the public sector is withdrawing from responsibility leaving more room for (and even inviting) other actors.

Local initiatives and responsibility are stressed more

In addition to public sector withdrawal, partnerships may profit from recent administrative reforms. Local level partnership arrangements are currently being formed as a result of the restructuring of services owing to government spending cuts, decentralisation of administration, reforms in state subsidies and the promotion of local democracy.

Since the mid-1980s reforms in public administration have been under way in Finland, which in practice have mainly meant decentralisation and the break-up of norm-related directives. Reforms in administration at local, provincial and central levels have taken place following official reports and various agreements. These have been in connection with norm-related directives, reviews of the state subsidy system, functional changes, greater powers of self-administration at the local level and the guaranteeing of citizens' participation (Kautto and Saari 1996). The basis for these reforms was the idea that central government control had become too distant and too complex and, to some extent, was seen to have undervalued local circumstances and the contribution of local people. Now in the 1990s the situation regarding administrative reform is such that the work of ministries is considered mainly to be that of planning and preparing new laws. Practical questions relating to the implementation of legislation are at the discretion of local authorities. This system is regarded as being an improvement in democratic decision-making and matters of citizens' participation. At the same time it signifies a shift in social responsibility from the central to the local level.

The most important reform resulting from this shift in focus to the local level has been the change in the government subsidies system. Since 1993 state subsidies have been determined numerically rather than being task-related. Under the previous scheme the central government determined, according to its strategic planning, a detailed provision of services and distribution of resources to each sector. With the new system local authorities may themselves decide how to allocate the money that is given to them.[5] As a result of these reforms the importance of local decision-making has grown.

The trends changing the status of the local authorities have also brought about a change in the relations of municipalities and voluntary organisations. Since the state subsidy system reform, the municipality itself can decide arrangements related to the production of services for its own area instead of having to obey the 'earmarking' directive style of government. Thus now, if a municipality can manage to organise its service provision otherwise than by financing it alone, its opportunities for channelling resources into further areas improve. The possibilities for bought-in services or taking advantage of any other schemes such as creating partnership-type alliances are greater, as the municipality becomes the control centre for local decision-making on a far larger scale than before. Voluntary organisations in this respect are a natural and already existing partner for such kinds of arrangement. Besides, such organisations have access to channels that the councils do not. An interest in foundations, associations and other legally independent organisations has grown, as local authorities can access outside funding only in cooperation with other independent bodies. Until now this interest has not led to any notions of partnerships as independent, legal entities, but it has certainly activated contacts between these partners.

Thus, the state no longer holds the reins when it comes to how money is spent, nor can it amend the amount of subsidy due to any single municipality once the rules for subsidies have been established. As the powers of decision-making having shifted more towards local government, funding-based

---

5 Nevertheless, certain obligations, as laid down in special laws to protect services, prevail.

project control is nowadays central government's only practical means of having some influence on development at the local level. From the point of view of planning and control this has underlined the importance of the Slot Machine Association as a system of discretionary aid.

In an interview we carried out for the partnership study in Finland, the executive director of the Association described its role as 'an additional aid organisation' which is today the only means of channelling resources 'earmarked' for new social problems. The benefits from the system also directly aid the local sector. Public services are slow to respond to new needs and rapidly growing challenges. Furthermore, through the resources of the Slot Machine Association, social problems with a strong moral dimension have been addressed constructively. SMA resources enable voluntary organisations to take risks and respond to weak signals. With such financial security, organisations can begin to act without relying on financial assistance or waiting for political approval from the municipality.

On top of the administrative reforms that seem to encourage local co-operation, the voluntary organisations have also revised their stance. The following trends may be observed:

- Voluntary work is integrated into public social policy, especially locally, and through cooperative networks.
- A number of the major social and health organisations act as important paid providers of services for municipalities. There are even cases where a municipality has commissioned its entire primary health care or part of it from a nationwide organisation (e.g. Folkhälsan, the Deaconess Institute in Oulu).
- Lobbying on behalf of a particular group or membership has become more common and important in the 1990s.
- Exerting other types of pressure, such as acting as society's conscience, may have become more prominent. This is suggested by the overviews and barometers measuring the wellbeing of the population and people's attitudes. Such barometers offer an alternative view on reality, especially with regard to the analyses supplied by public authority. Examples of this are the social barometer of the Finnish Federation for Social Welfare and Health, the health barometer of the Finnish Centre for Health Promotion and the Finnish Red Cross observatory on the underprivileged.

A recent study examined the 'state-of-the-art' of the 'civil dialogue', i.e. the frequency and quality of contacts between the public sector actors and the NGOs on the national as well as on the local level (Heikkilä and Karjalainen 1999). The study suggests that while voluntary organisations systematically keep contact with public actors, these contacts are regarded as inadequate, although they are said to have become more frequent in the 1990s. While the voluntary sector showed discontent both with the frequency of contact and the equality of interaction, such views were absent in the interviews with government officials, who felt on the contrary that there were sufficient contact forums for voluntary organisations and government to meet, and that the former were able to get their message across and exert influence.

In this same study a high-ranking official in the Ministry of Social Affairs and Health considered that, especially in the 1990s, voluntary organisations have been in special demand for two reasons. First, decentralisation of social security and the relevant decision-making has reduced the Ministry's ability to control social policy in a centralised manner. Consequently, voluntary organisations can assist in giving guidance to municipalities by providing information. This perspective also emerged in interviews with voluntary sector leaders. Second, in a decentralised situation voluntary organisations will assume a stronger role in safeguarding interests by acting as quality watchdogs.

These developments in the local authority and voluntary organisation sphere may be important for the future spread of partnerships in Finland. Decentralisation of decision-making power and the radical downsizing of normative control have made it a hard task to pursue social policy on a national level. Parallel to this, there have emerged or are emerging local social policies, a trend which may lead to great regional differences and inequality. This trend has meant especially the dispersal of social and health services, in addition to variations in service quality from one municipality to another. There is already debate on the fact that differences are beginning to emerge from region to region.

A perceived spread of exclusion?

Research in Finland on the growth of exclusion now faces the question of how to measure it. The popular idea is that exclusion spread during the economic recession of the 1990s, but how can this be verified? Studies of income distribution showed that this had remained relatively equal, the economic recession notwithstanding (Jäntti 1994). Yet the latest studies show income differences have somewhat widened (Uusitalo 1998). However, although differences in factor incomes have increased, the differences in disposable income have not grown much owing to income transfers.

An assessment of the growth of exclusion based on statistics does not reveal changes in people's personal life situations. A better view of the growth of exclusion is contained in recent information relating to the explosive increase in the number of recipients of income support and long-term reliance on it. Likewise, the rapid rise in the number of long-term unemployed can be seen as a clear indicator of marginalisation. Further information relating to over-indebtedness, food aid and the increase in demand for voluntary aid would indicate that the problem is becoming more acute. Solvency problems have become visible through changes in traditional relief roles. The activities of the Church, the Salvation Army and the Finnish Red Cross have become geared towards the basic needs of those in greatest need, and these tasks have also gained much publicity. (However, the media coverage may cause an optical illusion: in volume terms, the relevance of relief functions is marginal.)

As a consequence, the subject of exclusion has slowly been emerging in political rhetoric. The position of the long-term unemployed seems, in particular, to be crucial. Some argue that state-led welfare provision is relatively powerless in the face of the problems associated with modern hardships, although it functions well as a kind of collective insurance company. This line of thought highlights the significance of the unofficial sector and narrows down the role of the welfare state as the provider of material means of support. These trends may create both more room and more demand for partnerships.

New openings promote partnerships

If one considers that partnerships are essential tools in the current situation, the diffusion of partnerships would benefit from backing from national policy-makers. In fact, some new initiatives both at the rhetorical level and with the launching of a national partnership programme signal that the idea of partnership may be taking deeper root in Finland.

In November 1996 the President of Finland, Mr Martti Ahtisaari, gave a speech at a seminar arranged by the Employers' Federation (TT). His starting point was that the Nordic welfare state was in a 'coping crisis' and could no longer take social responsibility for all. He was demanding that employers take more responsibility so that consensus and partnership could become the basis of a new welfare society (Ahtisaari 1996).

The Minister of Labour, Mrs Liisa Jaakonsaari, has also promoted partnership and local initiatives for creating employment. In creating new employment opportunities, the Minister has often referred to the job creation possibilities in the 'third sector'. In May 1996 a one-man committee was assigned the task of making proposals for measures to promote local initiatives that would create employment among the older workforce and poorly educated unemployed. The appointment implied that the one-man committee should present one or several model(s) for promptly creating local level partnerships in Finland (Harjunen 1996).

Harjunen's report stressed that local partnerships are needed to complement macro-level economic and employment policies because they alone cannot put an end to unemployment. According to the report, prospects for partnership now existed in Finland. The report cited four reasons for this: the financing rules of EU programmes, the decentralisation of administration, the dissolution of public welfare services, and the dissatisfaction with public services. According to Harjunen there were signs of local activity already, although he admitted that existing partnerships existed mainly between the state authorities and local authorities. Great expectations were placed on the input of civil society. To promote partnerships the report

suggested a national partnership programme, that would contain 20 partnerships from different parts of Finland. These local partnerships have received
funding from the European Social Fund (ESF), indicating the impact of EU
resources. The programme was accepted, but as the partnerships chosen to
take part in it have only been in operation for less than two years at the time
of writing, it will be necessary to wait until the publication of the evaluation
report to learn of their success.

In the social welfare sector the notion of partnership has also entered
politics. It is interesting to note the similarities between the partnership
programme of the Ministry of Labour and the 'preventive social policy
programme' of the Ministry of Social Affairs and Health. The preventive
social policy programme aims to promote 'local innovative action models to
prevent social exclusion'. In this initiative, cooperation – both intersectoral
cooperation between public authorities and cooperation between different
partners – is elevated as the essential factor. However, according to the
evaluation report of the programme, most existing cooperation still happens
between public authorities (Pajukoski 1998).

A very recent example of a possible rise in the partnership-type model of
action in the field of extreme social exclusion, which also involves other than
merely public actors, is offered by the Hunger Groups and Food Bank offen-
sive initiated and organised by the Finnish Evangelical Lutheran Church.
The project was launched on the basis of a recognition that not all parts of
the population were doing well and recovering from mass unemployment
and losses of market income. There are a small minority of Finns still fighting
to gain control over the most fundamental external (material) preconditions
of their everyday life. In a way it is hard to understand and admit that in a
country (i) where the relative poverty rate remains around 3–4 per cent;
(ii) that holds the unofficial world record for equality of income; and
(iii) that holds sixth position in the UN Human Development Index ranking
(UNDP 1998), there are households and groups that are in need of food aid.
Most social policy observers are convinced that even the lowest level of the
safety net in Finland is relatively generous on the OECD scale and – more
importantly – it is tight, i.e. it is not leaking and its coverage is complete.
But the fact that this is not the case – for several reasons – gave rise to the
establishment of approximately 60 local food banks in local congregations
for delivering food aid, in a loose cooperation with the social welfare sector
of the municipalities.

More important, however, was that as part of this relatively large-scale
voluntary relief operation, the Church invited fourteen influential people to
establish a Hunger Group with the task of formulating a common perspective
on the reasons behind poverty in a welfare state and about the structural
measures to be taken in order to alleviate it. Clearly along the lines of a
national partnership, this group consisted of leading representatives of the
Central Organisation of Finnish Trade Unions (SAK), Confederation of
Finnish Industry and Employers (TT), representatives of major political

parties and some national NGOs. The group was chaired by the Bishop of Helsinki and the Speaker of the Parliament. This high-level group was assisted by an expert group of researchers and welfare officials. In December 1998 the Hunger Group released a statement that was directed to the government and the major political parties. The message was that the next government after the parliamentary election should prepare and implement a special programme for tackling poverty. This was seen as a high-profile demonstration on behalf of the most disadvantaged groups in the country. Interestingly, the current Prime Minister and the special group of ministers responsible for social affairs received a delegation from this national partnership and promised to pay more attention to the concerns stressed in the group's manifesto.

Conclusion: are partnerships taking root?

We started this chapter by showing how partnerships in Finland are rare and dependent on the public sector both in terms of partner coalition and funding. We argued that the rarity of partnerships is due to a uniquely large public sector that crowds out other actors from the welfare scene. Part of the explanation was sought in the normative principles of the Finnish welfare state, which were seen to be at odds with partnership features. A third reason presented was the relatively good situation that existed with respect to the spread of poverty and exclusion.

With the employment situation at present, in addition to the economic and governmental changes that have taken place, conditions for the development of new partnership-style cooperative models seem more favourable than before. Encouragement from key politicians and a national partnership programme may add fuel to the spread of partnerships. Welfare state solutions face criticism when it comes to both resourcing and action. The public sector is being reduced at the same time as there are more needs emerging and increasing demands for protection. The possible importance of partnership is accentuated partly by the fact that exclusion emerges as something to be addressed in a society burdened by unemployment. New ways to meet needs are sought after both as a means to get most out of the welfare state machinery (e.g. synergy from intersectoral cooperation) and in finding innovative ways to respond to local needs.

Thus, Finland seems to be in a situation where the efficiency of old policy models is being tested. It is still too early to make a final statement about whether partnerships will spread. The launching of a national partnership programme is still too recent to evaluate its success. Also, at this stage it is hard to assess the extent of the withdrawal of the public sector. For instance, empirical evidence about local developments tells another story: dogged by financial problems, local authorities have preferred to patch up their budgets by cutting down on bought-in services rather than pruning their own output

(Lehto 1995). Thus, against all odds there might be less room for cooperation between partners than before.

There are also findings that suggest stability rather than change has been the rule in Nordic social policy development (Kautto, Heikkilä, Hvinden, Marklund and Ploug 1999). A network of 20 Nordic academics assessing Nordic welfare state development from different angles concluded that the Nordic welfare states, at least until 1995, had survived the harsh economic conditions. Cuts that had been made appeared minor contrasted with the rising social expenditure created by unemployment, and comparative macro data about social policy confirmed that Nordic countries still stand as a group compared with other OECD countries. In some services, some of the unique Nordic characteristics had even been growing. There were no major changes for the worse in the population's wellbeing. These types of finding put the supposed cracks of the Finnish welfare state into a broader perspective and temper hasty conclusions about the end of the Nordic model.

It is also hard to tell to what extent there is an erosion of normative principles of the welfare state. Opinion polls at least suggest that the desire for equality among citizens has not vanished (Forma 1999b). Current criticisms of the welfare state in turn cannot be interpreted as a sign of a legitimation crisis. People both support and criticise the welfare state at the same time (Ervasti 1998). A further issue is the possible discrepancy between the opinions of the political elite and citizens, which Forma (1999a) has shown are often at a distance. Pekka Kosonen (1998) has questioned whether the politicians still agree on the normative principles supposed to be behind the Nordic social model. Having followed the development of the Nordic model since the 1970s, Kosonen suggests that the normative heritage may be changing. He argues that the goals of full employment and equality have substantially weakened, while public responsibility for welfare has also weakened, although universalism still seems to have support. But again here we cannot say anything definite about the politicians' adherence to the Nordic model.

Thus, when recent developments that signal that partnership may be more firmly established are contrasted with no or conflicting empirical evidence about the withdrawal of the public sector, weakening of the normative heritage and growth of exclusion, there appears to be no solid ground to characterise partnerships as revolutionary sociopolitical innovations in Finland. Social policy is increasingly localised, but only time will tell whether an increasing part of it will evolve in the form of partnerships.

References

Ahtisaari M (1996) 'Kohti yhteisvastuun ja mahdollisuuksien yhteiskuntaa' (Towards a society based on mutual responsibility and opportunities), Speech by the President of Finland on 20 November 1996 at an employers' seminar in Helsinki.

Alban A and Christensen T (eds.) (1995) *The Nordic Lights: New Initiatives in Health Care Systems*, Odense: Odense University Press.

Alestalo M and Uusitalo H (1986) 'Finland', in Flora P (ed.) *Growth to Limits. Vol. 1.* Berlin: Walter de Gruyter 197–292.

Anttonen A and Sipilä J (1992) 'Julkinen, yhteisöllinen ja yksityinen sosiaalipolitii-kassa – sosiaalipalvelujen toimijat ja uudenlaiset yhteensovittamisen strategiat' (Public, mutual and private in social policy – actors in social care services and new compatibility strategies), in Riihinen O (ed.) *Sosiaalipolitiikka 2017. Näkökulmia suomalaisen yhteiskunnan kehitykseen ja tulevaisuuteen* (Social policy year 2017. Perspectives on the development and future of Finnish society), SITRA, Porvoo: WSOY, 435–62.

Atkinson A, Rainwater L and Smeeding T M (1995) *Income Distribution in OECD Countries. Evidence from the Luxembourg Income Study*, Paris: OECD, Social Policy Studies No 18.

Baldersheim H and Ståhlberg K (1999) 'Regionernas Norden – från enhetsstat till utvecklingsregion' (Regions in the Nordic Countries – from Uniform State to Developing Regions) in Ståhlberg K (ed.) *Den nordiska modellen i en brytningstid* (The Nordic Model at a turning point). Copenhagen: Nord 1999.

Castles F G (ed.) (1993) *Families of Nations: Patterns of Public Policy in Western Democracies*, Aldershot: Dartmouth.

Castles F G (1998) *Comparative Public Policy. Patterns of Post-war Transformation*, Cheltenham: Edward Elgar.

Eriksson R, Hansen E J, Ringen S and Uusitalo H (eds.) (1987) *The Scandinavian Model. Welfare States and Welfare Research*, Armonk: M E Sharpe.

Ervasti H (1996) *Kenen vastuu? Tutkimuksia hyvinvointipluralismista legitimiteetin näkökul-masta* (Whose responsibility? Studies on welfare pluralism from a legitimacy perspective), Stakes Research Reports, Jyväskylä: Gummerus.

Ervasti H (1998) 'Civil Criticism and the Welfare State', *Scandinavian Journal of Social Welfare* 7: 288–99.

Esping-Andersen G (1990) *The Three Worlds of Welfare Capitalism*, Cambridge: Polity Press.

European Observatory on National Family Policies (1995) *Developments in National Family Policies in 1994*, York: University of York.

Forma P (1997) 'The Rational Legitimacy of the Welfare State: Popular Support for Ten Income Transfer Schemes in Finland', *Policy and Politics* 25 (3): 235–47.

Forma P (1999a) 'Welfare State Opinions among Citizens, MP Candidates and Elites: Evidence from Finland' in Taylor-Gooby P and Svallfors S (eds.) *The End of the Welfare State? Responses to State Retrenchment*, London: Routledge and Kegan Paul, 87–105.

Forma P (1999b) 'Eroding Solidarity – Growing Polarisation? Welfare State Opinions of the Well-off and Worse-off Finns during the Economic Recession', in Forma P *Interests, Institutions and the Welfare State. Studies on Public Opinion Towards the Welfare State*, Stakes Research Report 102, Jyväskylä: Gummerus.

Harjunen R (1996) *Paikallisen aloitteellisuuden ja kumppanuuden Suomen malli* (The Finnish Model of Local Initiative and Partnership), Helsinki: Ministry of Labour.

Heikkilä M (1990) *Köyhyys ja huono-osaisuus hyvinvointivaltiossa* (Poverty and depriva-tion in a welfare state), Sosiaalihallituksen julkaisuja 8/1990, Helsinki: VAPK.

Heikkilä M and Kautto M (1997) *Local Partnerships and Social Cohesion in Finland*. Stakes Reports, Saarijärvi: Gummerus.

Heikkilä M and Karjalainen J (1999) 'Leaks in the Safety Net. The role of civil dialogue in the Finnish inclusion policy', *Stakes Themes*, Helsinki: Stakes.

Hellsten K (1993) *Vaivaishoidosta hyvinvointivaltion kriisiin. Hyvinvointivaltiokehitys ja sosiaaliturvajärjestelmän muotoutuminen Suomessa* (From poor relief to the crisis of the welfare state. Welfare state development and shaping of social security system in Finland), Helsinki: University of Helsinki, Department of Social Policy, Research Reports 2.

Jaakkola J, Pulma P, Satka M and Urponen K (1994) *Armeliaisuus, yhteisöapu, sosiaaliturva. Suomalaisten sosiaalisen turvan historia* (Charity, Community Help, Social Security. The History of Finns' Social Aid), Helsinki: Sosiaaliturvan keskusliitto.

Jäntti M (1994) 'Tulonjako ja tulojen muutos laman aikana' (Income distribution and changes in incomes during the recession), *Talous and Yhteiskunta* 4: 64–72.

Kangas O (1993) 'The Finnish Welfare State – A Scandinavian Welfare State?' in Kosonen P (ed) *The Nordic Welfare State as a Myth and as a Reality*, Renvall Institute Publications 5, Helsinki: University Printing House.

Kangas O and Ritakallio V-M (1996) 'Different Methods – Different Results? Approaches to Multidimensional Poverty', *Stakes Themes* 5.

Kautto M and Saari J (1996) 'The Principle of Subsidiarity and Governance Structures of Social Policy in Finland', in Alestalo M and Kosonen P (eds) *Welfare Systems and European Integration, Proceedings from COST A7 Workshop in Tampere, Finland, August 24–27, 1995*, Tampere: Department of Sociology and Social Psychology, Series A:28, University of Tampere.

Kautto M, Heikkilä M, Hvinden B, Marklund S and Ploug N (eds.) (1999) *Nordic Social Policy. Changing Welfare States*, London: Routledge.

Kohl J (1981) 'Trends and Problems in Postwar Public Expenditure Development in Western Europe and North America', in Flora P and Heidenheimer A J (eds.) *The Development of Welfare States in Europe and America*, New Brunswick: Transaction Books, 307–44.

Kosonen P (1998) *Pohjoismaiset mallit murroksessa* (Nordic models at a turning point), Tampere: Vastapaino.

Kuhnle S and Selle P (eds.) (1992) *Government and Voluntary Organizations*, Aldershot: Avebury.

Lehto J (1995) 'Kunnallisten sosiaali- ja terveyspalvelujen muutossuunta 1990-luvun talouskriisin aikana' (Changes in local social and health care services during the economic crisis of the 1990s), in Hänninen S, Iivari J and Lehto J, *Hallittu muutos sosiaali- ja terveydenhuollossa?* (Change and its control in municipal welfare and health care in the early 1990s), Stakes Reports 182, Saarijärvi: Gummerus.

Lehto J, Moss N and Rostgaard T (1999) 'Universal Public Social Care and Health Services?', in Kautto M, Heikkilä M, Hvinden B, Marklund S and Ploug N (eds.) *Nordic Social Policy. Changing Welfare States*, London: Routledge.

Matthies A-L (ed.) (1991) *Valtion varjossa. Katsaus epävirallisen sektorin tutkimukseen* (In the shadow of the state: a review of research on the unofficial sector), Helsinki: Sosiaaliturvan keskusliitto.

OECD (1997) *OECD Statistics CD rom*, Nov 1997, Paris: OECD.

Pajukoski M (1998) *Mitä muuttui? Ehkäisevän sosiaalipolitiikan kuntaprojektin osaprojektien arviointi* (What did change? Evaluation of sub-projects under the preventive social policy project), Sosiaali- ja terveysministeriön selvityksiä 3, Helsinki: Edita.

Rauhala U (1991) *Köyhyys ja huono-osaisuusongelman lähtökohdista ja ratkaisuyrityksistä* (On starting points and solutions concerning the problem of poverty and deprivation), Helsinki: Ministry of Social Affairs and Health, Planning Department Publications 1991: 7.

Ritakallio V-M (1995) *Köyhyys Suomessa 1981–1990. Tutkimus tulonsiirtojen vaikutuksista* (Poverty in Finland. A study on the effects of income transfers), Stakesin tutkimusraportteja 39, Saarijärvi: Gummerus.

Ritakallio V-M and Salavuo K (1989) *Hyvinvointiongelmat ja sosiaalihuolto maaseutukeskuksessa* (Social problems and social welfare services in a rural centre), Turku: Turun yliopisto, sosiaalipolitiikan laitoksen julkaisuja, sarja A:28.

Social Affairs and Health (Ministry of) (1995) *Social Security* 1995: 2, Helsinki: Ministry of Social Affairs and Health, Department of Finance and Planning.

Tuomikoski H (1989) 'Hyvinvointivaltion huono-osaiset' (The worse-off in a welfare state), in Karisto A, Takala P, Hellsten K, Helminen I and Massa I (eds.) *Sosiaaliset riskit, tutkimus ja päätöksenteko* (Social risks, research and decision-making), Helsinki: Helsingin yliopisto, Lahden tutkimus- ja koulutuskeskus.

UNDP (1998) *Human Development Report 1998*, United Nations Development Programme (UNDP), New York: Oxford University Press.

Uusitalo H (1998) 'Laman aikana tulonjako säilyi entisellään, mutta laman jälkeen erot ovat kasvussa' (Income distribution remained as it was during recession, but differences are increasing since then), *Yhteiskuntapolitiikka*, 5–6: 425–31.

Vaarama M and Kautto M (1998) *Social Protection for the Elderly in Finland*, Stakes, Saarijärvi: Gummerus.

Vaattovaara M (1998) *Pääkaupunkiseudun sosiaalinen erilaistuminen* (Residential Differentiation within the Metropolitan Area of Helsinki, Finland – Environment and Spatiality), City of Helsinki Urban Facts, Research Series 1998: 7, Hämeenlinna: Karisto.

Wilensky H (1975) *The Welfare State and Equality: Structural and Ideological Roots of Public Expenditures*, Berkeley: University of California Press.

4 Local partnerships and social exclusion in France

Experiences and ambiguities

Patrick Le Galès and Patricia Loncle-Moriceau

Introduction

'Partnership', what a strange word in French! It sounds very much like a term that is derived from EU jargon and then reinterpreted to describe a variety of experiences or to serve policy goals that have to change, or at least be seen to change.

The partnership approach is a concept that is alien to the tradition of state control in France, to the crucial political legitimacy of local mayors (in 36,000 communes) and to the division between public and private, particularly from the legal standpoint. It follows that if partnerships are defined in the specific sense used in the European Foundation research (see Benington and Geddes, Chapter 1), they are unlikely to be found in France on a regular basis.

Nevertheless, the use of the term has spread. It took hold some years ago and usually points to forms of cooperation between social actors and organisations from different backgrounds. The challenge to the State and more generally the challenge to the relationship between the State, local authorities, firms, voluntary associations and various other agencies has paved the way for an explosion in the number of partnerships of all types, particularly but not exclusively in the area of social policy. This indicates on the one hand an attempt to modernise (whatever that means) public policies and the delivery of programmes and services, and on the other hand, it is a way of reformulating previous forms of collective mobilisation which pre-dated the emergence of partnerships in the French social and political sphere.

The term is used most frequently to describe partnerships either between public and private organizations particularly in the area of economic development (urban projects for instance) or between different public sector bodies in the area of social policy. There are at least two reasons for this development (Le Galès 1995a):

- Traditional state policy tools have been found wanting in various respects: they have not been effective, have lacked legitimacy and resources have become increasingly scarce. Public/private partnership is one of several means of structuring forms of organised action based on joint intervention, which might complement or replace intervention by the State, local authorities or public agencies. This type of action is sometimes part of a neo-liberal approach which seeks to reduce the role of the State and allow private players to exert some control over public action or to introduce a market-oriented system.

- But the term is sufficiently vague to cover a large number of informal arrangements or diverse agreements, in particular in the opaque world of social policies. Here the situation in France is still characterised by the traditional primacy of the State and for this reason we need to consider under the heading of partnership much more than the kind of arrangements that exist in fields such as town planning and urban renewal.

To explain these developments it is necessary firstly to emphasise the influence exerted by the State and its pre-eminence in French society, and secondly to establish a link between the challenge to the role of the State and the emergence of the partnership approach, in particular as social and urban policies have had to cope with rising poverty.

The background to the emergence of the partnership approach in France: challenge to the *dirigiste* system and the rise of poverty

The centralised voluntarist state

For a long time the *dirigiste* system that operated in France was one of the features of 'French exceptionalism'. The French State and its bureaucratic and political elites played a key role in the economic development of the country, its remarkable reconstruction after 1945, and its industrialisation and urbanisation (Dyson 1980). In other words, France displayed several of the classic attributes of a dirigiste state: the fundamental position of the State in society, its disregard for local authorities, the voluntary sector and commercial interests which were inevitably archaic; its belief in the common interest, the superiority of the State and centralised economic planning; the dependence of large companies on the State and their protectionist tendencies; the homogeneity and voluntarism displayed by the elite in the senior echelons of the civil service; and the strong centralist tendencies and the relative historic weakness of trade unions and employer organisations.

From 1945 to the mid-1970s there was almost no reference in France to the partnership approach. The all-pervading influence of the State inevitably precluded any discourse or practices that were closely or remotely akin to partnership. France had few social partners who could have devised compromise arrangements on social issues without the intervention of the State. Recourse to the State was a permanent feature of French life, not only to act as a referee in the case of conflicts, but also to intervene directly in social issues.

This meant that a term such as a public/private partnership had little meaning as the central position of the State goes hand in hand with the public sector's mistrust of, and even contempt for, the private sector. The interests of society as a whole, the long-term vision, and the moral high ground emanated from the public sector. French public law is a good example of this philosophy, originally drafted as it was to counter the market-oriented approach. It reflects this concern for the moral virtue of the public sector by discrediting the market and private companies (Caillosse 1993). In contrast, there was an enormous increase in the number of *sociétés d'économie mixte*, which were a combination of both the public and private sector, the French version of the mixed economy but under State control.

The same is more or less true in the social policy field, but some nuances have to be noted. The implementation of social policies in France in the 1930s changed the nature of social welfare: even though some forms of an assistance-based approach did remain they were destined to play merely a residual role from then on. The development of the social sector into a centralised órganisation based on the concept of risk was confirmed with the introduction of a general system of social security in 1945. The reform, partly inspired by Beveridge, was comprehensive: incorporating previous legislation within a general plan, filling the gaps and eliminating inequality in social protection. The organisation of the system was based on three principles: standard insurance cover, the extension of cover to new groups of beneficiaries and a widening of social protection (Palier 1999).

The results of economic growth and the institutionalisation of the welfare state raised hopes of a permanent eradication of poverty. In 1953 the system of assistance became social assistance (Rosanvallon 1990), signalling an intention to move towards a 'residual' form of social provision. Various population groups considered 'at risk' on the grounds of poverty or exposure to moral danger were identified: single mothers, the disabled, the elderly, and young people in difficulty were to be the subject of greater protection, which involved placing them in specialised institutions where they were supervised by highly qualified specialist staff. Instruments of social assistance were set up: for example the creation in 1958 of the Protection Judiciaire de l'Enfance en Danger (Legal Protection for Children at Risk), in 1964 the Direction Départementale de l'Action Sanitaire et Sociale (Departmental Offices for Health and Social Provision). These were backed up by the intro-duction of a range of allowances paid to families, housing and single-parent allowances, the granting of which depended upon a predetermined resource ceiling.

Within this context of growth and a strong impetus from the centre, the State organised its services on a sectoral and regional basis so that it could implement its policies effectively, voluntarist though they might be. At the local level the external services of the State, the Directions Départementales et Régionales de l'Action Sociale (Departmental and Regional Social Services) acted as intermediaries. However, even during the initial development of the welfare state, i.e. during the period of 'rigid centralism', the various administrations did allow the establishment of institutions which were innovative in terms of their legal status and which were called upon to play an important role in the development of facilities and social welfare. There were also examples of 'joint management', which could be interpreted as tentative steps towards partnership. In addition, many other associations and voluntary sector organisations have developed at the local level in a wide range of areas (social, sport, cultural, leisure, etc.), funded primarily by grants from the local authority.

Joint management experiments have also been tried at both national and local level, which in our view presage the use of the partnership approach, for instance in the 1960s in the Ministry of Youth and Sports, or in different cities, for instance Grenoble, Lille or Rennes where partnership initiatives were undertaken in different policy fields (e.g. social policies, culture).

Changing times: the rise of poverty and decentralisation reforms

From the mid-1970s onwards several developments converged which served to question the validity of certain aspects of a centralised approach to public policies: the crisis in the welfare state, the urban crisis and decentralisation policies resulted in a withdrawal/redefinition of the role of the State. As social policies came under economic pressure, attempts to reduce inequality were initially slimmed down and then abandoned. At the same time there was increasing criticism of the welfare state: critics variously denounced the pernicious effects of welfare dependency, benefit cuts and the endemic cost question. They even challenged the validity of the centralised state, arguing that it was ineffective, remote from local decision-making centres and technocratic in management style, and that greater authority should be given to civil society and to local authorities.

The rise of poverty

At the same time there was a growing awareness of forms of 'new poverty' which had previously been unknown or marginal in France, thanks to the work of an association called ATD Quart Monde (Aide à Toute Détresse – Help to Those in Distress in the Fourth World). This organisation was the result of an initiative by Christian activists in run-down suburbs (Jobert 1981). The discovery of 'new forms of poverty' in the 1980s accelerated the review of state intervention (Paugam 1991; 1994).

The growth of unemployment and of those dependent on minimum subsistence allowance is shown in Tables 4.1, 4.2 and 4.3. Table 4.1 shows long-term unemployment trends, while Table 4.2 shows the current distribution

Table 4.1 Unemployment in France since 1970

Year	1970	1980	1990	1998
Numbers unemployed (ILO definition)[1]	530	1,492	2,205	3,050
Unemployment rate	2.5	6.4	8.9	11.8
Female unemployment rate	4.3	9.5	11.7	13.8

Source: INSEE

[1] Numbers in thousands. The ILO definition of unemployment includes people who are looking for a job; those immediately available for work; and those who have found but not started a job.

Table 4.2 Unemployment by gender and age group, 1997

	Unemployment by gender[1]					
Age group	Men Numbers	Rate[2]	Women Numbers	Rate	Total Numbers	Rate
15 to 24	301,525	24.6	307,162	32.8	608,687	28.1
25 to 49	999,271	9.9	1,120,641	13.4	2,119,912	11.5
50 and over	222,409	8.0	200,578	9.2	422,987	8.5
Totals	1,523,205	10.8	1,628,381	14.2	3,151,586	12.3

[1] ILO definition.
[2] The unemployed as a proportion of the working population.

of the unemployed, and Table 4.3 shows the recent growth in numbers on benefits.

This discovery of 'new forms of poverty' prompted new ways of concept-ualising the phenomenon progressively described as 'social exclusion'. These analyses have underlined the difficulties for public policy in addressing a social problem whose solution appears to be more linked with the economic arena than with the political one. Thus public action has had to adapt its objectives and its means of tackling poverty and exclusion within an uncertain frame of reference that now includes the labour market. Three

Table 4.3 Revenu Minimum d'Insertion (Minimum Subsistence Allowance) bene-ficiaries

Year	1993	1993–4	1994	1994–5	1995	1995–6	1996
No of beneficiaries	678,450		783,435		820,115		882,047
% change		15.5		4.7		7.3	

Source: CNAF
NB Figures are for Metropolitan France for December of each year.

types of interpretative analysis can be distinguished that help to understand different dimensions of this phenomenon (Autès 1995):

- An analysis in terms of 'social disqualification' has been developed by Serge Paugam (1993). This focuses on the link between mainstream society and excluded groups, and the means of involving them. Paugam stresses social representation within the welfare system and the effects of its classifications on individuals.
- An analysis of the 'social de-insertion' of poor people (de Gaujelac and Leonetti 1994). These authors reveal the process of 'de-insertion'/ exclusion of fragile populations and its different stages: the 'ruptures' stemming from initial and subsequent events, and the marginalisation and decline of such groups. Within the phenomenon of social de-insertion there is an important symbolic dimension due to the way in which society seems unable to restore value and identity to such people.
- Finally, an analysis of the transformation of the social structure that leads to the development of the phenomenon of 'disaffiliation'. Robert Castel (1995) associates the erosion of the welfare system based on the generalisation of the wage-earning class, with a growing 'disaffiliated' population, and the seeming inability of public policy to influence this phenomenon.

Other authors (Lenoir 1974; Martin 1997) demonstrate how the phenomenon of social exclusion does not constitute a generalised process, but on the contrary concerns more particularly certain social groups such as young people and single women. These analyses reflect increasingly visible phenomena (which receive wide media coverage), such as the rise of poverty and violence within disavantaged areas (Bachman and Leguennec 1996). From the beginning of the 1980s, awareness progressively emerged of the extent of ongoing changes, and especially that of two elements: the weakness of social relationships and links within neighbourhoods that had structured the associative networks during the 1960s and 1970s; and a deep generational gap around the urban riots. One of the consequences of this crisis was, of course, the growth of the Front National, particularly in urban areas (Perrineau 1998; Mayer 1999; Le Galès and Oberti 1992).

The restructuring of public policies and decentralisation reforms: opportunities and constraints for partnership

State restructuring has become the new mantra for policy-makers and commentators alike and in its own way the French welfare state has also been confronted with pressure for change for all sorts of objective and subjective reasons (Palier 1999). Pressure has applied to the restructuring of social policies, the relations between national, local and regional authorities and the redefinition of the nature of social work with excluded groups. Partnerships are one part of these attempts at coping with new problems.

The rise of local social policies (in parallel with the decentralisation reforms of the early 1980s) and the development of the social dimensions of urban policy are particularly related to the rise of poverty and the restructuring of the State. Decentralisation reforms paved the way for the increasing role of *départements* and to some extent communes and regions, in social policies, and increased the financial and legal 'room for manoeuvre' of elected politicians at different levels.

These developments had two obvious consequences: the rise of different initiatives including attempts to develop some sort of local systems of welfare and, most importantly, a major fragmentation of public intervention (between the State, its decentralised services and the various specialist agencies and management bodies). It also resulted in power struggles and conflicts in the relationship between public authorities at various levels, i.e. commune, département and region (Mabileau 1991; Faure 1994; Lorrain 1993; Le Galès 1995b).

This issue of political legitimacy, reinforced by the legislation on decentralisation, has made it difficult for partnership (as defined in the context of this research project) to emerge in France (although in itself this is neither good nor bad). It is evident from our research that mayors not only claim local legitimacy but also feel deeply responsible for everything that happens in their communes. It is, therefore, 'natural' for mayors (and in most cases for other actors also), that elected representatives should retain control over partnerships, even if only at the formal level of the governing body, rather than at the operational level. Local elected representatives are often distrustful of 'partnerships' that might escape their control and that might give away resources and power to hostile interests and form a base for possible political rivals. In most cases, the external legitimacy of the European Union is required before they can be brought into partnership arrangements where partners have real margins for manoeuvre.

The main actors represented in partnership-type structures come from the public sector

The public sector

The public sector in France is extremely extensive and complex and a single partnership may well have numerous representatives from the public sector. There are many examples of so-called partnership which are no more than cooperative arrangements between partners from various organisations belonging to the public sector. The State may be present in the form of representatives from the various levels of the prefecture (General Secretariat for Regional Affairs, the Sub-prefect in an urban area, etc.), the Ministries of Education, Justice, the Interior, Urbanism and Planning, members of DATAR (Délégation à l'Aménagement du Territoire et à l'Action Régionale), or the Délégation Interministérielle à la Ville (Interministerial

Urban Agency located within the Ministry of Social Affairs). Local authorities may be present in the form of the various levels in the area (regions, départements, communes), plus structures involving more than one commune (urban communities, districts, associations of communes), or structures within individual communes (project managers, community council representatives). The status of individual public sector representatives may vary considerably: elected representatives, national or regional civil servants, or local officials.

The State and local authorities have developed an extremely positive rhetoric about partnership: partnerships resolve conflicts and give the impression that resources are being mobilised, while the risk of non-decision or deadlock is accorded less significance. However, the reality of public sector participation in initiatives is not always that clear. The autonomy of their representatives is often largely theoretical; if a decision is required the authority given to representatives is often extremely limited, which means that they must systematically refer back to their parent organisation, which acts as a restraint on what can actually be achieved. In addition, partnership projects and the mechanisms for the allocation of public funding are organised in such a way that partners invariably have very little time to prepare their applications, and submissions must comply with an extremely complex list of formalities, both of which represent a very considerable constraint. Moreover, certain examples of the attitude adopted by the State towards such initiatives leaves the observer extremely cynical about whether they really do wish to act as facilitator.

For instance, in the case of the Contrat de Ville partnership in Lille (discussed more fully below), some attitudes of the State representatives appeared unproductive. Whereas local authorities were involved beyond their legal obligations, the State representatives tended to exit or offer only a limited engagement. In fact, the spread of partnership experiments is often stopped by inner logics of 'conflictual cooperation', and by rivalries between different parts of the public sector. On the other hand, there are examples of more fruitful attempts at the involvement of the State, such as the GALCOB (Local Action Group for Central Western Brittany) partnership where several public agencies created new structures on the territorial basis not of the département but of the GALCOB area.

Semi-public organisations play a key role

Social security offices, the Mutualités Sociales Agricoles (MSA – Agricultural Friendly Societies) and the offices responsible for social housing are frequently active in partnership projects, representing the semi-public sector. These organisations operate a policy of openness and thus give priority to ensuring a degree of coherence between their interventions and those of regional authorities and external services of the State. They play an extremely important role in social affairs in terms of expertise and finance.

Some facilities are the result of joint funding by the public and semi-public sectors, e.g. the Social Centres (funded by the municipal authorities) and CAF (Caisses d'Allocations Familiales) in urban areas, or by communes and the MSA in rural areas. Social Centres, despite a wide diversity of projects which reflect their specific geographic location, funding and professional approach of staff, play a key role in certain areas developing a partnership approach to combat social exclusion. In our case studies, these semi-public organisations proved their capacity to respond, in a locally distinctive way, to the needs of ongoing partnership experiments, and were often among the most active organisations in combating poverty.

Voluntary sector: extreme diversity

There are approximately 730,000 voluntary associations in France, of which about 120,000 employ paid staff, providing in the region of 1.3 million jobs. The French voluntary sector is financed primarily by the public and semi-public sectors: national associations and federations tend to be financed by the State and local associations by regional authorities and the CAF. The French voluntary sector is extremely diverse. At the national level there are large federations of associations that intervene in specific areas of social policy. These large federations, the majority of which were created after the Second World War, are active for example on issues of delinquency (Association Nationale de Sauvegarde de l'Enfance et de l'Adolescence – National Association for the Protection of Children and Young People), against exclusion in rural areas (Aide à Domicile en Milieu Rural – Help at Home in Rural Areas) and the struggle against poverty (ATD Quart Monde), etc.

These associations are represented on a central body: UNIOPSS (Union Nationale des Oeuvres et Organismes Privés Sanitaires et Sociaux – National Association of Charities and Private Organisations for Health and Social Provision). UNIOPSS was founded in 1947 in response to the new social security system, which the private organisations saw as a threat to their existence. Some 140 national associations are now members of UNIOPSS and it provides co-ordination and technical support and represents the interests of its members in contacts with public institutions. As part of its efforts to combat social exclusion it runs a publicity campaign based on the idea of a national pact to combat exclusion which would stimulate initiatives involving political, socioeconomic and economic actors. It organises seminars on the subject and disseminates information widely among policymakers: local elected representatives, UNEDIC (the umbrella organisation for ASSECIC, the bodies responsible for managing local unemployment insurance funds), the Social Security, the Centre National du Patronat Français (National Federation of Employers), and the Centre des Jeunes Dirigeants (Federation of Young Managers). Since 1988 the main priority of UNIOPSS has been to 'refine partnerships in order to widen the scope of the solidarity approach...by positioning itself between government and the market'.

At the local level there is also an extremely diverse voluntary sector. The initiatives developed by local associations are often more horizontal and less sectorial and intervention tends to be at the level of the commune or the individual district in a town or city. Associations find themselves in a delicate situation towards local authorities because they are often funded by them. Nevertheless, they play a role in stimulating and implementing well targeted programmes towards disadvantaged groups. In this respect, associations can take on quasi-public service missions, although in other cases their role remains more uncertain and fragile.

As part of the struggle against exclusion it is important to emphasise the key role played by voluntary associations working with young people and in the area of popular education. This tradition, which owes its origins to both the youth club movement and the activities of the Popular Front in 1936, has evolved since the 1980s and is increasingly active. The associations for young people and people's education operate at various levels: they intervene either directly at the community level where they participate in partnerships, or in training initiatives which adopt practices of social integration and develop qualifications designed to increase employment opportunities for groups with problems. Thus, the participation of the Fédération Léo Lagrange of Nord-Pas-de-Calais in the implementation of the Contrat de Ville in Lille has been highly significant in the evolution of the role of popular education towards social exclusion. The Federation was involved in several initiatives such as the 'chantiers d'insertion' and 'régies de quartier' providing training for very excluded young people.

During the last five years, a number of associations representing excluded groups have appeared at the margins of partnership experiments. Many of them, such as AC! (an association for action against unemployment) and le DAL (an association campaigning for the right to housing) are developing new arguments and norms of collective action in these fields, compared to the classical repertory, including direct forms of contestation (on the model of associations of the fight against AIDS such as ACT Up) such as the occupation of administrative offices, hunger strikes, and indictment of public authorities. By this means, such associations are beginning to play a significant role of 'counter-power'.

The representation of the voluntary sector in partnerships raises questions of ambiguity very similar to those that apply to public sector representation. Initially the large national federations were strongly resistant to the development of such arrangements. From their perspective the broadly-based consultation process, which was an essential requirement, represented a threat to the privileged relationship that they had enjoyed for several decades with public bodies. However, confronted with the growing trend towards a partnership approach, they have gradually come round to the idea.

In contrast, local associations were apparently much more sympathetic to the partnership approach from the outset. It gave them an opportunity to gain recognition for their work at grass roots level, a legitimacy which undoubtedly had been difficult to secure within the earlier 'mixed' structures (public sector–voluntary sector) set up after the end of the Second World War which favoured national associations.

However, despite public pronouncements that are extremely favourable to the partnership approach, an analysis of the actual participation of the voluntary sector reveals that things have been far from easy. The status of individual voluntary sector representatives varies and this impacts on the weight of any decision taken by a partnership structure – whether, for example, an individual representative is a member of the association's salaried staff or an unpaid volunteer. Similarly, account has to be taken of the relative position of strength or weakness of the representative in his/her own association. Finally, partnership-type initiatives have resulted in co-operation between associations that were previously either unaware of each other's existence or were in actual competition. For example, secular and religious associations have found themselves at the same negotiating table, a development that has gone largely unrecorded. This face-to-face approach may be accepted by voluntary organisations at local level, which are exposed to similar difficulties during the course of their work and so do not find it difficult to understand each other and grasp the need for a partnership approach. However, the same cannot necessarily be said of their leaders who tend to be more steeped in the ideology of an individual association.

Limited but innovative participation of social partners

The third group of actors in partnership-type initiatives consists of trade unions and employer organisations. Although participation by social partners at national level remains extremely modest, there have been several examples of extremely innovative experiments at the local level.

It is still an exception for employers to be involved in partnerships established to combat social exclusion. However, attempts have been made to create a network of company directors in connection with the 'solidarity funds' and return-to-work projects for the long-term unemployed. There have also been attempts to form specific partnership relations with the local agencies for the employment of young people. In addition, employers are sometimes active in partnerships financed by European funds.

The participation of trade unions is also extremely localised. French trade unions, which are suffering from declining membership (unionisation in France is the lowest of any OECD country), are not used to intervening in the struggle against social exclusion. They have traditionally concentrated primarily on the world of employment and have adopted diverse positions with regard to the necessary response to social exclusion and a recognition of the crumbling of the traditional employment environment which it seems to herald (traditional at least with regard to the perceptions on which they have based their struggles). Only the CFTC (French Christian Workers' Confederation – a small Catholic trade union) and the CFDT (French Democratic Confederation of Labour) consider that action against social exclusion has a degree of legitimacy in as much as the phenomenon challenges their whole system of operation constructed as it is around the notion of a contract of employment. At the national level they work in co-operation with COORACE (Coordination des Organismes et Associations de Demandeurs d'Emploi – co-ordinating body for organisations and associations for job seekers), the Fondation de France (Foundation for France), and the Fédération Nationale d'Accueil et de Réadaption Social (National Federation for Care and Social Readjustment). These campaigns bring together a certain number of partners including intermediary associations and the mutual banking networks. Things are changing quite rapidly, however, and most trade unions now play an increasing role.

The emergence of partnerships to combat poverty: experiments and limits

The problems associated with poverty and the urban crisis, the perceived need to control spending on social provision, the impact of the transfer of responsibilities under decentralisation, but also the change of government in 1981 and the simultaneous search for new methods of understanding social problems, resulted in profound changes to social and urban policies.

Urban policies represent an important turning point in the approach to social issues. Within the context of urban riots and of economic and social crisis, they introduced new tools of comprehensive public action in the 1980s. Various experiments in urban policy have now been implemented in France for two decades and have been a major source of partnership initiative, from the Développement Social des Quartiers programme to the Contrat de Ville (City Contract) and urban pacts (Le Galès and Mawson 1995). For instance, the Contrat de Ville initiative was established in 1989 to bring coherence to the various interventions that had been introduced over the years to respond to neighbourhoods in crisis. The idea behind the Contrat de Ville was to link the State and a local authority (if possible a group of local authorities) within the framework of a contract negotiated by the two partners. This provided a fertile ground for the rise of partnership.

Partnership, usually at local level, to bring consistency to public action

Within the global Contrat de Ville, initiatives are institutionalised into contracts and then into framework agreements. The purpose of such contracts and agreements is to co-ordinate intervention by the State (and its various central and local agencies) and by local authorities (at different levels).

This 'partnership' approach to urban policy (and also to policies for young people and various aspects of social policy) is primarily to achieve consistency in public intervention in a given area by recourse to a partnership which is made up of various public sector partners at central and local level. Other partners are subsequently involved during the development and implementation stages. However, it is unusual for private associations to be signatories to an agreement or contract. In the main, the partners involved in specific actions are usually quasi-public bodies controlled by the State or local authorities, such as the offices responsible for social housing (HLM) and the social security offices.

This means that multi-sectoral partnerships (in the sense defined in the European Foundation research) are almost non-existent at the formal level. On the contrary, the partnership approach is used for the implementation of public programmes, initiatives and contracts. This 'partnership' is subject to control by the State or local authorities to whom it also owes its legitimacy. The new generation of social policies almost invariably use the partnership approach, but it seems to us that a new myth has developed within this systematised approach. When one reads the policy literature, recommending the use of the partnership approach but never defining it, one wonders what part ritual plays in what has become a veritable vogue. This is all the more so because the partnership approach, although it undoubtedly does deliver the advantage of a global approach, contains numerous complexities and ambiguities and as such is not necessarily a very effective tool. This is evident, for example, in the strong impact that the partnership approach has had on the models and practices employed by social workers (Ion 1992). The main social work professions listed in France are social workers, youth workers and the co-ordinators of sociocultural activities. These professions have developed their own approach based on their respective histories and thus each profession does not necessarily have the same capacity to adapt to the partnership approach. The first two categories have had considerable problems in grasping the partnership approach: the model adopted by their professions was based on a personal relationship with 'clients', on a degree of professional confidentiality, on considerable autonomy in terms of their relationship with the institutions that employ them, and with conflict limited solely to professional issues. These new initiatives, which operate on the basis of an approach that is contrary in every respect to this tradition, represented a significant challenge to the model adopted by these professions. In contrast, the coordinators of sociocultural activities have been better able to respond to this development: their work, a more recent development and less structured than that of other social workers, has prepared them better for a joint approach where intervention is often acted out in the public domain. Thus, although the partnership approach does facilitate an interaction between various professional approaches and a wider understanding of social problems, the learning process that professionals have to undergo before they can participate in this type of work is not necessarily automatic.

There may be resistance to what is perceived as a criticism of their own efforts and these feelings may sometimes be stronger than the will to evolve.

It should also be noted that alongside the emergence of a formal partnership approach the various partners have maintained innumerable informal networks for some considerable time, so that many decisions are actually taken jointly through consultation with social actors from a broad spectrum. These networks may very well exist alongside formal partnerships. They may, depending upon the circumstances, be what facilitates the development of a partnership (when members of a network decide to formalise some of their priorities).

This kind of French-style partnership arrangement responds to a multiplicity of demands: the need to address the dysfunctionality highlighted by reports produced at the beginning of the 1980s (in particular the compartmentalisation and centralisation of social issues), the increase in all forms of exclusion, and a commitment to the idea of reductions in public expenditure. This national orientation sympathetic to the partnership approach also created a bridge to EU funding programmes which favoured a similar approach.

The various European programmes introduced in France have encouraged the development of local partnerships in a wide range of locations and policy areas. Programmes such as LEADER, LEDA and Poverty 3 have made a partnership approach a condition of funding. Partnership has become a key criterion in the reform of the Structural Funds and everybody has had to adapt, more or less reluctantly, to benefit from the Funds (where they apply). The existence of this requirement has made it possible to assemble partners who might otherwise not have found the necessary forum or felt the need to participate. The transnational exchanges undertaken by partners within the framework of European programmes have been perceived as an important means of facilitating access to innovative experiments in other countries and a more objective approach to one's own area of intervention. The involvement of players in European programmes can allow them to overcome any resistance which might be displayed by the organisations to which they belong (irrespective of what that organisation might be), by giving them a new legitimacy and a certain detachment from their normal decision-making forums. However, European programmes, due to their complexity, their lack of transparency and the requirement for regular evaluations, sometimes act as a focus for the irritations of the actors at grass roots level who castigate the technocrats and the wasted use of resources.

Contrasting experiences: the Contrat de Ville de Lille and the Association Européenne pour le Mantois-Val de Seine

Case studies of the Contrat de Ville de Lille and the Association Européenne pour le Mantois-Val de Seine reveal something of the involvement of different sectors and the interactions between them. The nature of the partnership approach, the weight of the different private and public actors involved, and the prominence given to excluded groups, mean that these are two contrasting partnership experiments.

When the Contrat de Ville initiative was launched by the Délégation Interministérielle à la Ville in 1989, Lille was one of 13 pilot areas proposed by the State. In fact, Lille and its agglomeration exhibited all the characteristics associated with the partnership experiment: a serious situation with regard to unemployment, immigrants and young people, and population concentrations in depressed neighbourhoods. The Contrat de Ville is built around a strong intermunicipal institution: the Communauté Urbaine de Lille (CUDL), created in 1967, which groups together 86 communes and 1.1 million inhabitants. This institution was headed by Pierre Mauroy, the former Prime Minister and the socialist mayor of Lille.

With the support of the Nord-Pas-de-Calais region, the partnership experiment was extended to the level of the agglomeration under the management of the CUDL. This represented a local political consensus around action against social exclusion from the Left to the moderate Right. The Lille Contrat de Ville also benefited from a deeply rooted associative network in the area. The Contrat was focused on action against exclusion in the fields of housing, early childhood care, educational achievement, care of people with disabilities, and delinquency; culture and health; training and economic insertion; the town and university; public transport; and new communication technologies.

The partners in the Lille Contrat de Ville come from two main groups: representatives of public institutions (from each level of local authorities and from the State to the municipality), and associations from sectors dealing with social exclusion (from leisure to those concerned with preventive action and from national associations to those in the area). However, despite its social aims, the partnership experiment appeared to be largely closed to representatives of excluded groups. The very local associations of groups such as immigrants and young people that could enable such representation were grouped together in broader representational arrangements. Moreover, the lack of significant participation of social partners in the partnership represented a major weakness, despite the fact that Lille's old tradition of philanthropy among textile employers might have provided a basis for such involvement.

The implementation of the Contrat de Ville de Lille involves a programme of concerted actions to which institutions and different public, associative and commercial organisations provide financial and human resources. While it is true that participation by some associations is more or less obligatory because their grants are partly dependent on it, nevertheless their participation in the Contrat de Ville requires other actors to confront different values and ways of working, which in turn can change their conceptions and practices in tackling social exclusion. Consequently, the partnership experiment has permitted the emergence of new networks, greater solidarity between inhabitants and a greater transparency of public action. It has been particularly effective in the sphere of housing, and initiatives concerning early childhood and young people have also borne fruit. Those involved have identified benefits from the process in terms of the promotion of a better image of the areas concerned, prevention of delinquency and drug addiction, and the reinforcement of feelings of identity and diminution of the perception of barriers between different social groups. Nevertheless, some weaknesses must be underlined: the rapid turnover of local actors, the 'corporatism' of some partners who experience the need for consensual action as an attack on the integrity of their organisation, and the persistence of some vote-catching practices. Beyond these aspects, the limited involvement of the business sector appears to be the main weakness of the Contrat de Ville, particularly in terms of efforts at economic integration.

In the case of the AEMVS (European Action for Mantois-Val de Seine, a local partnership within the European Poverty 3 Programme), the partnership process was less dominated by public actors or at least by their institutional logic. The area of Mantois-Val de Seine, located within the wider industrial periphery of Paris with an economy structured around the motor industry, is characterised by many social and economic difficulties and exclusion processes, with high levels of poverty, unemployment, youth delinquency, drug addiction, and high numbers of immigrant families.

The AEMVS was set up in 1989 in order to access funding from the European Poverty 3 programme. The first objective of the initiative was to group together, around the notions of action against poverty and exclusion, a wide range of local partners (political, social and economic). The Poverty 3 Programme was unusual in that it came direct from the European Commission, without passing through the institutions of member states. Poverty 3 was extremely flexible, requiring little in the way of predetermined attainments, but this tended to lead to ambitious projects which lacked feasibility because they were not related to the local reality. This area, which had been the site of many experiments in transversal public policies since the beginning of the 1980s, is characterised by the limited institutional influence of the municipality and the State at local level.

The first aims of the AEMVS were to promote both the partnership approach and collaboration between municipalities in the field of action against exclusion. Consequently, the partnership was headed by locally elected representatives from the participating communes with a representative of the sub-prefect. The association included a technical team and a project manager, an assistant and coordinators of various portfolios. These were articulated around the following areas of intervention: environment and heritage; employment and professional insertion; educational achievement; early childhood care; housing for young people; living conditions and international exchange; and evaluation.

While the partnership involved a large number of diverse organisations, there was only a weak commitment on the part of national public authorities and businesses. Broadly speaking, the main actors were the local elected representatives, leaders of local associations, social workers, public or para-public institutions at the local level (i.e. the various external services of the State, the Social Security Office), the Chambers of Commerce, individual company executives, and representatives of local residents. The dis-advantaged groups themselves (women, immigrants, young people with problems) were consulted through the specialist working groups established with regard to training, schooling and housing. Links were also established with other specialists as required by the needs of an individual portfolio. In our view, the methods of working developed by the partners involved in AEMVS reveal evidence of considerable expertise and/or technical skills. However, this was not always well received by all concerned, even though strong emphasis was placed on communication and the evaluation of initiatives.

After the initial tentative steps the AEMVS adopted an extremely prag-matic approach. Its main aim was to ensure success for a variety of initiatives that emanated from the grass roots level and was characterised by a willing-ness to pursue a partnership approach within a multi-commune framework and an institutional weakness resulting from the limited local base of the project. The AEMVS sometimes acted as the main funding agency, but on other occasions it provided residual funding for measures to combat social exclusion; it might either initiate action or implement it; it might act as a technical adviser offering considerable expertise or as an innovator; or it might lobby on behalf of the partnership.

The AEMVS achieved a number of its objectives relating to action against social exclusion. Its partnership approach tended to be exercised most effec-tively at the sectoral level, within the specialist working group of technical experts and local people and not at the executive level of the Association, which consisted of elected representatives from Mantois-Val de Seine. The exit strategy adopted by AEMVS, which concentrated more on continuity for successful portfolios and less on a more general analysis of the problems of social exclusion, confirms this. Although the Association was heavily criticised by many for its technical nature and its lack of transparency, some interesting initiatives were implemented and although fragmented they did bring together a diverse range of actors (social workers, employers, targeted groups, etc.). The structures that survive from AEMVS are responsible for some extremely positive initiatives, which, provided they can rise above local power struggles and financial difficulties, can remain meaningful instruments both in terms of the use of the partnership approach and action against exclusion. The Achilles heel of AEMVS and its successors arises from the omnipresence of local elected politicians in this partnership structure. Changes in the make-up of elected councils and the differing political sensitivities of individuals means that an 'end-of-year exam', the results of which are fairly unpredictable, is inevitable each time there is an election.

Strengths and weaknesses of the partnership approach

On the basis of the French experience it seems to us that several issues must be highlighted.

Partnerships make it possible to identify problems which are all too often hidden, in particular through the participation of women, immigrants and local residents in the development and implementation of projects in a systematic way. This was the case with the Développement Social des Quartiers (DSQ) policy. In Lille, Mantes and other locations, a partnership provided an opportunity, albeit incomplete, to mobilise new actors from the voluntary sector which has gained an expanded role and has benefited from additional resources. A partnership may represent an area of freedom where the participation of local residents and groups traditionally disadvantaged in terms of representation can be developed. This aspect is the subject of intense debate in France at the present time, a debate which divides those who wish to maintain the Republican model of integration and those who argue for a measured acceptance of the reality of the community in order to encourage the mobilisation of immigrants. Partnership models may possibly represent an avenue of reconciliation or at least a relaxation in the French system which would make it possible for local and community associations to take responsibility in a more systematic way without precluding a relationship, even one with tensions, with local elected representatives. Partnerships, particularly within the framework of European programmes, have given a legitimacy to small and medium-sized associations with a strong local base, which can, therefore, rise above the barriers created for example by the disintegration of communities.

Partnerships facilitate innovation and experimentation, although this is not without its difficulties and resistance. The examples of Lille, Mantes and GALCOB provide concrete evidence of this: initiatives and programmes, even political projects, have been developed and implemented which are different, even very different, from what has previously characterised French social policy. Even if innovation has its limits, the link between partnership and innovation is clearly evident from our case studies. As part of a more decentralised approach to social policies, partnerships may provide an opportunity, even if they remain under the control of the elected representatives, of public action which avoids in part the bureaucratisation inherent in attempts to achieve territorial coherence between the various organisations of the State at national and local level and the local authorities.

However, risks and problems associated with partnerships have also emerged. In management terms a partnership is a difficult structure. The organisation of joint action by various partners, with resources which are sometimes limited and with methods of working which are very different, raises a considerable number of problems which have been well documented in all studies on this issue. A key factor in the success of any partnership is, therefore, an ability to attract individuals who have or acquire the 'soft skills' that allow partnerships to function and progress. Our research shows that this has not always been the case. Partnerships also attract a certain type of professional who flourishes in a partnership but who paralyses it at the same time. Some professionals, with a flair for relationships and networks, position themselves at the heart of a partnership for the wrong reasons: to satisfy their obsession with the culture of meetings, to enjoy congenial contacts with a range of very diverse partners, and to give the impression of causing a stir. This contributes to the opaqueness of initiatives and confusion about objectives, of partnership as an amorphous collaboration which prevents clear reporting and results in nothing happening on the ground. We met this type of professional in several of our case studies. They are more formidable because their flair for networking and relationships reinforces their position, which can be difficult to challenge because the complexity of a partnership and the differences between certain players can allow the person at the centre considerable latitude. Rigorous evaluation in a partnership can be a challenge to those in charge. Expressed directly, a partnership always runs the risk of turning into a quagmire of public action without clear responsibilities.

As partnership is difficult to implement and as elected representatives are often required to justify projects and exceptional expenditure, the consequent pressures may result in a strengthening of the stronger partners, e.g. large national associations at the expense of smaller associations with good local roots, in the name of efficiency. The age-old conflict, common to any organisation, between efficiency and internal democracy, is particularly tricky in the context of partnerships. Thus, for reasons such as that 'results are required', there is a risk that initial good intentions or more fragile interests or target groups may end up being marginalised.

The way in which partnership in France, in particular in its contractual form such as the Contrat de Ville, is seen as a way of developing consistent public policy in a given territory leads to similar problems. Because of the rules governing public accounts these partnerships promote the development of a complex bureaucratic structure which represents an additional barrier to the mobilisation of local residents and small associations. Partnerships in France find it difficult to escape from a technocratic excess.

Employer organisations in France remain reluctant in many cases to participate in partnerships (the case of GALCOB is an interesting exception). There are at least two reasons for this. On the one hand, local employer associations in France, irrespective of whether they are chambers of commerce and industry or the regional employer organisations, are relatively weak and their control over their members is similarly very weak. Without exception their ability to act within the framework of a partnership is limited. On the other hand, the directors of large companies have always considered social action to be a public matter: that is why the State is there, it does the job relatively efficiently and the relatively high level of taxes compared with other European countries (even if many find them unjustified) is justified by social policies pursued by the State. In other words, as the State plays such an important role in France it is not for companies to concern themselves with social issues. Even if this position is in the process of change, it remains firmly rooted at the present time.

The (often justified) importance that partnerships place on innovation and communication may also conceal cut-backs in other programmes, or a wider lack of success in other respects of partnership. The French case shows that there is a danger of rushing headlong towards innovation and communication in order to conceal fundamental inadequacies.

A further risk, which goes hand-in-hand with the emphasis on the multi-dimensional nature of partnership and its objectives, was given concrete form in the case of Mantes. Although all agree that there is a need for multi-dimensional action, its limits are rarely questioned. Too often the reference to a multidimensional approach to the struggle against social exclusion serves as a pretext to justify anything and everything in terms of action and to justify spreading funds too thinly, selecting the wrong partners and a lack of strategy and priorities.

Conclusion

Partnerships to combat poverty (as defined by the European Foundation research and in France) may be a good idea. However, this does not mean that they should be cited systematically as the ideal solution in all cases. Partnerships often go hand-in-hand with the activities of social and partici-patory regulation, whereas their impact in terms of action, medium-term strategies, continuity and political choices is relatively disappointing. In this respect, support/control by public authorities may be essential to guarantee the durability and relative stability of the partnership.

Partnership has considerable potential. In France, the State and the local authorities (e.g. the association of mayors in France) could encourage a development of the partnership approach, which would go hand-in-hand with greater room for manoeuvre and experimentation at local level, includ-ing an increase in financial flexibility within an accounting framework slightly less strict than that which applies to public accounts.

However, the advantages of the partnership approach are not such that would justify a major retreat by the State from an involvement in social issues, or that the State should act solely as a financial regulator. Neither should local authorities be pushed aside: the promotion of competition between partnerships and local authorities would be counterproductive.

References

Alphanderi E (ed.) (1990) *L'insertion*. Syros: Paris.

Andre C and Delorme R (1983) *L'Etat et l'économie, un essai d'explication de l'évolution des dépenses publiques en France, 1870–1980*. Seuil: Paris.

Ascher P (1994) Le partenariat public-privé dans le (re)développement, le cas de la France, in Heinz W op cit.

Autes M (1995) Y-a-t-il des exclus? L'exclusion en débat, Lien Social et Politiques *Revue interdisciplinaire d'action communitaire*, no. 34.

Bachman C and Leguennec N (1996) *Violences urbaines ascension et chûte des classes moyennes à travers cinquante ans de politique de la ville.* Albin Michel: Paris.

Bailleau F (1987) *Le travail social et la crise.* IRESCO: Paris.

Caillosse J, Duran P and Lascoumes P (eds.) (1993) Piloter l'action publique, avec ou sans droit, *Politiques et Management Public* 13, 2–67.

Castel R (1995) *Les métamorphoses de la question sociale, une chronique du salariat.* Fayard: Paris.

Delahaye V (ed.) (1994) *Politiques de la lutte contre le chômage et l'exclusion, mutation de l'action sociale.* ENA, La Documentation Française.

Delarue J M (1991) *Banlieues en difficultés: la relégation.* Syros: Paris.

De Swaan A (1995) *Sous l'aile protectrice de l'Etat.* Presses Universitaires de France: Paris.

Donzelot J (ed.) (1991) *Face à l'exclusion, le modèle français.* Esprit: Paris.

Donzelot J (1996) Les transformations de l'intervention sociale face à l'exclusion, in Paugam S (ed.) *L'exclusion: L'etat des savoirs.* La Découverte: Paris.

Dubet F and Lapeyronnie D (1992) *Les quartiers d'exil.* Seuil: Paris.

Dubet F, Jazouli A and Lapeyronnie D (1981) *L'Etat et les jeunes.* Presses Universitaires de France: Paris.

Dubet F (1987) *La galère, jeunes en survie.* Fayard: Paris.

Dyson K (1980) *The State Tradition in Western Europe.* Martin Robertson: Oxford.

Faure A (1989) Le trousseau des politiques locales. *Politix*, No. 7–9.

Faure A (1994) Les élus locaux face à la décentralisation. *Revue Française de Science Politique* 44, 3, 462–89.

Fragonard B (1993) *Cohésion sociale et prévention de l'exclusion.* Commissariat général au plan, La Documentation Française: Paris.

de Gaujelac J and Leonetti I (1994) *La lutte des places.* Paris: Desclée de Brower.

Heinz W (ed.) (1994) *Partenariat public-privé dans l'aménagement urbain.* L'Harmattan: Paris.

Ion J (1992) *Le travail social à l'épreuve du territoire.* Privat: Toulouse.

Ion J and Tricart J P (1986) *Les travailleurs sociaux.* La Découverte: Paris.

Jazouli A (1995) *Une saison en banlieue, courants et prospectives dans les quartiers populaires.* Plon: Paris.

Jobert B (ed.) (1994) *Le tournant néo-libéral en Europe.* L'Harmattan: Paris.

Jobert B (1981) *Le social en plan.* Les Editions ouvrières.

Jobert B and Sellier M (1977) Les grandes villes: autonomie locale et innovation politique *Revue Française de Science Politique* 27, 2, 205–27.

Le Galès P (1995a) Politique de la ville en France et en Grande-Bretagne, volontarisme et ambiguités de l'Etat. *Sociologie du travail*, 37, 2, 249–75.

Le Galès P (1995b) Du gouvernement urbain à la gouvernance urbaine *Revue Française de Science Politique* 45, 1, 57–95.

Le Galès P (1996) *Partenariat public-privé et développement territorial*, Editions Le Monde: Paris.

Le Galès P and Thatcher M (ed.) (1995) *Les réseaux de politiques publiques.* L'Harmattan: Paris.

Le Galès P and Mawson J (1995) Contract versus competitive bidding, rationalization of urban policies in Britain and France, *Journal of European Public Policy* 2, 2, 205–42.

Le Galès P (1993) *Politique urbaine et développement local, une comparaison franco-brittanique* L'Harmattan: Paris.

Le Galès P, Oberti M and Rampal J C (1993) Localité et vote Front National à Mantes La Jolie, *Hérodote*.

Le Galès P and Oberti M (1992) L'AEMVS dans le Mantois Val-de-Seine: un diagnostic de localité, *Locatude*.

Le Goff V (1995) *Intervention européenne et partenariat: les nouvelles formes du développement rural, le cas du Centre Ouest Bretagne*, Final Dissertation, Institut d'Etudes Politiques de Rennes.

Lenoir R (1989) *Les exclus*, Le Seuil: Paris.

Lorrain D (1993) Après la décentralisation, l'action publique flexible. *Sociologie du Travail* 35, 3, 285–308.

Mabileau A (1991) *Le systeme local en France*, Montchrestien: Paris.

Martin C (1997) *L'après-divorce, lien familial et vulnérabilité*, Presses Universitaires de Rennes: Rennes.

Mayer N (1999) *Ces français qui votent Le Pen*, Paris: Flammarion.

Muller P (1992) Entre le local et l'Europe, la crise du modèle français de politiques publiques *Revue Française de Science Politique* 42, 2, 275–97.

Palicot M C and Thibout L (1995) *L'Europe et la lutte contre l'exclusion, Emergence de nouvelles formes d'insertion*, Racine Editions: Paris.

Palier B (1999) *Réformer la sécurité sociale*, Thèse de doctorat de science politique, IEP: Paris.

Paugam S (ed.) (1996) *L'exclusion, l'état des savoirs*, La Découverte: Paris.

Paugam S (1994) *Les pouvoirs locaux à l'épreuve du social*. Unpublished report, Paris: Institut de la Decentralisation.

Paugam S (1993) *La société française et ses pauvres*, PUF: Paris.

Paugam S (1991) *La disqualification sociale, essai sur la nouvelle pauvreté*, PUF: Paris.

Perrineau P (1997) *Le symptom Le Pen*, Paris: Fayard.

Rosanvallon P L (1990) *L'Etat en France de 1789 à nos jours*, Seuil: Paris.

Ruegg J, Decoutere S and Mettan N (eds.) (1994) *Le partenariat public-privé, Un atout pour l'aménagement du territoire et la protection de l'environnement?* Presses Polytechniques et Universitaires Romandes: Lausanne.

Sociologie du travail (1995) Special edition, *La Ville: habiter, gouverner*, Vol 37, No. 2.

Theret B (1995) *L'Etat, la finance et le social. Souveraineté nationale et construction européenne*, La Découverte: Paris.

Warin P (1992) *La politique de la ville, peau de chagrin. Contrats et conventions*, PIR-Villes.

Wuhl S (1992) *Les exclus face à l'emploi*, Syros: Paris.

5 Grass roots local partnerships in the Federal Republic of Germany

Instruments for social inclusion and economic integration?

Karl Birkhölzer and Günther Lorenz

Introduction

This chapter focuses on grass roots local partnerships in the Federal Republic of Germany (FRG) that are active in regeneration and employment policies. While not necessarily being known as 'partnerships', but working in a similar way, German local partnerships normally take the form of an association, including partners from all three sectors (public, private and the not-for-profit/community sector). A short historical survey on social and economic development including a characterization of social exclusion is followed by descriptions of three case studies representing the characteristic types of partnership.

In conclusion, the authors highlight the strengths and weaknesses of local partnerships and will make the case for area-based, community-led approaches.

The socio-economic context of local partnerships in Germany

Our chapter first identifies the specific dimensions of poverty and exclusion in Germany, and of the national context of social policies. It specifically describes the social policy developments and institutions with reference to poverty and social exclusion after the Second World War particularly since the 1980s.

In the 1950s, there was mass poverty following the war. Economic and employment policies became the main means of reducing poverty, and in the 1950s and 1960s were extremely successful. In the 1970s, however, excluded groups, especially migrants, emerged as a social problem, demonstrating that exclusion could not be solved solely by economic growth and income support. The debate on 'New Poverty' (Bahlsen, Nahielski, Roessel and Winkel 1985), beginning with the profound structural changes in the early 1980s, led to new approaches in social policy, one of which was the

partnership approach, though in a 'prototype form'. However, public awareness of new forms of partnership strategies – e.g. private-public partnerships
for urban regeneration, or national alliance concepts such as the 'Alliance
for Jobs' – is still very limited, although there is a growing interest among
local authorities in this approach.

Local partnerships in Germany before and after unification

Then, drawing on examples, we analyse and evaluate the ways in which local
partnership initiatives have developed, with detailed reference to their objectives, structures and outcomes. We outline the development of social partnership in West and East Germany, from the classical tripartite (corporate)
approach in the West and the enterprise-based partnership in the East via
the recent National Alliances to the local partnership approach.

Local partnerships in Germany: local economic restructuring 'from below'

Finally, we offer brief conclusions concerning the contribution that a
partnership approach makes in Germany. Drawing on three case studies –
'Kommunales Forum Wedding' in Berlin, 'Ökospeicher' in the Land of
Brandenburg and 'Entwicklungszentrum Dortmund' in the Ruhr region –
we focus on specific features of partnership strategies which seem predominantly to be developed in Germany. In short, the local partnership
approach here focuses on combating local and economic exclusion 'from
below', through local employment initiatives and economic regeneration
activities. We conclude with an assessment of the different partners' involvement in the diverse partnerships, and of the contribution of the partnership
approach in promoting social and economic cohesion, and contrast this to
the potential that could be developed under certain conditions.

The socio-economic context of local partnerships in the Federal Republic of Germany

Social and economic exclusion in Germany

For our definition of social exclusion we have followed the study by Ball,
according to which social and economic change has brought not only benefits
but also – for many population groups – disadvantages. These groups include
young people without vocational training and/or without employment
prospects; women on whom fall additional demands for family care; people
who have to live in socially and economically run-down regions and districts;
the unemployed and those facing unemployment; and people who cannot
participate in social and economic life on account of physical disabilities
(Ball 1994). The group of people marginalized or socially excluded in this

way in Germany has grown in size since the mid-1970s,[1] and reunification in 1990 added an East/West economic and social disparity to the existing duality between the 'rich south' and the 'poor north', which had existed in pre-unification West Germany.[2] In unified Germany there has been a dual socio-economic structural crisis in East and West since the beginning of the 1990s: while an increasing structural crisis in western Germany has consolidated basic unemployment at around 9–11 per cent of the potential labour force, significant developments have been taking place in the former German Democratic Republic (GDR), in that large areas are falling into crisis in an irreversible process that cannot be tackled with the traditional instruments of economic, labour-market and social policy.[3] Whereas immediately after unification almost all working people in the former GDR were affected or threatened by unemployment, this region, too, is now experiencing the emergence of a dualism, in that unemployment and poverty are becoming concentrated on certain regional and social problem groups.

Poverty and social exclusion now affect not only the traditional crisis regions of the West hit by sectoral restructuring in shipbuilding, steel or coal-mining, or geographically peripheral regions. Social exclusion now appears equally in newly impoverished rural regions, particularly in the Eastern Länder, and in the inner cities of many conurbations.

In 1996, 4.6 million people asked for assistance from the Welfare Departments of the local authorities (Sozialamter) and 2.7 million received welfare benefits (Sozialhilfe – HzL). This means an increase of 250,000 beneficiaries compared with the previous year. Around 12.3 million people lived on income below the poverty line of DM 1000 net (Hunfeld 1998; Becker and Hauser 1997). This increase in poverty was accompanied by mass long-term unemployment. Whereas in 1990, 1.9 million of the population were unemployed, by 1996 the number had doubled to 4 million. At the same time, the duration of unemployment has risen from 29.7 per cent in 1990 to 33.3 per cent in 1995 (Friedrich and Wiedemeyer 1998).

If the phenomenon of social exclusion is analysed in terms of the life-situation approach proposed by Doring, Hanesch and Huster (1990), we find four important dimensions of social exclusion:

1 This led to the coining of the term 'new poverty' in Germany, which unleashed a furious debate on whether this was really a true description of the German situation. Politicians, in particular, criticized the use of the term, claiming that the Federal Republic's social security system was still 'intact'.

2 Regional unemployment statistics already shortly after unification in the FRG show a wide disparity between the West German Länder in 1990, ranging from 13.5 per cent for Bremen to 4.1 per cent for Baden-Württemberg.

3 Regional unemployment statistics show a wide disparity between the West German and East German Länder in 1998, ranging from 8.8 per cent in the West to 15.9 per cent in the East (BA Information Nov 1998 from 10/12/98). The average unemployment rate at the same time was 10.3 per cent, according to the BA statistics. The EUROSTAT employment survey only stated an unemployment rate of 9.3 per cent at the same time.

- low income;
- poor living conditions;
- lack of training and jobs;
- under-provision of social services.

Low income

In 1992, 10.1 per cent of the population of Germany were living in 'income poverty';[4] the percentages were 7.5 per cent for the West and 14.8 per cent for the East. Although there is a levelling-out tendency in average incomes as between East and West, there has nevertheless been a significant increase in 'income-poor' population groups in the new Federal Länder (1990: a rise of 3.3 per cent; 1992: a rise of 5.8 per cent).

Living conditions

In 1990, almost every fourth person in the GDR lived in substandard accommodation; in 1992 it was still every fifth person. The standard of dwellings between East and West differs substantially: whereas in 1992 some 2.2 per cent of West Germans still lived in accommodation without their own bath and WC, the figure for East Germans in the same year was 13.7 per cent. This, therefore, is one reason for the frequent inclusion of projects for the homeless and improved housing and housebuilding projects in the present partnership agendas.

Training and jobs

Up until reunification the unemployment rate in West Germany had remained relatively steady since 1975 at 7.5 per cent. After reunification it increased dramatically and currently hovers around the 9–11 per cent mark for the whole of Germany. From 1992 up to and including 1995, since the world recession, the unemployment rate has climbed to new heights, and when 'hidden unemployment' is taken into account the absolute number of unemployed is greater than it was before the seizure of power by the Nazi party in 1933.[5] From 1990 to 1992 over 4 million jobs disappeared, leaving 43 per cent of all households affected by at least one case of unemployment, short-time working or participation in job creation schemes (Arbeits-BeschaffungsMaßnahmen) in 1992 (Friedrich and Wiedemeyer 1994).

The physical and social consequences not only reduce the self-esteem of those immediately affected, but also accelerate the break-up of family and

---

4 The 'income-poor' are, by definition, those people who are entitled to 'subsistence aid' (social assistance).

5 Friedrich and Wiedemeyer (1994) assume an effective unemployment rate of 30 per cent (p50).

social ties. Unemployment is now the main reason for social assistance claims. The use of social assistance benefits, which were not originally intended for the unemployed at all, is a sign of the structural disintegration of the German social system.

Social services

The unemployed, whose numbers are steadily increasing, chiefly comprise people with health problems, the over-55s, and people who have not completed their training. In eastern Germany, in particular, it is the families with many children and thus principally children and young people who are most affected by poverty. The rate of those suffering multiple social under-provision among couples with more than three children was 40.2 per cent in the East and about 22 per cent in the West. Single mothers form a major group of the poor in the new Federal Länder. There is a clear correlation between their membership of this group and their massive exclusion from the labour market. People who can no longer earn their living – the sick, pensioners, and people with disabilities – not only experience financial hardship, but also suffer from the effects of the irreversible social downgrading to which they are condemned.

Despite a levelling-out of average living conditions as between East and West, there has been no improvement – even in relative East/West terms – in the conditions of the affected East German population groups; rather, in both halves of the country there has been general growth in the number of persons excluded from the convergence process (Hanesch *et al*. 1994: 37). Besides the material deprivation suffered by these socially excluded people, a subjective feeling of deterioration in psychosocial and physical health is a decisive factor in the overall pattern of decline. Although the experience of social exclusion varies widely from one individual to another, those affected – especially in the former GDR – blame the politicians for what has happened.

The partnerships we have examined mostly attempt to tackle the dimensions of social exclusion identified in the 1994 Poverty Report (Hanesch *et al*. 1994) – income poverty, poor living conditions, lack of training and jobs, and under-provision with social services – in a holistic way.

The historical and political context of partnership

Until the reunification of the two German states in 1990 there were two different contexts for partnership in Germany.

The original Federal Republic of Germany (West Germany) from the time of its foundation after the Second World War provided the classic example of social partnership in Europe. The state seldom interfered with the collective bargaining autonomy of trade unions and employers; until the early

1970s state intervention was the exception. The social partnerships in question developed at national level (concerted action), regional level (collective agreements) and plant level; in the latter case, works councils traditionally negotiated agreements on behalf of the workforce with the corporate level (plant agreements). This was linked to the concept of 'co-determination' or employee participation in companies. In a historic compromise between capital and labour, which had its roots in the wartime experience, a post-war consensus came into being, which developed into the concept of the 'social market economy'. During the economic crises of the 1960s and 1970s this process of integration slowed down and stopped, until by the early 1980s at the latest the social consensus at national level and employee participation rights in companies started to be eroded.

This has led to the debate on the modernization of the welfare state, in which the social partners, depending on their position in the socio-political landscape, have adopted widely differing stances: whereas the federal government and to some extent the Land governments and also the greater part of the private sector regard the restructuring process as one of 'conversion' or 'rebuilding', the trade unions, most of the municipalities and districts and also the voluntary sector complain that the welfare state is being 'dismantled'.

The concept of social partnership in western Germany is confined almost exclusively to the private sector, including the trade unions, and public sector corporations. In addition, there is a concept, derived from this, of tripartite equal partnership; this applies to the 'self-governing' bodies and systems such as:

- the Federal Employment Service (Bundesanstalt für Arbeit) and the unemployment insurance system;
- social security (statutory health insurance funds, statutory pension schemes, etc.);
- the Federal Institute for Vocational Training (Bundesinstitut für Berufliche Bildung), etc.

In this case, employers' and employees' organizations and government representatives are represented on these institutions' governing bodies. These social partnership institutions do not include any partnerships falling within our own definition, which includes the voluntary and community as well as the public and private sectors.

In the GDR the term 'partnership' was not used as such. It was held that the working class ('the people') owned the means of production and therefore it would have been absurd to speak of social partnership. Nevertheless, there were forms of social partnership between companies and young people or the elderly, which promoted social cohesion. For example, there were sponsorship agreements between schools or universities and companies to familiarize young people with working conditions. Similar individual partnerships were created by the internal company trade unions with retired employees and with schools and universities.

Current developments in local partnership

The present economic and social situation in Germany is characterized by the emergence of structural crises in the economy and in society as a whole. At the same time the government's economic and social policy has for many years been at the limits of its scope for intervention, with the result that the social partners in particular now find themselves again having to make their own contribution towards relieving the situation. Besides various models for redistributing work, an 'Alliance for Jobs', in which the social partners form a strong counterweight to the politicians, has recently entered the debate. Overall, the effects of the work redistribution policy vary from sector to sector and from region to region, with the result that the necessity for and the importance of local partnerships increases from the bottom up.

The 'Alliance for Jobs', proposed in 1995 by Germany's largest single trade union, IG Metall, aims to create jobs for the long-term unemployed and trainees through wage restraint and a reduction in overtime. Participating in the negotiations to turn the proposal into reality at both national and regional level are employers' organizations, trade unions and regional governments. IG Metall's proposal envisages that 100,000 jobs and 10,000 apprenticeships could be created by a reduction of 250 million hours of overtime. The 'Alliance for Jobs' was revived after the election of the Schroeder government as an 'Alliance for Jobs, Training and Competitiveness'.

In the early 1980s developing urban and rural crises led to the beginnings of local partnerships. The local partnership approach has become internationally known through a study on the regeneration of deprived urban areas (Froessler 1994; Froessler, Lang, Selle and Staubach 1994; Staubach 1995). However, whereas these partnerships focused largely on physical planning questions, the partnerships examined in our own study were mainly initiatives with a socio-economic background and focus, and were the product of 'bottom up' or 'grass roots' initiatives. Such initiatives – which do not (yet) usually call themselves partnerships – may be either:

- initiated by local authorities in crisis regions; or
- initiated by employees in crisis-hit industrial sectors, some of which can rely on a degree of support from trade unions; or
- local initiatives which at least include the socially excluded and therefore also include women's and foreigners' groups in their work (sometimes with the aid of EU programmes and policies).

In crisis regions, recognition of the need for self-help and grass roots initiatives is gaining ground because neither the private sector – through investment – nor the public sector – through intervention – are achieving a decisive or comprehensive turnaround. There are as yet no regional or national programmes to foster these beginnings, with the result that these partnerships do not have to have any formal structure, and nor can they rely on special promotion programmes. This explains their flexibility but also their lack of adequate resources. They sometimes go under the name of Round Tables (Runde Tische), local alliances for jobs (Lokale/regionale Bündnisse für Arbeit) or regional fora (Regionales Forum). Initiative is often taken by intermediary organizations, motivated by the fact that politicians have not yet had much success in harnessing local resources to combat unemployment, poverty and social exclusion.

Many of these partnerships are concerned mainly with creating jobs, others with ecological and regional regeneration, and a few have purely social objectives. Some of them use the creation of their own companies (e.g. social enterprises, whether with a private sector or not-for-profit status) to implement their intentions or else include among their partners social enterprises (companies that carry out socially useful work). A number of the social enterprises are set up by local authorities as Kommunale Beschäftigungsgesellschaften or are supported by Länder governments through social enterprise support schemes (Birkhölzer and Lorenz 1998a, b; Birkhölzer 1998).

A number of local partnerships were established on the basis of EU programmes, for example under the Poverty or LEDA programmes. These were important in ensuring that social cohesion became an important theme and also in bringing 'the community' into social policy-making at the local level. However, partnerships of this kind, in which the socially excluded have a genuine say, are very thin on the ground. Apart from a few positive examples, the socially excluded population groups are represented by the large welfare organizations, which regard their users as 'clients'.

The role of particular sectors in local partnerships

The public sector is represented in such local initiatives by municipal, district and Land government. In a few cases federal organizations (public-law bodies) are also represented. From the voluntary sector there is a wealth of societies and associations, including both the major welfare organizations and also local and regional initiatives, projects and associations. Many initiatives are set up 'from the bottom', from local forums or are founded or co-founded by local authorities (such as the Regional Forum for Jobs in Berlin-Kruezberg).

Apart from a few initiatives by employees (e.g. EWZ, Dortmund and FNP, Kiel – see Birkhölzer and Lorenz 1996), the cases and examples investigated by us reveal very little involvement by trade unions in local social policy partnerships and no involvement at all by employers' organizations. This does not mean, however, that there was no involvement on the part of the trade union members themselves. In the Wedding Communal Forum (see below) and other cases, trade union groups from companies have been involved in the creation of partnerships and in their subsequent work even when they received no support from their organization for activities of this kind. The example of the Communal Forum also shows that small firms and social enterprises can be included in partnerships if a voluntary organization is leading the partnership. The 'Ökospeicher', again discussed below, is a special case in that there the role of the private sector is relatively strong because 'ecological' (i.e. ecologically oriented) companies initiated the partnership. In an initiative in Heidelberg, social enterprises were leading actors in a local initiative.

As might be expected from the great extent to which women are affected in multiply deprived areas, their participation at grass roots level – particularly in the locality-related partnerships – is especially marked. Although combating women's disadvantage or promoting their advancement are not usually expressly stated as objectives in the relevant agendas, women play a leading role in the majority of the cases that we have studied (for example, as managing directors). In addition, we have found that in most cases local initiatives do include specific projects to assist women, such as the FRIEDA women's centre in the EU Poverty 3 partnership in Friedrichshain, and various projects to assist girls and women in Wedding, (both in Berlin). The latter also includes several other projects that reflect the high proportion of Turkish inhabitants in the locality.

With reference to ethnic groups, it is important in the German context to distinguish between economic immigrants (Gastarbeiter), who have largely become socially integrated into the community, and political asylum seekers and refugees from war zones. The second group and also the new illegal immigrants from eastern Europe have not become integrated at all. The national organizations of ethnic minorities are barely represented in the partnership initiatives that we have studied. Nevertheless, representatives of the first group do participate as individuals in partnerships, particularly locality-related ones, or are 'clients' for the corresponding social organizations. The problems of the second group are represented even less in the organization and policies of existing partnerships.

Examples of local partnerships in Germany: local economic regeneration from below

Despite the relatively limited nature of local partnership-based initiatives to combat social exclusion in Germany, some examples that are of wider relevance and interest do indeed exist and will be discussed here.

Kommunales Forum Wedding (Wedding Communal Forum), West Berlin

The Wedding Communal Forum (KFW) was set up in 1988 in an urban neighbourhood in the Wedding district of West Berlin. Wedding was formerly one of Berlin's major industrial centres but has now been almost completely de-industrialized, which has led to high rates of unemployment and a high incidence of deprivation among its inhabitants.

In its legal structure the partnership is a non-profit association. It currently has some 40 formally registered member organizations including 60 to 70 active persons and represents a broad spectrum of local institutions and organizations in the private, public and voluntary sectors. The partnership has a written constitution based on the ideas of economic self-help and local development proposed by the 'Local Economy' Interdisciplinary Research Group (IFG 'Lokale Ökonomie'); the latter organization provides supervision, training and evaluation services for the partnership.

Represented in the KFW as members are District Council staff and elected representatives, the churches, cultural and youth associations, training and employment initiatives, tenants', foreigners' and women's organizations, and works and staff councils. Social enterprises and private sector businesses are also involved in the activities. However, although the initiative for the creation of the Community Forum came from trade unions and works councils, these have increasingly withdrawn from the partnership's work.

The KFW's activities started with the opening of a local 'action bureau' in a disused and partly contaminated factory (the former Rotaprint printing works). The work takes place at three levels. Once a month a communal forum is held at which all the relevant actors and people affected come together to discuss various local problems. The forum has given rise to a number of working groups, some of them dealing with sectoral problems (e.g. unemployment, housing, women, the environment, ethnic minorities), others working more at local level in deprived neighbourhoods using deficit and resource analyses and planning techniques developed at grass roots level. Finally, there is a coordination office, which initiates joint action programmes and organizes a range of employment projects in cooperation with the Berlin Senate department responsible for employment and women.

The guiding philosophy of the Communal Forum is that social cohesion should be promoted by bringing together organizations and institutions which normally work on different levels; mobilizing 'ordinary people' as experts on local needs; and creating jobs by meeting local needs and making use of local resources. The main thrust of the work is to make use of largely untapped skills and experience by building new cooperative relationships and identifying new fields for employment through an analysis of the area's needs and resources. With the help of a planning process designed to mobilize the local community, the aim is to create new jobs that will help to improve the quality of life in the area. A feature of the KFW is that it did not start by acquiring or receiving funds, but it commissioned unemployed people to build up the necessary structures and search for funds.

This informal partnership is now complemented by the constitution of the Lokale Partnerschaft Wedding (1997), which was shortly followed by the Lokale Partnerschaft Prenzlauer Berg in East Berlin. Their agenda is the improvement of life quality through new jobs. Both partnerships are members of the Europe-wide REVES Network of towns and villages supporting the social economy.

Ökospeicher ('Eco-Warehouse'), Wulkow bei Boossen, Frankfurt/Oder

The municipality of Wulkow near Frankfurt an der Oder in Brandenburg lies some 80 km east of Berlin. With a population of only 150, Wulkow is a small village near the Polish border whose principal economic activity before reunification in 1990 was agriculture. Farming was nevertheless in decline, with the resultant social consequences, and the East German authorities planned to resettle the inhabitants in other regions. In 1989, 28 inhabitants were still employed in agricultural cooperatives, but by 1991 all of these had become unemployed. Faced with the prospect of being resettled, the Wulkowers had two options: either to abandon their village or to fight for its future. In 1990 the inhabitants mounted an initiative to revitalize their locality.

They set up a partnership-based initiative that included almost every inhabitant: farmers, commuters (most of them working in Frankfurt an der Oder), the mayor, traders, the school, and the church. Ökospeicher is a registered association (e.V.) which acts as a local development agency and coordinates all economic and social activities in the locality. Issues affecting Wulkow are discussed by various specialist groups and dealt with through the association and – at political level – through the municipality. The association has a written constitution and there are also local planning regulations and a paper entitled 'Wulkower Weg' ('The Wulkow Way'), which argues from a holistic standpoint that, in order to be viable, villages need not only agriculture but also other trades, and that ecological transformation is the key to success.

The first step was to reconstruct an old, disused four-storey warehouse (hence the name 'Ökospeicher' or 'Eco-Warehouse'), which was converted into a multi-functional building. It now houses a market, workshop and office space, a training and communication centre, a restaurant and a space for conferences and exhibitions. At the same time a local plan for the creation of a model village operating on sound ecological principles was developed. The Ökospeicher attracted, and continues to attract, not only visitors, politicians and experts from both Germany and abroad, but also partners from outside the village. New ideas were developed, leading to a series of demonstration projects of sound ecological development, and in 1993 the partnership was awarded the German environmental prize.

The objectives of the Ökospeicher association are set out in its standing rules: Ökospeicher e. V. supports the ecologically oriented management of the land and ecological developments in agriculture, business, energy utilisation, architecture, art, culture and tourism. A further objective is the proportion of training, environmental education, and participation in research, all of which should result in the development and shaping of an ecologically sound economic area. The overriding aim of the initiative is to safeguard the continued social existence of the village. This required the creation of a new economic base, which was planned and put into effect by working groups organized on the basis of a number of specializations. There are three elements to this integrated 'cure and prevention' plan:

1   Creating jobs and income. In 1989, before reunification, 57 per cent of the population of Wulkow were in paid employment, but by 1991 this figure was down to 33 per cent. The losses were not only of jobs and income, but also of important elements of infrastructure: the local cafe, postal sorting office and cooperative store had all closed. The initiative has now brought 11 new businesses into being. Besides the re-opened cafe, these include the operator of the market; a water management and fish breeding business (using, among other resources, the restored village pond for fish breeding); an engineering firm that designs wind power units etc; firms growing and selling herbs; and an Institute called 'Copses in Agriculture', which engages in open air growing experiments and is building up a tree nursery. All these businesses are geared to the locality's own natural and man-made resources.
2   Measures to improve housing quality. These involve both owners and tenants in renovating and refurbishing the housing stock within quality regulations laid down by the municipality.
3   Redesign and maintenance of the landscape. This is being achieved by planting the castle park, gardens and avenues, and laying tracks and paths for cyclists and walkers.

Perhaps the best illustration of the multidimensionality of the initiative is the work taking place in the 'eco-warehouse'. This building accommodates a number of new businesses, together with organizations involved in village development; is the site of the weekly produce market and of a new communication and cultural centre for the local region; and generates ideas and coordinates activities for the ecologically oriented regeneration of the village.

Ökospeicher e.V. is a non-profit association with 150 formally equal members. The membership includes many Wulkow villagers plus individuals and institutions from outside, including the European University Viadrina in Frankfurt/Oder and several Brandenburg colleges. Of the 150 members,

50 are businesses, 14 are educational institutions, 16 are institutes and 70 are individuals. There was an original intention that all Wulkow villagers should be members of the association. This had to be abandoned because in the beginning only a limited number were interested enough to be involved. There is, however, a higher level of participation in projects such as the sale of home-grown produce in the market or the preparation of village festivals. The members of the association work on an honorary basis: Ökospeicher e.V. is financed by a small subscription by all members. Specific projects are financed from earnings and grants. For example, the market in the 'eco-warehouse' is funded by the traders, who pay a levy of 5–10 per cent of their turnover. In addition, grants have been obtained from various charitable foundations, especially for experimental projects.

The Wulkow initiative is of wider relevance due to the way in which the local partnership came into being not as a result of an initiative by government, or even by a disadvantaged population group and its partners, but in response to the threatened exclusion of a whole municipality. Social exclusion was therefore tackled by restructuring an entire local community, with ecological transformation seen as the key instrument for building a self-sustaining community. The success of the 'Wulkow Way' can be attributed to a number of factors:

- a multidimensional approach and interdisciplinary methods;
- an open and democratic partnership structure with clearly defined general objectives;
- an easily recognizable locality and participants strongly motivated to reverse the process of exclusion.

The inclusion of all three sectors – public, private and voluntary – not only indicates the openness of the initiative, but also permits extensive use of local and external resources. There has also been a good balance between the role of the management board in formulating overall strategy and the work of specialist groups and companies. It is also important that the local municipality has adopted a cooperative posture and has not tried to dicate the course of events.

The Wulkow model cannot be regarded as universally transferable, in the sense that the community consciousness of the residents was an important precondition of its success. Nonetheless, it does serve as a model for other intermediate employment creation initiatives in rural areas.

Entwicklungszentrum (EWZ) (Dortmund Development Centre), the Ruhr

Dortmund, Westphalia's largest city (580,000 inhabitants), is home to a number of different industries, particularly in the iron making and processing and chemical sectors. The city is situated in the ex-industrial conurbation of the Ruhr, in which falling demand has led to a slump in sales and the closure of many mines.

The North Rhine-Westphalia association of the German Federation of Trade Unions (DGB) commissioned the University of Dortmund and the local branch of the DGB to organize a local employment initiative. In 1985, on the basis of work by this working group, the 'Association for the Creation of the Dortmund Development Centre – Eastern Ruhr Model' was founded.

The members of this association are the city's economic promotion office, the DGB, the trade unions IG Chemie, IG Bau and IG Metall (chemicals, construction and the metal industry respectively), socially committed institutions and training projects. The partnership is run by active trade union members in alliance with the district and Land authorities. An innovation consultancy formed by some of the founders of the EWZ supports the development of services and products in the private and public sectors.

Existing programmes and institutions are used to:

- develop socially useful and ecologically sound products and processes;
- identify employment opportunities in socially useful fields with a view to creating jobs;
- provide future-oriented training;
- persuade universities and technical colleges to take an interest in the needs of employees and the unemployed.

Existing resources are used mainly for converting former industrial sites to other uses. At both the EWZ's old and new site the objective is the further-ance of social cohesion through product development, advice to tenants, training for the unemployed, and work with foreigners.

Conclusion

Local partnerships can have a number of functions (Walsh, Craig and McCafferty 1998):

- a brokerage role (usually in the form of a foundation); or
- an intermediary organization (e.g. as a local or regional agency); or
- as a service provider (e.g. as a project development agency).

The partnerships studied by us in Germany tend to fall into the last two cate-gories. They often fulfil the double function of intermediary organization and project development agency, because their initiators and managers have founded them on the basis of quite specific ideas for dealing with certain problems.

All three examples demonstrate (and other examples of local partnerships in Germany indicate) that managements partly act as enablers of projects, thus helping to promote social cohesion, and partly participate in specific projects as members of associations or managing directors.[6] This involvement in the day-to-day running of partner projects, although it may in individual cases inhibit the creation of more far-reaching strategies, is nevertheless a stimulus to continued attempts to try out innovative approaches to specific problems as they arise. The arm's-length position of brokers or agencies would tend to favour an attitude that left the partnerships in the position of mere resource distribution centres and constituted an additional layer of power. Involvement in the day-to-day running of projects has the drawback, however, that it does not create the same aura of impartiality that is enjoyed by an organization that is not directly linked to the projects it supports.

The problems of local partnerships to promote social cohesion take many different forms. We can discuss them under the categories of initiation; division of powers; management structures; resources; political influence, and effects on social exclusion.

Most of the partnerships examined here have been founded by 'bottom-up' initiatives by the voluntary sector.[7] In the case of the EU initiatives such as the Poverty 3 project in Friedrichshain, the municipalities have been either the initiators or the co-initiators of the partnerships. Partnerships on the model of the British 'City Challenge' and similar programmes, which have come into being as a result of national or regional programmes or initiatives, do not exist in Germany owing to the absence of such programmes. Accordingly, it is noticeable that an increasing number of German initiatives that apply the partnership approach are based on European programmes.[8]

Most of the partnerships, by reason of their grass roots origins, have democratic and *egalitarian structures*, although a distinction has to be drawn between the formal and informal levels. For example, in the case of Ökospeicher (and to a certain extent the Wedding Communal Forum) there are no formal structures for decision-making on the basis of equal representation at general meetings of the association's members. Yet for this reason none of the working groups (and the same is true of the Dortmund EWZ) are required to comply with formal instructions from above, but are allowed to operate relatively independently within the limits set by the association's standing rules. This autonomy can sometimes lead to excessive

---

6 The managers of the KFW coordination office create the social infrastructure and administer job-creation projects, the chairman of the management board of Ökospeicher employs socially excluded people through the association's project alliance, and the managing director of the Dortmund EWZ leads training projects.

7 For the purposes of the present study we have used the term 'voluntary sector' (freigemeinnütziger Sektor) to cover both voluntary and community organizations. Community organizations pursue the interests of a specific local community and/or its inhabitants, whereas voluntary organizations in the narrower sense are those welfare, social and cultural organizations that are not part of the public sector and are not connected with a specific locality.

8 The Wedding Communal Forum, in cooperation with the representatives of other Berlin initiatives, is currently soliciting European funds to finance its partnership work.

independence,[9] although some partnerships have overcome the problem by more fully integrating the partners.

Management structures and skills are required that are flexible enough to cope adequately with actual circumstances and projects. But management's coordinating function must not be so extensive that it restricts the autonomy of working groups and projects. Most partnerships have only a joint administrative office, which is usually staffed by one or more of the partners. Coordination of projects within a partnership is usually informal, being exercised by key individuals or cooperation associations.[10] Attempts to disengage the organization of the partnership work from that of the direct project work have so far failed for lack of resources.

Since no special *resources and programmes* are available at national and regional level for partnerships, the partnerships have to rely on a wide variety of other programmes and a great deal of volunteer work. Although volunteer work is regarded as extremely desirable, a number of activities nevertheless require paid professional work. This applies to both general management and project management. There are insufficient funds to finance partnership management for the full term of its existence. Some partnerships counter this by piecing together a number of short-term employment programmes, others make use of liberally financed pilot projects or increased collaboration with partners who have access to greater resources.

As partnerships to promote social cohesion are so small in number in Germany, they cannot be expected to have much *influence on other policy measures* at the present time. As a result, there is a general lack of awareness of this subject in Germany. However, conversations with some politicians at Land and federal level who have already come into contact with partnerships indicate that they consider the partnership approach to be efficient. The result is that an increasing number of partners in the public sector are participating in partnerships. It can be envisaged that lack of budgetary funds will make this approach more attractive,[11] because it helps to save net social costs owing to its subsidiary method of functioning.

Up until now there have been no systematic evaluations of *effects on social exclusion* apart from one made in respect of the Poverty 3 programme for Friedrichshain. We conclude from our observations, however, that – especially in the case of partnership projects whose objectives are linked to employment measures – this approach has made it possible for people to be reintegrated into society both economically and socially, at least

9 In the case of the Dortmund EWZ, for example, project managers acquired skills in the course of work on their projects and then left to work elsewhere.
10 Cf. the metaphor of orchestra and conductor quoted in connection with the Ökospeicher. The role of conductor can be played by key individuals or by coordinators. In the case of the Wedding Communal Forum, coordinators also fulfil the function of information-providers and organizers within the framework of the cooperation associations.
11 This is especially noticeable in Berlin.

temporarily. Since these measures usually last for only two years, the process is of only short duration and therefore increases the frustration of those affected if they are thrown back into unemployment and/or social isolation after the measures have come to an end.

The most important conclusion to emerge from our observation of the social exclusion problem and partnership structures is that one cannot generalize and say that poverty and social exclusion apply exclusively to specific social groups. The structural crisis of areas with multiple deprivation affects nearly all the population groups living there, albeit to differing degrees. In every case, people who are in any case disadvantaged suffer multiple discrimination which cannot be tackled by sectoral programmes aimed at specific target groups.

It is clear from these observations that action programmes and policies for local partnerships have to take place at local level or relate to a specific locality if they are to be efficient. The reasons for this are that, firstly, most people suffering from poverty and social exclusion are to be found in districts where crisis spots develop. Second, if a locality-related approach is used, certain social groups do not feel stigmatized: everybody in the locality, what-ever kind of social disadvantagement they suffer from – be it physical dis-ability, long-term unemployment, sex discrimination or membership of an ethnic minority – can then receive support designed to assist their social reintegration.

Since poverty and social exclusion both have multidimensional aspects, the many-sidedness of the different kinds of deprivation must be suitably taken into account. For the partnership structure, however, this means that all population groups must be included as far as possible. Our observations show that the inclusion of unemployed people, recipients of social assistance, women and foreigners[12] in local partnerships can be successful. The inclusion of self-help groups is proving difficult. The reasons for this are, first, the reluc-tance of some self-help groups to participate in partnerships, often fearing that the superior power of other partners will affect their own objectives. Second, some partners, especially from the public sector, consider that such groups are not professional enough to be allowed to participate in partner-ship projects. In contrast, programmes geared to specific target groups usually succeed in reaching only a small proportion of the socially excluded and even then only those who are both entitled to claim social benefits and competent enough to pursue those claims successfully. In order to reach the truly socially excluded, who have not benefited from previous programmes, locality-related initiatives may therefore be an important part of the answer. They can counter the separation or segregation of individual 'communities of interest' on the basis of ethnicity or gender and the exclusion of a social underclass from target group initiatives. An important issue, therefore, is to

12 There are very few foreigners in Germany's rural regions, however.

have monitoring by ethnic or other interest groups to ensure that people are not excluded from partnerships for ethnic or similar reasons. A further conclusion to be drawn for the role of local partnerships in Germany is that it is important to integrate not only all the population groups in a given district but also these people's social and economic objectives. Initiatives that tackle people's economic problems usually last longer and generate higher levels of activity than those confined to purely social or cultural problems.

In Germany, compared with the number and effectiveness of existing initiatives there is a huge potential not currently being realized for grass roots local partnerships. With a few exceptions, current economic regeneration and employment programmes do not support or comply with the partnership approach. Some of them – for example, the so-called ABM schemes – are not suitable for partnership approaches at all. We should draw on positive outcomes in Germany and on the European experience to enhance the effectiveness of existing initiatives and to initiate new partnerships in Germany.

References

Bahlsen W H, Nahielski H, Roessel K and Winkel R (1985) *Die Neue Armut.* Köln: Bund Verlag.

Ball C (1994) *Bridging the Gulf: Improving social cohesion in Europe.* European Foundation for the Improvement of Living and Working Conditions. Luxembourg: Office for Official Publication of the European Communities.

Becker I and Hauser R (1997) *Einkommensverteilung und Armut: Deutschland auf dem Weg zur Vierfünftel-Gesellschaft?* Campus: Frankfurt/Main.

Birkhölzer K (1998) A philosophical rationale for the promotion of local economic initiatives, in Twelvetrees A (ed.) *Community Economic Development: Rhetoric or Reality?* London: Community Development Foundation.

Birkhölzer K and Lorenz G (1996) *The Role of Partnerships in Promoting Social Cohesion: Research Report for Germany.* Dublin: European Foundation for the Improvement of Living and Working Conditions.

Birkhölzer K and Lorenz G (1998a) Allemagne: Les sociétés d'emploi et de qualification en appui à la réunification, in Defourny J, Favreau L and Laville J-L (eds.) *Insertion et nouvelle économie sociale.* Desclée de Brouwer: Paris.

Birkhölzer K and Lorenz G (1998b) Social Enterprises and New Employment in Europe: Germany, in Borzaga C and Santuari A (eds.): *Social Enterprises and New Employment in Europe.* Trento: Regione Autonoma Trentino Alto Adige.

Döring D, Hanesch W and Huster E-U (1990) *Armut in Wohlstand.* Frankfurt/Main.

Friedrich H and Wiedemeyer M (1994) *Arbeitslosigkeit – ein Dauerproblem: Dimensionen, Ursachen, Strategien.* Oplade: Leske & Budrich.

Froessler R (1994) *Stadtviertel in der Krise. Innovative Ansätze zu einer integrierten Quartiersentwicklung in Europa.* Institut f. Landes- u. Stadtentwicklungsforschung des Landes Nordrhein-Westfalen: Duisburg (ILS-Schriften; 87).

Froessler R, Lang M, Selle K and Staubach R (1994) *Lokale Partnerschaften. Die Erneuerung benachteiligter Quartiere in Europäischen Städten.* Birkhäuser: Basel, Boston, Berlin.

Hanesch W et al (1994) *Armut in Deutschland*. Rowohlt: Reinbek bei Hamburg.

Hunfeld F (1998) *Und plötzlich bist du arm: Geschichten aus dem neuen Deutschland*. Rowohlt: Reinbek bei Hamburg.

Staubach R (1995) *Lokale Partnerschaften zur Erneuerung benachteiligter Quartiere in deutschen Städten*. Arbeitsgemeinschaft Bestandserneuerung: Dortmund (Werkbericht der AGB, 35).

6   Catalysts for change

Public policy reform through local partnership in Ireland

Jim Walsh

Introduction

The Irish government has engaged in an experimental new localism in recent years, in an effort to address persistent problems of long-term unemployment, poverty and social exclusion (Walsh, Craig and McCafferty 1998). At the core of this new approach lies the establishment of over 100 local partnerships, which bring together state agencies, business, trade unions and community groups, to promote local socio-economic development in mainly disadvantaged rural and urban areas. Local communities play a lead role in these local partnerships, in terms of identifying community needs, harnessing resources and delivering new services. The European Union is also a key player in this local approach, both by providing most of the funding for local partnerships and through influencing the contents of the overall programme.

The local partnerships have been designed by government as catalysts to transform the policy framework for tackling unemployment and social exclusion based on three key innovations:

- the establishment of local multi-agency structures for planning and co-ordination;
- the involvement of local communities and social groups in decision-making;
- the promotion of local development and employment initiatives.

This intervention is supported at national level through public funding, interdepartmental policy co-ordination, ministerial leadership and social partnership endorsement. The policy reform promoted by the local partnerships has not been without controversy, however, due to their ad hoc administrative status, their weak linkages with local government, their multiplicity and lack of co-ordination, and their financial dependency on central government. Nonetheless, the local partnerships are clearly pioneering a new local dimension in an otherwise centralist system of public policy. This experimental era is now under threat from two main sources: the termination of EU Structural Funds in 1999, the main funding source for local partnerships to date, and their inclusion in a reformed local government system, with implications for their autonomy. The future direction of the local partnership approach is thus clouded with uncertainty. It is therefore an opportune time to reflect on the impact of local partnerships as innovative instruments of public policy.

There are some parallels between the Irish situation and other EU countries, where local partnership has been applied to varying degrees as a local response to problems of social exclusion, particularly in urban areas (Geddes 1998; Hughes *et al.* 1998; Madanipour, Cars and Allen 1998). What is distinctive about the Irish case is the concerted nature of the intervention, involving not only central government and the EU, but also the national social partners. In addition, Irish local partnership operates in an adversarial context of centralised administration and major economic restructuring. The uniquely innovative nature of this decentralised policy approach is reflected in a recent OECD commentary:

> The Irish initiatives...have happened upon a master idea: to apply the problem-solving techniques of work teams now being disseminated throughout the OECD economies to simultaneously increase the self-reliance of the vulnerable – be they individuals, going firms, or start-ups – and to provide them with skills increasingly regarded as necessary for employment in jobs and industries with a future...this outcome has begun to emerge with a speed and clarity of purpose in operation that is distinct from other efforts in the OECD to reform and connect economic development and welfare provision.
>
> (OECD 1996: 13)

Similarly, the Irish local partnership approach is seen as a pathfinder for EU efforts to promote local development and employment initiatives, including the recently launched territorial employment pacts, as a means of increasing employment and promoting social inclusion (Commission of the European Communities 1995; 1996; Department of Taoiseach 1996).

This chapter begins by outlining the origins and operation of local partnership as a local policy response to social exclusion. It then focuses on the institutional dimensions of this model of public policy reform, based on a concept of local governance. The chapter reviews the four key ingredients in the local partnership model: central government, partner agencies, local government and community participation. It concludes by visioning the future role for local partnerships, as they seek to remain at the cutting edge of public policy.

Origins of local partnerships

Local partnerships are a central government response to the concentrated problems of unemployment and poverty in discrete localities. While a spatial dimension to public policy is not a new departure, it has largely been utilised as a means of targeting resources at areas of special need. However, in the nineteenth century localised policies played a more active role in policy, such as the poor law system (based on local unions) and the Congested Districts Board, a government body set up to address poverty and over-population in the west of Ireland. Since then, the spatial dimension of policy has greatly declined, and now only exists as a residual feature in welfare schemes providing free school meals and top-up grants for schools in dis-advantaged areas. In other policy areas, spatial categories have been used to differentiate levels of grant aid, e.g. location of foreign industrial develop-ment and farm compensation payments (Walsh 1999). This new-found geographic emphasis in public policy in the 1990s represents a significant shift, and stems from a number of factors.

A new geography of poverty

The growth in poverty that occurred in the 1980s (Callan, Nolan, Whelan and Williams 1996) was accompanied by a new geography of poverty. Rising poverty levels had a distinct urban aspect, stemming from high rates of unemployment in local authority housing estates. These estates suffered both from the general increase in unemployment in the 1980s, especially among unskilled manual workers, and the targeted exodus of employed people from these estates under housing surrender grants. The resultant high rates of joblessness and poverty were described in numerous local pro-files and the concept of unemployment blackspots quickly assumed a policy importance, providing a 'prime facie case for the development of area-based programmes' (National Economic and Social Council 1990: 72). This view is reiterated in the National Anti-Poverty Strategy, where it states:

> As well as considering the three core issues of educational disadvantage, unemployment and income adequacy, it is also necessary to examine the consequences of high levels and concentrations of poverty which can lead to a threat to the social fabric of the country and incur high economic costs...There are areas throughout Ireland where there are concentrations of people living in poverty, often resulting in cumulative disadvantage. These are sometimes referred to as 'poverty blackspots'. It has been suggested that the experience of being poor and living in such areas is a qualitatively different, and usually worse, experience than being poor and living in a non-disadvantaged environment.
>
> (Government of Ireland 1997: 16)

The existence of a distinct spatial distribution was also a common theme in studies of socially vulnerable groups, such as travellers, drug addicts, lone parents and educationally disadvantaged children. This prompted calls in policy circles for the introduction of locally targeted interventions (e.g. Kelleghan *et al.*, 1995; Ministerial Task Force on Measures to Reduce the Demand for Drugs, 1996.)[1]

Local co-ordination of welfare services

There were significant developments within mainstream welfare policy that encouraged a greater local focus to the design and delivery of services. One key policy concern was to make service provision more effective through local co-ordination, especially in response to the multidimensional nature of many intractable social problems, as indicated by the newly-coined phrase 'social exclusion'. The concept of integration was central to two pilot programmes in the late 1980s: the Irish government COMTEC programme and the Third EU Poverty Programme (Bruton 1996). It also appeared in the report of a key government advisory body, the National Economic and Social Council, which offered the following critique of the prevailing policy response:

> Currently, social policies and services operate on a 'functional' or 'departmental' basis (health, social welfare, and others) without any coherent attempt to integrate services at local levels. Clearly, many low income communities are affected by the services, and receive resources from a range of state agencies – local government, health boards, the Department of Social Welfare, FAS [Foras Áiseanna Saothair – National Training and Employment Agency], for example. The scope for area 'renewal' and community based co-ordination must therefore be considerable. Evidence suggests that concerted, intensive programmes in small areas, containing elements of housing and environmental improvement, as well as retraining and employment schemes and 'outreach' health and educational projects, can have an impact over and above the separate effects of individual programmes. Furthermore, the more closely involved are local communities in the planning and delivery of area-based projects, the more they will reflect local needs and priorities.
>
> (NESC 1990: 74)

Similar demands for greater integration of services were enunciated in other policy reviews covering labour market, drugs, crime prevention and family

---

1 Of lesser importance in encouraging an area-based approach was a desire for better targeting of resources on those in need, as part of a general move away from universalism in social policy. This concern was particularly strong in the late 1980s, when the fiscal crisis was at its height and severe cut-backs in public expenditure were required (National Economic and Social Council 1990). In this context, spatial programmes provided a cost-efficient means of identifying and responding to the emerging social needs.

support services (e.g. Interdepartmental Group on Urban Crime and Disorder 1992; National Economic and Social Forum 1994 and Task Force on Long-term Unemployment 1995).

Local development and employment initiatives

From the mid-1980s, there was a growing awareness of the potential of local development and employment initiatives as a new source of jobs in both national and EU economic policy. Again, a state agency, in this case the Youth Employment Agency, was crucial in giving official support to local employment initiatives through the Community Enterprise Programme (O Cinneide 1985), while in Gaeltacht areas, some limited government support was provided for community co-operatives. Another government initiative in the late 1980s was the Area Programme for Integrated Rural Development, which fostered support for local economic development in a rural context. Subsequently, the policy merits of a 'bottom-up' model of economic development in fostering entrepreneurship, redistributing economic activity and facilitating local involvement in the development process were articulated in an influential government-commissioned assessment of the 1989–93 Community Support Framework (Economic and Social Research Institute *et al.* 1993). This approach received further support at the EU level through various policy reports in the early 1990s, which highlighted the importance of local development and employment initiatives in promoting job creation (Commission of the European Communities 1993; 1995). EU support was reflected in the Structural Funds, in particular in programmes such as LEADER, LEDA and EMPLOYMENT. Consequently, when it came to agree the community support framework between the EU and the Irish government, a key theme was:

> The importance of a local dimension to enterprise and employment creation and the importance of developing the capabilities of local communities to contribute to tackling unemployment and pursuing local development.
>
> (quoted in McCarthy 1996: 15)

Local development initiatives are seen as providing a means of integrating enterprise with welfare and economic growth with redistribution. Thus, local job creation in new sectors of the economy is a practical way of improving access to the labour market for disadvantaged groups. This welfare/enterprise nexus is particularly evident in the introduction of the Back-to-Work Allowance, a welfare scheme that allows the unemployed to retain welfare benefits while establishing micro-businesses.

Community as an official actor in policy

A sub-theme in the emergence of local welfare co-ordination and local economic policies, alluded to above, is the contribution that local 'communities' can make in policy implementation. Traditionally, community involvement has been something public policy has endured rather than embraced. Major community movements such as Muintir na Tire and credit unions have emerged, and more often faltered, without government support. At the same time, there is a considerable rhetoric in policy about community-based models of service provision, including information and advice (community information centres), labour market programmes (community training workshops, community employment programmes) and social services (community care) (McCashin 1990; O Cinneide and Walsh 1990).

In more recent years, however, community involvement in policy has extended beyond a notion of community as simply being a site for the delivery of services, to community as having a legitimate role in deciding what and how services are provided (Curtin and Varley 1995). This enhanced community role is particularly evident in the realm of anti-poverty policy, where community involvement is based on notions of empowerment and social inclusion. This understanding is associated with the work of the Combat Poverty Agency from the mid-1980s. The Agency, a statutory body, promoted community development as a strategy for involving disadvantaged groups in local decision-making, with the support of pilot initiatives such as the second EU Poverty programme (Cullen 1989; Combat Poverty Agency and Community Workers Co-operative 1990). Since, community development has also become evident in many areas of policy, such as in welfare ('community development programme'), education ('home-school-community liaison') and housing ('tenant participation in estate management'). At a national level, the government has included umbrella community networks such as the Community Workers Co-operative, the Irish National Organisation of the Unemployed and the Irish Travellers Movement in policy advisory bodies, and these were also party to the current social partnership agreement (Partnership 2000). This legitimisation of the community sector as an actor in policy is given explicit expression in a current government discussion paper on voluntary activity (Department of Social Welfare 1997; Government of Ireland 1996).

National social partnership

Social partnership, involving government, unions and business, has been a pervasive component of public policy in Ireland since the economic crisis of the late 1980s, despite the absence of any legal basis for this relationship. The primary motivation for social partnership is to enhance national competitiveness through careful management of the public finances, backed up by wage constraint and tax reforms. It has also been used, indeed increasingly so, to shape social policy. Hence, the emergence of local partnerships has been strongly associated with social partnership agreements based on the policy concepts outlined above. However, social partnership has not simply been a conduit for policy reform, but has also shaped the local implementation of policy. This occurred under the framework of the social partnership-brokered Programme for Economic and Social Progress (1991–3) (Government of Ireland 1991). Under a pilot area-based response to long-term unemployment, 12 projects were established involving government agencies and social partner representatives, together with local community organisations. This structure was explicitly chosen to replicate, at a local level, the perceived success of the national social partnership arrangement. In particular, they were designed to go beyond being a forum for policy discussion to acting as a mechanism for mobilising the resources of employers and trade unions, together with state and community groups, to meet agreed objectives. This initiative significantly deepens the involvement of employers and trade unions in policy design.

Local partnership: a new local policy direction

The current localism is thus very much the product of national policy reform, in response to the exigencies of persistent and concentrated patterns of unemployment and poverty. The elements of this local policy focus were experimented with through a number of pilot programmes in the late 1980s and early 1990s. These included the COMTEC programme, the Area Programme for Integrated Rural Development, the EU Poverty 3 programme, the Area-Based Response to Long-term Unemployment and the Global Grant for Local Development. These programmes were promoted both by the Irish government and the EU, and were based on a range of concepts including enterprise, social inclusion, partnership, participation, multi-dimensionality, strategic planning and capacity building. Subsequently, these ideas were formulated into a number of mainstream programmes with a local development theme and delivered by a variety of local multi-agency structures.

While there were also some isolated local examples of inter-agency networking, the impetus for local partnerships has come primarily from central government, with significant EU support. In particular, the social partnership agreement at national level has been the key framework for the emergence of local partnerships, under the leadership of the Department of the Taoiseach (prime minister) (line government departments have had lesser influence, such as agriculture, enterprise and social welfare). A variety of anti-poverty interests also helped to shape this local policy response, notably the Combat Poverty Agency. However, interests in spatial development, such as the Department of the Environment or regional and local government, have been conspicuous by their lack of input (this reflects the traditional weakness of spatial planning at urban, rural or regional levels in public policy). By contrast, the contribution of the EU is very apparent, both in providing the resources and the policy support for local intervention, and also in shaping its content, delivery and monitoring through formal agreements with the Irish government.

Operation of local partnerships

Local partnerships are an innovative and distinct institutional form in Irish public administration. Because of the national policy context in which they have emerged, local partnerships are structured around a number of defined operational characteristics:

- a formal institutional structure (typically a limited company, without share capital);
- membership from a diversity of interests, including public agencies, employers, trade unions, and voluntary and community organisations;
- a strategic approach to local planning and development;
- a strong emphasis on unemployment, poverty and social exclusion;
- limited financial autonomy, based on national government/EU funding.

There are currently in the region of 100 officially recognised local partnerships, operating under a variety of national and EU programmes, the principal one being the local development programme ('disadvantaged' sub-programme), which is part of the mainly EU-funded Community Support Framework. The aim of the sub-programme is:

> To counter disadvantage through support for communities which make a collective effort to maximise the development potential of their areas, which are capable of a sustained effort to implement a plan and which have committed an appropriate level of local resources, broadly defined, to that process.
>
> (Government of Ireland 1995)

The sub-programme has a budget of approximately £100 million and is divided into two operational strands: 80 per cent of resources go to 38 local partnerships in designated areas of disadvantage and 20 per cent go to 33 'community groups' (in effect, mini-local partnerships) in non-designated areas. The local partnerships are required to prepare local development plans, including measures on micro-enterprise, employment support, second-chance education, amenity and environment projects and community development. The sub-programme also has an equal opportunities theme, focusing on women, travellers (an ethnic minority) and people with disabilities. Additional support for local partnerships is provided under EU programmes such as LEADER (34 local partnerships), URBAN (three urban partnerships – in effect, maxi-local partnerships) and Peace and Reconciliation (this does not have a dedicated local partnership structure, but is heavily accessed by existing local partnerships to fund local development initiatives).[2] Some of the rural partnerships deliver both the LEADER and the local development programmes, while in urban areas six local development partnerships are also in the URBAN programme. Some minor funding is also provided from international government and private funds, e.g. International Fund for Ireland and the Ireland Funds.

At national level, support for local partnerships is co-ordinated by the Department of Tourism, Sport and Recreation, which took over responsibility from the Taoiseach's (prime minister's) Department, which initiated this approach (itself an indication of the central government support for local partnerships under the social partnership pact). There is also a minister of state with special responsibility for local development, who in turn reports to a ministerial committee on social inclusion. Funding for local partnerships under the local development programme is channelled through an intermediary body called Area Development Management (ADM), which also provides technical support to local partnerships, monitors their activities and facilitates networking and transfer of good practice. Other government departments and national agencies also have links to local partnerships, including the Department of Agriculture and Food, which directly manages the LEADER programme, and the Combat Poverty Agency, which oversees funding under the Peace and Reconciliation programme, together with Area Development Management. These linkages are co-ordinated by an interdepartmental policy committee. Finally, joint EU/national monitoring committees perform an overall supervisory role in the various programmes.

Local partnerships: a model of local governance?

Local partnerships are a public policy response to localised concentrations of poverty and unemployment. As government implants into the domain of local administration, they have a brief to develop new ways of working based on the three core themes of inter-agency networking, integrated local development and community involvement. In effect, they are a top-down model, intended to breathe new life and vigour into a previously residual domain of policy. The key questions then are how has this model taken root in local society, to what extent has it been adapted to local circumstances, and how has it improved the policy response to social inclusion? In this regard, local partnerships incorporate new relationships at two levels: a local horizontal linkage of state, business, trade union and community

2 The LEADER programme does not have an explicit social inclusion focus, but does lend limited support to community and social development measures. In addition, a number of rural partnerships combine LEADER and local development funding. Similarly, Peace and Reconciliation is not a specific social inclusion programme, but it does contain a number of social measures.

organisations; and a vertical engagement between this collective local interest and central government. These two sets of relationships are a uniquely Irish aspect of the local partnership approach. They reflect, on the one hand, the vacuum in local public administration associated with a heavily atrophied system of local government and, on the other hand, the longstanding centralism of the Irish state. As such, the institutional ramifications of local partnerships are:

> virtually unthinkable in any other western European state. In most, a fairly settled structure of administrative, representative and political authority, from central through regional to local government, would define the structure within which new initiatives for local economic development would occur and would probably exclude the developments seen in Ireland.
>
> (O'Donnell 1995: 227)

These new relationships have been presented as providing the basis for a devolved system of local governance (Adshead and Quinn 1998). Using Rhodes' (1996) definition of governance as 'self-organising networks' that mediate between government, market and civil society, they argue that local partnerships mark:

> a move away from a top-down, highly centralised policy formation. Increasing importance is attached to the creation of locally-based, bottom-up development strategies...The move towards governance has impacted on the policy output. Instead of concentrating solely on economic targets, such as industrial activity or sectoral growth, development is now seen as a multidimensional process with serious social and political, as well as economic implications.
>
> (Rhodes 1996: 219)

However, an alternative perspective might suggest that instead of local governance, a better description of local partnerships is as 'qualgos' (quasi-independent local government agencies). After all, local partnerships are the artificial construct of central government, imposed upon local agencies and controlled and funded by central government. To dismiss local partnerships like this would be to miss their potential for establishing their own independent dynamic, i.e. 'going native'. In Healey's (1998) analysis, the quality of local governance is dependent on institutional capacity, that is 'the capability of the collection of relationships through which governance tasks are accomplished' (Healey 1998: 66). This institutional capability for local governance and policy-making is dependent on four factors:

- the devolution of decision-making from central government to local partnerships;

- the willingness of partner agencies to engage in joint local planning and co-ordination;
- the linkages between local government and local partnerships;
- the impact of community involvement on local decision-making.

These four issues are now examined in greater detail.

The devolution of decision-making from central government

The patronage of central government has been critical to the emergence of local partnerships as an instrument of public policy. In effect, this relationship represents the life blood of local partnerships, which otherwise would not exist without the intervention of central government. A key issue is to what extent central government has decentralised decision-making functions to local partnerships, or whether local partnerships are a camouflage for reinforcing the traditional policy influence of government at the local level.

In the first instance, local partnerships are a decentralised mechanism for the local administration of EU Structural Funds for socio-economic development. The make-up, location and activities of local partnerships are orchestrated by central government through its control over the provision of funding, albeit channelled through an intermediary body, Area Development Management. This funding relationship is backed up by an elaborate monitoring framework for local partnerships. This includes a formal performance monitoring system, along with informal reviews by a plethora of government bodies, including government departments, monitoring bodies, an interdepartmental policy committee and a minister of state. This pattern of central government policy control over local partnership delivery of funds is evident in other policy areas, where local partnerships have been used to fund child-care facilities (Department of Justice, Equality and Law Reform) and community anti-drugs initiatives (National Drugs Strategy Team). Similarly, local partnerships have been used to distribute Peace and Reconciliation programme funds in the southern border counties and funds under the EU URBAN programme.

However, local partnerships have a broader policy mandate than simply the decentralised administration of public funding. Local partnerships are also expected to contribute to the policy-making process. There are three dimensions to this. The first is to improve the local delivery and co-ordination of mainstream policies through the involvement of state and other agencies in a partnership process of local decision-making. This acknowledges that while significant resources are available under the Structural Funds to support local development, these are modest compared to the resources committed under mainstream programmes to meet the needs of disadvantaged communities. (The realisation of this policy-shaping opportunity is discussed in the following section.) A second policy role derives from the partnerships' explicit remit to promote local experimentation and innovation. Arising from this demonstrative brief, it is expected that models of good practice will be disseminated widely in public policy. Indeed, there are a number of examples where central government has directly engaged with local partnerships to develop new policy initiatives. Various government departments have collaborated with local partnerships with regard to the development of employment schemes, guidance and counselling services, welfare-to-work programmes and early school-leaving measures. Local partnerships have assumed a similar policy innovation role in the implementation of the EU territorial employment pacts.

Despite the local partnerships' designated role in policy innovation, there is scant evidence of the government's capacity to absorb the lessons of local experimentation, except where it is directly involved in the process. As the recent OECD review remarked:

> The partnerships...are extraordinarily innovative, but they have been better at creating new things than at building stable institutions that embody and extend their innovations. In part, this is because the Irish state has been better at allowing innovation than at learning from its protagonists about how to generalise local successes and incorporate changes they suggest into the organisation of the functional administration. Thus, many experimental projects...may succeed, but the experiment as a whole may fail.
>
> (OECD 1996: 85)

Thus, despite the existence of ADM and the interdepartmental policy committee, whose briefs include acting as conduits for the exchange of local experience and national policy, the national policy impact of local partnerships has been limited. While the locus of policy-making remains at national level, central government is too clearly fragmented and remote to absorb the lessons of local partnerships. We can also point to the failure of local partnerships to adequately translate their experience and insights into the language and concerns of national policy. The one-sided nature of this local-central axis raises serious question marks about the policy-shaping capacity of local partnerships. It also highlights the policy vacuum that continues to exist at local level, a key element of which is the absence of a sub-national planning framework through which the policy impact of local partnerships can be filtered.

While the favour of central government has been crucial in energising local partnerships in an otherwise moribund system of local administration, this support has been less effective in achieving mainstream policy reform. The main policy platform for local partnerships is their effective local disbursal of EU Structural Funds. However, with the decline in the value of these resources post-1999, the significance of this support will also be lessened. In addition, there are mounting concerns at government level about local fragmentation and duplication arising from the multitude of local partnerships. Meanwhile, in order to protect and enhance their role as a local policy mechanism of government, local partnerships have established an umbrella organisation (PLANET) to provide a national representative voice.

The willingness of partner agencies to engage in joint local planning

As noted above, local partnerships are not designed simply to be local funders of development activity: they have a remit to promote local planning and co-ordination. The importance of this brokerage role is outlined by the Taoiseach (prime minister):

> A vital test of the success of the partnership approach will be the extent to which mainstream programmes are renewed and refocused as a result of the partnership process. For that reason, the state agencies represented on partnership boards must be active, willing and flexible participants in the process. They must overcome the difficulties which can exist when organisations which are hierarchically structured at national level come to address the problems of integration at the point of delivery...This will require commitment at senior level, a definite culture to support partnership and participation, openness as regards information on local plans and resources and, above all, a willingness to listen to the views of others, especially consumer interests in shaping operational policies.
>
> (Bruton 1995: 86)

A mandate of public service reform is therefore central to the remit of local partnerships, through influencing the spending decisions of state agencies on the one hand and shaping the employment opportunities in local business on the other. This is not simply a question of the greater efficiency of resources, but is also about prioritising social inclusion as a policy goal. Such a pluralist approach to local policy is heavily dependent on the willingness of the partners – state and business in particular – to collaborate under the partnership umbrella since, as ad-hoc non-statutory bodies, local partnerships have no legal policy remit.

The main tools in the armoury of local partnerships in meeting this challenge are twofold: use of own resources as leverage and informal agreements based on shared concerns. The extent to which local partnerships have used their resources to develop an active engagement with partner agencies is in part a developmental issue. Thus, in the early days, local partnerships concentrated in initiating activities using their own funding capacity, either through direct delivery or by contracting with intermediary (mainly voluntary) bodies. This was especially important in areas with a weak local infrastructure and was frequently encouraged by community partners as the most direct way of directing additional resources into their areas (Craig and

McKeown 1994). Over time, the focus has slowly shifted to working with partner agencies at a strategic level. This has entailed joint initiatives with partner agencies in the state or business sectors where the majority of resources lie in terms of services or access to jobs. This has involved the local partnership assuming an advocacy role 'from within', with a key role played by community interests.

Where local partnerships have sought to expand their influence on local policy-making, they have been frustrated by institutional obstacles. One is the limited policy autonomy afforded to local partner agencies in a pre-dominantly centralist state. For example, among state agencies, most policy decisions are made at regional (e.g. FAS, health boards) or even national level (e.g. Department of Social Welfare). Local offices serve largely to administer the local delivery of services designed and funded at higher levels. Even with locally focused bodies such as local authorities, three-quarters of their spending is pre-determined at central government level and their functions are also curtailed. This lack of local autonomy restricts the scope for a local input in decision-making to the margins of policy. Among the social partners the problem is more acute since their organisations have only a national focus, and are not constituted to act as local policy-making units. Other devolved structures such as local chambers of commerce, centres for the unemployed, or even local businesses, are less inhibited in this regard, though lacking the broader policy perspective.

A second difficulty relates to the functionalist brief and outlook in partner agencies, most of which operate from a national remit. It is hard therefore to instil a territorial focus to policy, especially when the regional and local aspects of planning are weak (no regional structures and rather depleted county bodies). Similarly, among the personnel who represent partner agencies on local partnerships, their primary motivation is the sectoral interests of nominating organisations, with their commitment to territorial concerns of secondary importance. It is also a problem where a senior official of a partner agency is selected as the link person so as to maximise local influence, their familiarity with and commitment to particular areas will be less than that at the local level. Imposing a local focus on what is by design a functional system of public administration is thus highly problematic. Interestingly, the one partner agency with the clearest commitment to local issues – local government – is frequently a weak player in local partnerships. This is in part explained by the fact that the local planning remit of local government is almost exclusively for physical development, such as housing, roads and other infrastructure (see below for a fuller discussion of the role of local government). Meanwhile, the brief of the social partners primarily relates to negotiating terms and conditions of employment, and they have a limited tradition of mobilising resources for community purposes, although this may change as a 'social responsibility' mentality is fostered within business and trade unions at the local level.

Nonetheless, local partnerships have made some inroads into local policy-making through informal networking and local alliances. These have mainly centred on employment issues and have usually involved the coming together of key personalities, rather than institutionalised commitments. For example, in a number of cases, local business interests have collaborated with local partnerships in targeting employment opportunities towards the long-term unemployed residents of designated areas. Similarly, certain individuals in state agencies have promoted joint initiatives with local partnerships. Also, under the URBAN programme, local partnerships have developed, in conjunction with local authorities, neighbourhood planning forums and local area plans. However, these agreements remain ad hoc and reliant on local partnership funding as the key carrot in encouraging local policy-sharing. Were this to diminish, then the limited capacity of local partnerships to shape local decision-making could be reduced. Meanwhile, the perceived failure of local partnerships to deliver on their brokerage mandate has led to a separate government initiative to promote the integrated delivery of public services in four disadvantaged urban neighbourhoods. The formula for locally 'joined-up working' clearly remains to be found.

The linkages between local partnerships and local government

A crucial ingredient in fostering a model of local governance is the relationship between local partnerships and local government. The expectation here is usually expressed as an innovative coming together of representative and participative democracy. Local government, as a democratically elected body, has traditionally assumed the lead role in representing the interests of local people in the policy process. However, over the years the role has greatly diminished, due to the limited functions of local government and, in addition, the curtailed powers of local councillors over executive decisions, leaving them to adopt a largely clientilist role in representing people (Barrington Committee 1991; Walsh 1998). In addition, local government was widely perceived as remiss in its management of public housing estates – its one clear function – leading to considerable tensions between residents and local government.

Not surprisingly, then, when local partnerships were established, local government was allocated a relatively minor role and elected officials were specifically excluded from participation (only officers were included). (This downplaying of local government was paralleled at national level by the bypassing of the Department of the Environment and Local Government from the government bodies overseeing local partnerships.) As a result, local partnerships have operated apart from, rather than in conjunction with, local government. The sole exception has been in urban regeneration partnerships, supported under the URBAN programme, where local government has negotiated an enhanced role on a par with other local actors, including local partnerships (though again, at national level, the Department of the Environment and Local Government is not the lead body). The URBAN exception reflects the strong physical orientation of this initiative, including improvements in the built environment and provision of community facilities. In addition to board membership and the provision of key technical input, urban regeneration partnerships also include elected representatives on their management boards.

While the weaknesses of local government can be used to justify its weak role in local partnerships, in the long term this marginalisation has given rise to major institutional difficulties in terms of moving towards a multi-agency model of local governance. Three main sources of tension have emerged between local government and local partnerships.

Local co-ordination of development efforts

One immediate source of tension is the lack of local co-ordination of development agencies, with the rapid expansion of local partnerships and other local development bodies (e.g. enterprise boards, tourism committees). This carries with it the dual dangers of resource duplication and fragmentation of policy. Local government has traditionally assumed the lead role in local (physical) development, though with limited resources and capacity to exploit this potential. In particular, the weak linkages between physical and socio-economic development initiatives are increasingly untenable due to the obvious overlaps between people and place poverty (e.g. estate management in public housing estates, urban regeneration in disadvantaged areas or access to public services, such as transport). In addition, the resources available to local partnerships (and not to local government) adds to local tensions between existing and new local development bodies.

Public accountability

Ensuring the local accountability of public funding, if not its actual allocation, has been a primary function of local government. This is reflected in the membership of elected members on a range of local government agencies, including the local authority itself, health boards and vocational educational committees. The exclusion of local politicians from local partnerships is seen by some as diminishing the public accountability by these bodies in their allocation of funds. Indeed, some commentators have raised the possibility of the corrupt use of these funds as a reason for channelling local development funding through local government (Fitzgerald and Keegan 1993). This claim has been given some substance with the revelation of unorthodox financial procedures in one local partnership.

Local democracy

The most serious point of conflict between local partnerships and local government exists in terms of local democracy. Local government is based on a traditional model of representative democracy. Local partnerships provide a challenge to the hegemony of this model with their promotion of the direct participation of local people in its decision-making processes. However, this is not an academic contrast, but is felt on the ground in terms of undermining the traditional brokerage role of elected members with local communities. It has arisen in a more acute way where community representatives on local partnerships have competed (often successfully) with existing members for election to local public office.

There have been a number of attempts to resolve these issues. The first was the establishment by central government of 'county strategy teams' to co-ordinate the work of local partnerships, local government and other local development bodies, under the framework of the local development programme. These consist of representatives of these various interests, including (somewhat belatedly) elected local representatives. In reality, the strategy groups are mainly confined to information-sharing and informal co-operation, and are explicitly not an executive structure for overseeing the activities of member bodies.

Following a change of government in 1994, it was decided 'to make local government the focus for working through local partnerships', as part of a wider programme of local government reform. To advise on the implementation of this decision, the government established a Devolution Commission (Devolution Commission 1996). The Commission subsequently suggested an integrated framework comprising regional authorities, local government and local partnerships. This would also involve the simplification of the existing range of local partnerships. Institutions at all levels would operate on the basis of an integrated multi-purpose development plan, which coincided with national and EU programmes. Horizontal linkages between local government and local partnerships would also be strengthened. While local partnerships would retain development functions in their own right, they would also be obliged to include elected councillors on their boards. In turn, local government would include representatives of local partnerships (and other community organisations) on their operational committees. As interim measures, it was proposed that local partnerships should include elected representatives on their boards of management.

Before the government could act on the recommendations of the Devolution Commission, the Department of the Environment and Local Government published its own proposals on reform of the relationship between local government and local partnership in a white paper entitled *Better local government, a programme for change* (Department of the Environment 1996). As might be expected, this proposed a more formal integration of local partnerships and local government than that envisaged by the Devolution

Commission, with a clear prioritisation of local government through a sub-committee structure, headed by a director of community and enterprise development. The committee would have an equality of membership between elected representatives and local partnerships, and the chair would be an elected representative. However, there was considerable opposition to this approach and, following a change of government, it was effectively stalled. However, one element of the reform package was established – the strategic policy committee – and many partnerships have secured representation on these bodies.

In 1998, a fourth initiative (a task force) to advise on the integration of local partnerships and local government was announced. This task force recommended a model of local governance, based on principles of partnership, democratic legitimacy and community development (Task Force 1998). The key element would be new 'local development boards', linked to but separate from local government. These boards would prepare local development plans, which would provide a strategic framework for local partnerships, local government and other development bodies. It also proposed a rationalisation of agencies and functions, a strengthening of the community development remit of local government (via expanded local area committees), and the inclusion of elected representatives on partnerships. This framework is now in the process of implementation.

In effect, what is now being implemented is a new local structure to co-ordinate the efforts of a wide range of bodies, include local government and local partnerships, but not formally link them in any way. Whether this new structure will actually work will depend on the capacity to combine a traditional model of local representation with one based on community consultation and participation. A second question mark over this now relates to the control of resources under this new structure, in particular those provided by central government and the EU, and whether these will be channelled through local government or be allocated directly to local partnerships. A third concern is how a social inclusion agenda will be retained within a broad development approach, especially one based on local capacity building.

The impact of community involvement on local decision-making

The active involvement of local residents in promoting and implementing local initiatives is a core element of the local partnership approach. This theme is in keeping with a wider policy emphasis on community empowerment in recent years, which is in turn premised on emerging notions of active citizenship and participatory democracy (Powell and Guerin 1996). Hence, incorporating residents in local policy processes is not only undertaken for practical gains (e.g. better decision-making, more sustainable impact), but is also part of a broader policy agenda to recognise voluntary action. This emerging policy framework is outlined in a recent government discussion paper on voluntary activity, which states:

> There is a need to create a more participatory democracy where active citizenship is fostered. In such a society, the ability of the voluntary and community sector to provide channels for the active involvement and participation of citizens is fundamental. An active voluntary and community sector contributes to a democratic, pluralist society, provides opportunities for the development of decentralised institutional structures and fosters a climate in which innovative solutions to complex social problems and enhancement of quality of life can be pursued and realised.
>
> (Department of Social Welfare 1997: 24)

This vision of 'community empowerment' is based on local communities contributing to the design and implementation of policy. Linking disadvantaged communities into the mainstream of policy-making is a major departure from traditional state-community relationships. There is already evidence of community empowerment in specific policy sectors, e.g. tenant participation in estate management or parental involvement in schools. However, none have the same level of commitment to it as is exemplified by local partnerships. To what extent then have local partnerships fostered community empowerment?

In the first instance, community involvement in local partnerships covers a variety of actions. This includes at one extreme consultation with the community on their needs, through a community survey for example. At the other end of the continuum, there is community participation in the decision-making level of a local partnership, as a board member. In between, there are other forms of involvement such as the provision of services, tenant participation in estate management and community planning forums.

The pinnacle of community involvement is through membership of the management structure of local partnerships. The standard formula here is six community directors out of a total of 18, i.e. one-third. In some cases, however, this community representation has been increased to 10 community directors. In addition, many community representatives are involved at other levels of local partnerships. This involvement clearly provides the opportunity for a significant input in decision-making in local partnerships. However, there are a number of problems to be overcome. One relates to the management culture and procedures within local partnerships. The governance model of local partnerships is influenced by (a) the legal status of a private company with individual directors, and (b) a management ethos drawn from the worlds of business and public administration. These attributes are particularly unsuited to the experience of community activists and may in part explain the high turnover in community representatives as they struggle to come to grips with an alien management format. The voices of 'minority' groups, such as women, travellers and people with disabilities, are also under-represented in local partnerships, despite a proviso that a minimum of 40 per cent of board members are female.

A second issue relates to the representative nature of community involvement in terms of selection and accountability. In the early days, the procedures for selecting community representatives were rather ad hoc and informal, with the result that certain community groups had a monopoly over the choice of representative. This also encouraged a tension between community groups over the allocation of resources on a geographic basis. Over time, selection procedures have been refined and now take place under the auspices of community fora, which contain both geographic and sectoral groups. These fora also provide the basis for feedback to the community. However, there still remain two major difficulties. One relates to the exclusion of elected political representation on the board of local partnerships. The second is the centralist nature of local partnerships, which inevitably transfers decision-making capacity to an elite of professional community activists.

Community involvement in local partnerships also has a programme dimension. First, there is a network of community directors drawn from all the local partnerships. This network provides training and support for community directors, and also elects representatives on to the board of Area Development Management (ADM). A second tier of support is provided by sectoral bodies, such as the Community Workers Co-operative, the Irish National Organisation of the Unemployed, Pavee Point and Irish Rural Link, which play a technical role in supporting community involvement in local partnerships. In addition, these organisations are also represented in the monitoring and implementation framework for local partnerships, e.g. the board of ADM. Finally, community involvement in local partnerships has, over time, been matched by the involvement of the community sector in national policy-making fora, such as the National Economic and Social Forum. More recently, the sector has been recognised by government as a social partner, as part of the national social partnership agreement.

Conclusion

Local partnerships are an innovative approach to public policy for two main reasons: the process of instituting a form of local governance and the product of reducing unemployment and social exclusion. This chapter has focused on the former, primarily because of the unique institutional context in which local partnerships operate in Ireland. The output is also important in terms of enhancing the quality of life in excluded communities and groups. The main achievements of the main local development programme after two years (end 1997) are impressive:

- 4,400 micro-enterprises, employing 7,800 previously long-term un-employed;
- 9,500 people placed in employment;
- 16,000 children on preventive educational projects;
- 8,600 adults participating in education and training programmes;
- 200 amenity and environmental projects;
- 500 groups and communities benefiting from community development (Area Development Management 1998).

However, it is the institutional dimension that holds the greatest promise in terms of delivering a long-term and sustainable policy impact in terms of social inclusion. Local partnerships are attempting to revolutionalise social policy from the bottom up, based on a model of local governance. Their principal weaknesses in this regard are their lack of local political clout, a reflection of their add-on status to existing systems of local administration, in particular local government, and their dependency on central government for mainstreaming their innovative policy reforms. The recently announced government national anti-poverty strategy, which seeks to put poverty at the heart of public policy, could help to create a more benign environment for local partnerships. Similarly, the new links to local government may give local partnerships the democratic credibility they have lacked to date, and also help to integrate strategies for people-based and place-based development. Against this, the uncertainty over continued funding threatens the lifeblood of local partnerships, while the bureaucratic-sounding new structure of local development boards may restrict the unique developmental remit of local partnerships. Finally, the models of community governance associated with local partnership may provide the basis whereby traditional structures of local democracy can be invigorated and renewed.

References

Adshead M and Quinn B (1998) 'The move from government to governance: Irish development policy's paradigm shift', *Policy and Politics*, 26, 2, 209–25.

Area Development Management (1998) *Reaching Out to the Excluded, A Summary Report On Progress In 1997*, Dublin: Area Development Management.

Barrington Committee (1991) *Local Government Re-organisation and Reform*, Dublin: Stationery Office.

Bruton J, TD (1995) 'Putting Poverty 3 into policy', in *Putting Poverty 3 in Policy*, Proceedings of conference on the Third EU Poverty Programme 1989–1994, Cavan: Department of Social Welfare.

Callan T, Nolan B, Whelan C and Williams J (1996) *Poverty in the 1990s*, Dublin: Oak Tree Press.

Commission of the European Communities (1993) *White Paper on Growth, Employment and Competitiveness*, Luxembourg: Office for Official Publications of the European Communities.

Commission of the European Communities (1995) *A European Strategy for Encouraging Local Development and Employment Initiatives*, COM (95) 273.

Commission of the European Communities (1996) *First Report on Local Development and Employment Initiatives*, Working Paper, SEC (96).

Combat Poverty Agency and Community Workers Co-operative (1990) *Community Work In Ireland: Trends In The 80s, Options For The 90s*, Dublin: Combat Poverty Agency and Community Workers Co-operative.

Craig S and McKeown K (1994) *Progress through Partnership. Final evaluation report of the PESP pilot initiative on long-term unemployment*, Dublin: Combat Poverty Agency.

Cullen B (1989) *Poverty, Community and Development*, Dublin: Combat Poverty Agency.

Curtin C and Varley T (1995) 'Community action and the state', in Clancy P, Drudy S, Lynch K and O'Dowd L (eds.) *Irish Society: Sociological Perspectives*, Dublin: Institute of Public Administration and the Sociological Association of Ireland.

Department of the Environment (1996) *Better Local Government, A Programme for Change*, Dublin: Stationery Office.

Department of Social Welfare (1997) *Supporting Voluntary Activity. A Green Paper on the Community and Voluntary Sector and its Relationship with the State*, Dublin: Stationery Office.

Department of the Taoiseach (1996) Local development: The Irish experience, the European context, Dublin: Proceedings of European Presidency Conference on Local Development.

Devolution Commission (1996), *Interim Report*, Dublin: Stationery Office.

Economic and Social Research Institute, DKM Consultants, Boyle G and Kearney B (1993) *The Community Support Framework: Evaluation and Recommendations*, Dublin: Stationery Office.

Fitzgerald J and Keegan O (1993) *The Community Support Framework: Evaluation and Recommendations*, Dublin: Stationery Office.

Geddes M (1998) *Local Partnerships: a Successful Strategy for Social Cohesion?* Dublin: European Foundation for the Improvement of Living and Working Conditions and Luxembourg: Office for Official Publications of the European Communities.

Government of Ireland (1991) *Programme for Economic and Social Progress*, Dublin: Stationery Office.

Government of Ireland (1995) *Operational Programme for Local Urban and Rural Development*, Dublin: Stationery Office.

Government of Ireland (1996) *Partnership 2000*, Dublin: Stationery Office.

Government of Ireland (1997) *Sharing in Progress. A National Anti-Poverty Strategy*, Dublin: Stationery Office.

Healey P (1998) 'Institutionalist theory, social exclusion and governance', in Madanipour A, Cars G and Allen J (1998) op cit.

Hughes J, Knox C, Murray M and Greer J (1998) *Partnership Governance in Northern Ireland*, Dublin: Oak Tree Press.

Interdepartmental Group on Urban Crime and Disorder (1992) *Report*, Dublin: Stationery Office.

Kelleghan T, Weir S, O Hulachain S and Morgan M (1995) *Educational Disadvantage In Ireland*, Dublin: Department of Education, Combat Poverty Agency and Educational Research Centre.

Madanipour A, Cars G and Allen J (1998) *Social Exclusion in European Cities*, London: Jessica Kingsley.

McCashin T (1990) 'Local communities and social policy', in Combat Poverty Agency and Community Workers Co-operative (1990) op cit.

Ministerial Task Force on Measures to Reduce the Demand for Drugs (1996) *First Report*, Dublin: Stationery Office.

McCarthy D (1996) 'An overview of local development in Ireland', in Department of the Taoiseach, op. cit.

Ministerial Task Force on Measures to Reduce the Demand for Drugs (1996) *First Report*, Dublin: Stationery Office.

National Economic and Social Council (1990) *A Strategy for the Nineties: Economic Stability and Structural Change*, Dublin: National Economic and Social Council.

National Economic and Social Forum (1994) *Ending Long-term Unemployment*, Dublin: Stationery Office.

O Cinneide S (1985) 'Community responses to unemployment', *Administration*, 33, 2, 231–57.

O Cinneide S and Walsh J (1990) 'Multiplication and divisions: trends in community development in Ireland since the 1960s', *Community Development Journal*, 25, 4, 326–36.

O'Donnell R (1995) 'The National Economic and Social Council perspective on local development issues', in *Putting Poverty 3 in Policy*, Proceedings of conference on the Third EU Poverty Programme 1989–1994, Cavan, 1995, Department of Social Welfare.

OECD (1996) *Local Partnership and Social Innovation*, Paris: OECD.

Powell F and Guerin D (1996) *Civil Society and Social Policy*, Dublin: A and A Farmer.

Rhodes R A W (1996) 'The new govenance: governing without government', *Political Studies*, 44, 4, 652–67.

Task Force on Long-term Unemployment (1995) *Interim Report*, Dublin: Stationery Office.

Task Force on the Integration of Local Government and Local Development Systems (1998) *Report*, Dublin: Stationery Office.

Walsh J (1998) 'Local development and local government: from fragmentation to integration?' *Local Economy*, 12, 4, 329–41.

Walsh J, Craig S and McCafferty D (1998) *Local Partnerships for Social Inclusion?*, Dublin: Oak Tree Press in association with the Combat Poverty Agency.

Walsh J (1999) 'The role of area-based programmes in tackling poverty', in Pringle D, Walsh J and Hennessy M (eds.), *Poor People, Poor Places. A Geography of Poverty and Deprivation in Ireland*, Dublin: Oak Tree Press in association with the Geographical Society of Ireland.

7 Partnership and local development in Portugal

From 'globalised localism' to a new form of collective action

Fernanda Rodrigues and Stephen R Stoer

Introduction

Reference in recent years to the principle and mechanism of partnership in policy programmes, particularly in the area of social and economic policy, has prompted an analytical interest in the subject. The extent, diversity and increasing complexity of processes and situations of poverty and social exclusion within the European Union has led to a reappraisal of the causes of exclusion and ways of promoting social cohesion. Partnership has been identified and tried out as a means of realizing the potential of agents, organizations and resources at different levels, from the local to the transnational.

The concept of partnership has indeed become part of the jargon of international organizations and finds its predominant meaning very much attached to socio-economic models identified, above all, with the Anglo-Saxon world.[1] Thus, in a period of 'the detraditionalization of societies' (Giddens 1990) or 'reflexive modernization' (in the words of Beck, Giddens and Lash 1994), the emergence of a preoccupation with the concept of partnership appears to be related mainly to the promotion of market-friendly social relations in the context of a system of global governance where 'deregulation', 'competition' and 'privatization' are key words (Samoff 1996; Dale 1996). Here partnership functions, using Santos' phrase (1995), as a 'globalized localism' (i.e. the successful globalization of a given local phenomenon – in this case, as the vehicle of a revised, neo-liberal, version of modernization theory).

On the other hand, partnership also develops as a working concept in a climate of cosmopolitanism and the increasingly multicultural nature of

---

1 See, for example, the study by Geddes (1997) where the history of partnership and public policy in the UK is briefly traced. In contrast to the 1980s, where 'partnership predominantly involved the public sector providing mechanisms and incentives which would encourage the private sector to take the lead in local regeneration', 'the policies of the 1990s have to some degree recognised the limitation of that approach, and have introduced a more inclusive conception of partnership' (Geddes 1997: 7).

societies. It thus appears as a response to the development of new forms of solidarity and cooperation in an international context where social exclusion has become a major concern. To this extent, it may be seen as a new strategy for collective action to promote social cohesion. It may be argued, for example, that partnership is developing as an important element in the formation of a growing consensus at the international level that demands the emergence of a more egalitarian world order. In fact, concepts such as 'partnership', 'network' and 'territorialization' are part of the language of new forms of solidarity in a context of 'action at a distance'.

It is in this context that the challenge of partnership is felt in its appeal for the construction of a bridge for joining disparate social relations in light of the corporatist organization of societies; it thus works to enhance the collective representation of isolated individuals and 'minority' groups. It may also signify a subtle way of socializing production and distributing power in a situation of the concentration of power and increasing distance between citizens and the sources of such power. Finally, partnership can appear as a link between dimensions at a time of the increasing compartmentalization of political, economic and social spaces.

In a country such as Portugal, it is a mixture of 'new' (contractual) and 'old' (more informal) forms of solidarity that makes up the context in which the study of partnership takes place. Relating these two forms simultaneously may constitute added value for struggle in Portugal against social exclusion in the sense that the homogenization of social relations, a central facet of the modernization process in 'core' countries involving the removal of difference from the centre to the margins of the system, has developed in Portugal at the same time as cultural pluralism has increasingly taken the form of an assertion of a diversity of norms and values.

The national policy context

The orientation of Portuguese social policy and of initiatives in the field of development has been subject to considerable outside influences, both from Europe and from international organizations, since the mid-1960s. Portugal's accession to the European Union has resulted in even stronger outside influences as regards social policy, although the principle of subsidiarity has been invoked both to justify certain measures at national level and in the conception, design and format of many initiatives.

The situation in Portugal can be more easily understood if we bear in mind the context of inadequate provision of public services and the considerable limitations of compensatory mechanisms. These circumstances also explain certain groups' restricted access to many goods and services (such as housing, health and education). The goods and services produced by the market are often beyond the reach and means of these groups.

The past 25 years have seen significant changes in the conception and provision of welfare in Portugal. The changes that have taken place over this period have exhibited both similarities and differences in comparison with other European countries. For example, in Portugal it was not until the early 1970s that the State began to serve as a central provider in the field of welfare policy, complementing the important initiatives developed in this area by non-profit organizations such as the Private Institutions for Social Solidarity (IPSSs). This new orientation had the potential of over-turning the long-standing tradition whereby the State served mainly as a supplementary provider. Until 1970, the most important initiatives were implemented by agents, groups or organizations with varying organizational profiles (some of them dependent upon primary solidarity networks based on relationships among relatives, friends and neighbours).

The political changes that began in 1974 led to official recognition of the need to gradually establish a universal welfare state. If we compare the Portuguese context with others, it is interesting to note that Portugal began discussing the establishment of a universal welfare state in what might generally be perceived as adverse circumstances, that is, at a time when welfare states throughout the world were being contested and in a period marked by economic recession. While, in other countries, debates and orien-tations were being ruled by principles of individualism and civil and private responsibility and action, the trend in Portugal, in coincidence with (and in part due to) the changeover of the political regime, was towards State responsibility, collectivism and the virtues of public action.

The scope of the measures instituted covered an enormous variety of investments: the creation of an integrated social security system, to replace the then separate insurance and welfare systems; various risks and situations associated with work (for example, maternity, infancy, occupational acci-dents and illnesses); and the establishment of the basis for a national health system. Just one month after the change of regime in 1974, the minimum wage was introduced, though not for all workers but only for those officially employed in the industrial, service and commercial sectors.

Despite these changes, whose practical implementation was restricted by various internal and external pressures, the result, rather than a polarization of State intervention and private initiatives (almost exclusively non-profit-making because of the then restricted role of the market), was primarily the development of a welfare system that was based on these two pillars of support, on a relationship of 'cooperative companionship' between the State and the non-profit-making private sector (a period of development whose influence can still be felt today).

Portuguese society has been described by some social analysts as being semi-peripheral in the international context, which is a reference to the existence of socio-cultural and economic features that are typical of an intermediate level of development, with consequences as regards both the trajectory and form of development of production and social reproduction (Santos 1990). In Portuguese society, a fairly weak welfare state co-exists with a strong welfare society. Given these features, some authors argue that it is more appropriate to describe Portugal as having a welfare system (irrespective of its level of integration) rather than as being a welfare state, where State measures, initiatives and benefits account for the majority of social provisions (Gould 1993). Similar to the rates in other countries in southern Europe, social expenditure (in 1993) accounted for approximately 20 per cent of GDP (with the level being 30 per cent or more in other, more industrialized, countries).

If we consider the fundamental features of welfare in Portugal over the past two decades, we can identify three periods with the following main characteristics:

- A significant increase in policies to distribute wealth, either by means associated with work (i.e. direct pay), or by means of social policies (i.e. indirect pay). Indeed, since 1974, the Portuguese state has been changing its approach, developing not only as a financing agent but also as a direct – albeit limited – producer of social provisions.
- The early 1980s (a period influenced by the prospect of inclusion in the European Union) saw the emergence of certain trends towards the gradual restriction of social rights and a move towards the 'recommercialization' of goods and services.
- Portugal's accession to the European Union, with its tangible impact on the assessment and reorientation of social provision (which, generally speaking, had never moved beyond an embryonic phase).

The 1980s saw the development of certain trends towards privatization in the field of social policy. These trends were reflected in two main orientations: (i) promotion of a review of the Constitution to facilitate the penetration of market provision in the social sphere, and (ii) the transfer of some social facilities and benefits to private management. In Portugal, privatization in this domain took place mainly on the basis of non-profit non-governmental organizations, strongly subsidized by the State. In the mid-1990s, political objectives of social policy reform re-emerged, above all in education, health and social security. The enunciation and development of reform measures demonstrated the need for a new logic based on partnership.

Both these orientations were relatively successful in sectors such as education, health and social security. In the area of social services, the vast majority of facilities were transferred to private non-profit-making organizations. The purpose of these measures was, on the whole, to contribute to the reshaping of the welfare state and they were linked with the aim of repositioning the issue in the context of cuts in public social expenditure. In Portugal, there might also have been an additional reason associated with the State's inability to meet all needs in these areas. In other words, the State's efforts to promote (and even financially support) action by various agents in this context was a question of survival and the securing of legitimation. This is linked with the politicized issue of the degree of autonomy of some non-profit-making initiatives, given their (legal and financial) dependence on the State. In Portugal, there are good grounds to believe that some non-profit-making organizations are supported by State contributions, while others survive on their own resources and are, therefore, in a position to develop a more autonomous strategy.

For each of the periods we have mentioned, it is important to analyse the relationship between the curent legal structure as regards social provision in the country and the political and institutional practices developed to apply the range of benefits provided for by law. The past few years have seen some clear legal progress, which means that we can now include Portugal as one of the countries with a more advanced legislative framework (a development that has been strongly influenced both by the recent political changes and by the pressure deriving from Portugal's accession to the European Union). Despite this improvement, however, the degree to which this legislation has been implemented is rather more restricted, a fact that has contributed to a hiatus, with at least two consequences: (i) the doors that have been opened concern hopes and expectations rather than real rights, and (ii) there has been a tempering and postponement of the very necessary (though never achieved at national level) general internalization of basic rights, as the social and political condition for effectively establishing appropriate living and working conditions.

Partnership in Portugal: origins and historical development

Having only recently been invoked as a principle or basis for action in Portugal, the concept of partnership has not yet been subjected to analysis on its own account: that is, in connection with, but at the same time going beyond, the policies with which it is associated. An analysis of the origins and development of partnership in Portugal enables us to identify two main arguments. On the one hand, there is the claim that the principle of partnership is not part of Portuguese history and that Portuguese rural traditions, based on small property units (small holdings), particularly in the north, far from promoting cooperation and partnership, have given rise to a tradition of mistrust and territorial demarcation among neighbours. On the other hand, there is another approach whereby partnership, or 'parceria',[2] is perceived as part of an ancient tradition that can be traced back to the right of association, which has been recognized in Portuguese law since the nineteenth century. The origins and development of the 'misericórdias'

---

2 According to the *Dicionário de Língua Portuguesa* (sixth edition, Porto Editora, 1987), 'parceria' means 'a group of individuals with a common interest'. Mention should also be made of the definition of 'parceria' according to Portuguese rural tradition where to work 'em parceria' refers to a form of work organization based on sharing agricultural produce between worker and owner.

(charitable organizations) have contributed over the years to the consolidation of cooperation in the form of, more or less informal, partnerships. These
charitable organizations, set up within the framework of the Catholic
Church, have traditionally negotiated the provision of social services with a
highly centralized State apparatus. During the period of dictatorship
associated with Salazar's 'Estado Novo' ('New State'), a period during
which the boundaries between Church and State were at their most tenuous,
such 'partnerships' were a supplement to State (non-) action in the social
sector. This course of development has meant that, at the political level, the
concept of partnership in Portugal has, in more recent times, come up against
concepts and practices reminiscent of the failed corporatist project of the
'Estado Novo'.

The formal(ized) definition of partnership (which translates into
Portuguese as 'partenariado') emerged in Portugal mainly as a result of
programmes sponsored and promoted by the European Commission, particularly those associated with economic and social policy. Participation in
most European social programmes required involvement in transnational
partnerships which acted as a prerequisite and therefore condition of
development. This influence has meant that the initial reaction in Portugal
has been to perceive partnership as cooperation among 'partners' in the
various countries of the European Union. It is, therefore, seen as a transnational phenomenon within a (mainly) European framework.

The idea of partnership as more informal cooperation among people
and/or bodies with shared objectives and interests (parceria) concerned to
promote local development emerged in Portugal in the 1960s. The work
undertaken by the economist Manuela Silva, firstly within the Gabinete de
Estudos Sociais (Centre for Social Studies) and later as director of the Serviço
de Promoção Social (Service for Social Promotion),[3] in the promotion of
community development is an example of this form of cooperation. At stake
was the development of an alternative approach to the model that perceived
development merely in terms of economic growth – a model that was at that
time very much in fashion in the western world.

This can be seen as one of the first experiences of partnership in Portugal
over more recent years – an experiment that not only challenged the dominant model in vogue in the area of social policy but that also clashed with
the authoritarian political regime. This experience promoted the notion
(shared by few others at the time) of development as a multidisciplinary
activity, based on experimental projects that took participation and cooperation as their working philosophy. The central idea was based on identifying
local leaders (or 'forces vives') who were seen as potential catalysts of
change and encouraging these individuals and the local population to
develop their own initiatives: 'The technique of community development

---

3 State department linked to the Ministry of Health, which was set up in 1965 and abolished by
the regime in 1972.

implies a joining of forces by local populations and the public authorities, with a view to improving the economic, social and cultural situation of a municipality or region' (Silva 1964: 498).

During this same period, which was marked by heavy pressures, both internal and external, with respect to changes in socio-economic conditions and the prevailing model of development, various references were made in official documents concerning both the advantages of, and ways of introducing and following, a more cooperative approach (both intra- and inter-sectoral). This approach was taken up in the preliminary documents for the fourth Plano de Fomento (National Development Plan)[4] and also underpinned the setting-up of the Conselho Superior de Acção Social (Higher Council for Social Action) (in an attempt to promote the organic articulation of the following sectors: work, health, social advancement and social security).

In the early 1970s, despite the final desperate attempts of a moribund regime to kill off this experiment of multidimensional community development, new schemes arose under the stimulus of the revolutionary period of 1974–5. In the belief that 'the social roots (of a new societal project) are more readily found at local level' and adhering to the new conception of social policy based on the 'culture of partnership and association', Alberto Melo, Director-General of Life-Long Education (between November 1975 and July 1976), promoted partnerships among government departments and local independent associations.

This was partnership for the 'establishment of a new system of adult education – or even a new system, or "anti-system" of general education'. Melo later claimed that the relative success of this partnership could be attributed 'to the exceptional situation in which Portugal found itself, with the eruption of popular enthusiasm when the armed forces seized power in April 1974 and the temporary power vacuum that followed the demise of the dictatorial regime, and to the education initiatives launched by members of the Direcção Geral de Educação Permanente (DGEP – Directorate-General of Life-Long Education)' (Melo and Benavente 1978: 37).

Although partnership as 'parceria' was the predominant approach in the mid-1970s, gradually, and particularly with Portugal's accession in 1986 to what was then the European Economic Community, partnership as 'partenariado' became hegemonic during the 1980s. The sudden emergence of EC programmes and funds and the growing requirement that the notion of partnership be included and present even in project plans led to a period of frenetic activity: from one day to the next it became vital to 'find'

4 In this document, the definition of the intended model of development argues for the need 'to ensure that the action of economic agents...is in compliance...with recognition of the following:...the meeting, to a greater degree and under better conditions, of the collective need for education, cultural activities, health care, social security, housing, transport and communications' [by the State].

partners. At the same time, the word 'partnership' ('partenariado') became a key word that appeared in most official documents on social and economic policy. And so emerged a new voluntarism in social, economic and cultural development. Critics of this voluntarism suggested not only that the Portuguese State was incapable of establishing the necessary conditions to promote the contractual and cultural adjustment of Portuguese society (and that the hypertrophy of State normalization would persist instead), but also claimed that partnership would develop as a central concept in a neo-liberal project of a new 'market-friendly' political economy (Santos 1993).

In the late 1980s and early 1990s, various agreements on incomes and prices, health and safety at work and vocational training were signed by the Portuguese social partners (including the setting up of the Permanent Council for Social Harmony – Conselho Permanente de Concertação Social – in 1984). And thus, in addition to the impact caused by Portugal's accession to the European Community, there was also a trend towards formal cooperation, even though, as Mozzicafreddo (1994: 114–15) points out, 'the points of reference shared by the social partners were basically the close relationship between pay and inflation, or, in other words, moderation in the growth of real pay and, above all, the strong concern, at least until 1992, to preserve jobs and safeguard the main aspects of labour legislation'. However, the worsening socio-economic conditions, in the context of the European recession which began to be felt in Portugal in the early 1990s, restricted the signing of wide-ranging agreements by the social partners, in favour of more piecemeal 'concertations', limited in their scope and/or the number of actors involved.

In the face of this situation, various ideas were put forward as ways of overcoming the 'crisis'. In 1990 a national anti-poverty programme was launched, drawing on the three key principles of the Third European Anti-Poverty Programme: partnership, participation and multidimensionality. The creation, in 1991, of a new Direcção-Geral de Acção Social (Directorate-General of Social Action) was announced as being part of the trend towards the re-articulation of the social dimension with economic policy, with emphasis on actions planned in a partnership context, in line with developing European policy on partnerships. In November 1991 it was further proposed that 'advantage be taken of coordinated action – partnerships':

- partnership means cooperation among institutions and networking;
- the complexity and inter-relationship of social problems cannot be tackled by the functionalist approach currently being taken by organizations;
- the time has come to create a partnership culture, a concerted and co-ordinated way of operating, that is based on recognition of the complementarities and co-responsibility of organizations, both public and private.

(Madeira 1992)

In 1993, as part of a package of measures to deal with housing problems, the Programa Especial de Realojamento (PER – Special Rehousing Programme) made explicit reference, as a basic requirement, to the need for local initiatives to function on the basis of agreements involving the Central Administration and local authorities, and with provision being made for complementary agreements with other State services and non-profit-making social-solidarity organizations (such as the Instituições Privadas de Solidariedade Social – IPSSs – Private Social-Solidarity Institutions) for the provision of social facilities.

Mention might also be made of the logic underlying the Second Community Support Framework (1995–9), which makes express reference to the various partners' contributions, distinguishing between those responsible for executing various measures and others more directly involved as beneficiaries. In programmes that have recently been launched, it is intended that the recently appointed Comissões Técnicas de Acompanhamento (technical monitoring commissions) will be broadly representative, involving various partners, as well as providing a multi-disciplinary and multi-sectoral perspective. This feature is most noticeably present in integrated action programmes combining investments under various policies. A recent example is the Guaranteed Minimum Income programme (Rendimento Mínimo Garantido), which began in 1996 and which adopted a formal partnership orientation (based on signed agreements of participation) involving diverse partners, both public and private, from social, economic and cultural spheres.

On the basis of the argument so far, it can be suggested that the key issue for the 1990s, as regards partnerships in Portugal, has been the articulation of the more European, and more official, concept of partnership with the definition that is more closely bound up with its associative roots and is based on local culture(s) – in other words, articulation of 'partenariado' (formal partnership) and 'parceria' (informal partnership). It is possible to identify some interesting examples of this articulation, some of which will be described below. It is also important to note that the concept of partnership has developed unevenly in Portugal, which makes the study of partnerships in various contexts (rural, urban, semi-rural) absolutely vital. As the co-ordinator of a local development agency in Alentejo, in southern Portugal, commented: 'in some ways, it might be said that capitalism has yet to reach this part of the country...We do not have a strong entrepreneurial tradition, which obviously affects people's understanding of what partnership might mean in this area' (Rodrigues and Stoer 1997: 11).

Partnership and the fight against poverty and social exclusion in Portugal

Our analysis has enabled us to identify the main orientations that have, over the past few decades, motivated and shaped the mechanisms for cooperation in socio-economic development and in actions concerning poverty and social exclusion. An important point of our analysis is the identification of features of the Portuguese situation that reveal the tradition of a centralized State, despite (and sometimes because of) poor social provision. One of the outcomes of this tradition has been the production, by this State, of mechanisms of social control rather than scenarios of concertation with other agents, which has made it difficult to develop a constructive relationship between the State and other social actors. It is important to note that this centralized approach has co-existed with a 'welfare society', essentially based on relatively informal, small solidarity networks. The strong presence of social initiatives associated with the Catholic Church has more recently been complemented by other grass roots initiatives in the field of social provision, such as the cooperative movement and community associations. However, despite the contribution that these initiatives have made in terms of the number and range of activities they have undertaken, their existence is heavily dependent on State support – a fact that raises doubts about the real autonomy and identity of some 'other' interests represented in partnerships. The parallel existence of these two major groups of initiatives has led to the development of cooperative relationships that might best be described as 'inter-institutional'.

The – still incomplete – consolidation of the welfare state in Portugal has been based on three distinct and interconnected tendencies: a movement towards the recognition and consolidation of social rights; a movement towards the regionalization of measures and policies (a trend common to other national contexts but, in the Portuguese case, also justified by the specific nature of socio-economic imbalances in the country); and a movement away from fragmented policy perceptions and interventions towards an integrated conception of measures and initiatives in the field of social policy and local development. This means that, in addition to the vital strengthening of the State (the body that sanctions and defends rights), another focus is emerging, concerned with the facilitation and promotion of locally based and often multidimensional and multi-disciplinary initiatives. As has been pointed out, Portugal's accession to the European Union has been a key factor in strengthening, or even imposing, multi-sectoral, multi-partner initiatives. Virtually all actions to combat exclusion or promote social cohesion and, of course, all investments associated with European programmes, are now based on criteria concerning the institutionalization of partnerships, accentuating more formal and (supposedly) binding forms of collaboration.

Despite recent economic growth, Portugal is still one of the least industrialized countries in Europe and poverty affects a high percentage of the population (between 25 per cent and 30 per cent of the total population, according to recent data). Indeed, 'although economic growth and the creation of more wealth appear to be a necessary condition for the continued and sustained improvement of social wellbeing, they are not, in the end,

enough, particularly for the most disadvantaged members of the population'
(Ferreira 1994). There are profound inequalities in Portugal between the
various population groups and regions. For example, some 53 per cent of
the poor are pensioners and 35 per cent are employed people, calling into
question the capacity of both wages and pensions as the traditional means of
guaranteeing a safety net capable of sustaining a decent standard of living.
For some time now, inadequate levels of State provision have themselves
been a cause of poverty for a significant number of Portuguese citizens.
Some 70 per cent of pensioners receive less than the national minimum
wage (approximately 300 Euros/month) and 50 per cent receive only up to
one-half of the minimum wage. Effectively, poverty is less a question of a
lack of resources and more one of poor distribution of resources. In comparison with other member states of the European Union, and in the context
of a relatively low unemployment rate (though the rate has been rising over
recent years), 60 per cent of the unemployed (95 per cent of whom are
young people) receive no unemployment benefit and the average unemployment benefit is less than the minimum wage.

Thus, in Portugal poverty is a structural problem which, because of the
number of people involved and the uneven distribution of resources in the
various parts of the country, is leading to a situation in which, in various
local contexts, poverty and social exclusion are currently affecting most of
the local population (Rodrigues and Henriques 1994). Given the features
described above, poverty and social exclusion entail a combination of old
and new problems, which can in part be related to the specific trajectory
and features of the Portuguese social and economic climate and its welfare
regime, which has also been going through a period of simultaneous crisis
and consolidation. Given the severity of poverty and the significance of
rising unemployment, central issues are not only debates on specific aspects
of poverty, but also a discussion of more general policy orientations with
regard to the basic model of development, in a country that is part of the
European Union but is still failing to achieve basic levels of provision, thus
putting at risk the consolidation of basic human and social rights.

Partnership in action

Our research studied partnerships in a variety of geographical locations and
with different origins, although with common aims of action against social
exclusion. The first of these was the partnership developed by the 'Project
on the Historical Area of Sé and São Nicolau' in the city of Oporto in the
north of the country. This is an area of the city that in spite of its historical
significance (recently accorded the status of a 'world heritage site' by
UNESCO) has been traditionally marked by poverty and social exclusion,
including considerable physical dilapidation. Given the characteristics of
this area, considerable attention has been given to it, particularly since
Portugal's entrance into the European Union, within the scope of a pilot

programme for urban renovation. This area was also targeted within the framework of both the European Poverty 2 and Poverty 3 programmes. The 'Project on the Historical Area of Sé and São Nicolau' originated in a state department (the Regional Social Security Office) during the Poverty 2 programme. We found in the project a pronounced vertical (top-down) partnership developing, in its first phase, as an attempt to focus on members of specific target groups (the elderly, women and youth) and, in its second phase, as an attempt to expand its focus to embrace the whole area. Due to its relatively formal nature and predominantly vertical organization, we classify this model as 'partenariado' or 'formal partnership'.

Our second case study was centred on a partnership in a semi-rural area (that is, a 'transition' area, in which agricultural activities co-exist with developing small and medium-sized industrial enterprises) where there is considerable local solidarity, though mainly among individual or small groups, and where resources are notoriously inadequate. We have characterized the partnership promoted by ARCIL – Association for the Rehabilitation of People with Special Needs in Lousã – as 'parceria' or 'informal partnership'. This more horizontal, bottom-up partnership emerged directly from perceived local needs interpreted by local citizens with the help of professionals and has organized its development on the basis of these needs, while also making the most of, and adding value to, local resources.

The third study is of a project based on a regional development association (Association 'IN LOCO') working in a depressed rural area where the aim has been to establish an interface with the region of which it is a part (the Algarve) and its industrial, tourism and service activities. It is a model that we have described as oscillating between 'partenariado' (a formal partnership that takes advantage of outside resources, at times adopts a vertical approach and is concerned to guarantee the effectiveness of investments) and 'parceria' (a more informal partnership, which is based on processes that are more relational and less contractual and which is oriented towards the development of localities as a whole). The uniqueness of this project lies in its essentially horizontal development, even in the context of processes that were originally designed to be applied vertically. We analysed the way in which this mixed model makes it possible to operate, in a tension-laden context, a local-development approach that takes account of 'local populations and outside professionals...grass roots organizations and the public services...long-standing traditions and modernity...*and* the requirements of the enterprise approach and of social solidarity'.

Remembering the characteristics attributed to Portuguese society, which generally define it as a country whose situation is somewhere between that of central and peripheral, we can see the potential for defining on the basis of this situation a type of cooperation that oscillates between what are sometimes very disparate needs. An implication of this is the need for a partnership structure that is based on investments as varied as:

- the building of bridges between cultures (oral/written, urban/rural, local/ global, masculine/feminine), which demands a communication-based approach or, to use the words of Paulo Freire, 'dialogic relations';
- the promotion of local cultures;
- the capacity to make people aware of difference;
- the capacity to mediate (between authorities, statuses, interests and world views) and to stimulate local dynamics;
- the adoption of an ethical approach that remains constant over time and produces trusting relationships based on considered reflection among 'peers'.

Evidence from our three case studies shows that, from the start, partnership in action in Portugal has to deal with the 'over-representation' of the State in Portuguese society (particularly in light of the relatively recent experience of dictatorship in the form of the 'Estado Novo'). In Oporto, for example, as stated above, the organization of the Sé and São Nicolau partnership was initially in the hands of the Regional Social Security Office. Later it changed hands to become centred in an independent Foundation, which, nevertheless, was still led by a strong body of State representatives. According to some of our interviewees, this led to the inclusion of certain dominant factors right from the outset: on the one hand, the introduction of a partnership process without any prior analysis of what this might mean and, on the other, a political culture of limited participation. These determining factors produced limitations which were, in particular, reflected in the limited representation of the local population by the partners involved: as one project worker stated, 'the project design served as a point of arrival, when it should have served as a point of departure, rather than being imposed on local partners'. This model of partnership, focused on remedying deficient social infrastructures, suffers from the fact that only rarely is the very concept of partnership taken seriously at the moment of its conception.

In addition, public services in Portugal tend to use the term 'partnership' without matching it with a clear framework of guidelines concerning its practical application. It is probably this sector more than any other that has appropriated the term, but it tends to be a passive appropriation (both in terms of the distance between words and deeds and because this sector's behaviour pattern is to wait to be asked to cooperate rather than to actively promote cooperation). However, the various public services do seem to demonstrate differing levels of involvement, which may be associated with their specific field of intervention and/or the background and experience of their agents. By way of example, it may be noted that, according to our case studies, the social security sector emerged as being more likely to develop partnerships than the Institute of Employment and Professional Training, which was open to partnership but in the habit of waiting to be approached. The main reasons for this differing institutional behaviour may be associated with the broader field of action of the one sector and the more specialized field of action of the other, or it may have to do with the fact that the background and experience of officers and collaborators weighed differently in the two institutions.

Despite the different understandings of the meaning of the term 'partnership', the underlying approach currently being taken by the local authorities in Portugal is to act as promoters of local cooperation. This was particularly clear in the case of ARCIL where the town council was considered *potentially*, as far as partnership is concerned, as 'the backbone of it all'. The importance thus attributed by ARCIL to the local authority derives not only from the town council's ability to mobilize financial resources, but also from the significant symbolic recognition that local authorities confer on the institutions and organizations with which they enter into partnership. The expansion of their area of competence (without any equivalent increase in funding), associated with the natural proximity of local interests and needs, is probably a good reason for the local authorities beginning to seek cooperation. It should, however, be noted that the local authorities' traditional lack of power (in a very centralized State) has contributed to the poor image and presence of local action in Portugal; in other words, local action flourishes in a context of strong local authorities that define the areas of intervention, priorities and forms of cooperation.

Informal relations in small communities are very often a vital ingredient for setting up a platform for cooperation. In this respect, we note the experience of a coordinator in a local semi-public service who said that the fact that she lived in a neighbouring town and was not locally integrated meant that she could not use previously established relationships to help her coordinate local services, which was her job. In this case, contact with ARCIL allowed a bridge to be built to provide the coordinator with access to local agents on the basis of what we have called a 'formal partnership of informal partners', that is, cooperation that is developed both by means of formal coordination (which tends to be more vertical) and by taking advantage of more informal cooperation processes (which tend to be more horizontal). However, it should be pointed out that, in addition to ARCIL's role in facilitating and bringing partners together, other factors also have an impact on the success of these initiatives, whose realization depends, in particular, on the characteristics of local institutions and agents, both as regards the degree of flexibility in their organization and operation and as regards the availability of local specialists.

In general, the traditional social partners (employers and trade unions) are notably lacking in the composition of social partnerships to combat social exclusion – as one might expect due to the fact that 'Portuguese society does not have a tradition of formal, centralized and autonomous organization of well-defined sectoral social interests...capable of generating strong social partners in permanent conflictual dialogue between themselves and the State' (Santos 1994: 63). Employers' interest in cooperation has a notoriously corporatist bent and they are mainly interested in increasing transnational collaboration, in the business world. The trade unions have a general interest in the issue but are very reluctant to expand their traditional field of intervention. They are, however, beginning to create various spaces for the consideration of social exclusion. Overall, it might be said that these partners' positions are similar in that they do not participate in local partnerships, although they have different interests in relation to the issue of social exclusion, with the subject being much closer to the heart of the trade unions. For employers, combating social exclusion is just one element of the overall (but non-specific) context in which they plan their initiatives.

Interesting here is the partnership experience of 'IN LOCO'. In the contracts undertaken by this association with local partners, including local and regional business enterprises, two approaches to development emerged as underlying the various projects and partnerships: one approach was more concerned with the impact of development on national revenue (with emphasis being placed, in the Algarve, on 'urban and resort-based tourism'), while the other was oriented more towards integrated rural development (with advantage being taken of, for example, 'rural tourism'). What we have, therefore, are two trends: one more systemic and sub-paradigmatic and the other more anti-systemic and paradigmatic, with the first emphasizing local development that is oriented mainly towards, and reliant on, general economic growth, and the second focusing on development based on local need and potential, attentive to the life-world and constructing a path based on realizing the potential of possible articulations and bridges, rather than on producing dichotomies.

Indeed, 'IN LOCO' has played a crucial role in managing these two approaches, by ensuring that the principles expressed and defended by it within the second approach can be operated through strategies of action and research that take full advantage of the resources generated for the partners by the first approach. The balance created between different interests depends on a conception of development that is oriented towards social cohesion – an orientation that has been at the heart of the association's simultaneous promotion of 'formal partnerships of formal partners' (partnerships based on 'partenariado') and 'formal partnerships of informal partners' (partnerships based on 'parceria').

There is little doubt that in the community-based sector (in which we include institutions responsible for providing services, local associations and groups, and local development agencies) local partnership is seen as having a broad range of meanings and implications. Positions range from one extreme to the other, with some seeing partnership as being dependent on and subordinate to local processes and others seeing it as being able to lead local dynamization processes and even (under agreement) assuming responsibilities, including responsibility for promoting the launching of local development projects. The diversity of composition, resources and skills in this sector is matched by different levels of involvement in the processes of setting up and running schemes at local level. It should be pointed out that two of our case studies concerned two associations (ARCIL and IN LOCO) that also function as local development agencies, which indicates the potential of initiatives coming from this sector for the processes of mobilization and intervention.

There is also a question of the visibility and representation in partnerships of specific interests, such as ethnicity and gender. With the exception of projects that identify these interests as targets for their activities, it can be concluded that the visibility of specific groups is not particularly compatible with a global, integrated approach. There are signs that issues concerning differences of gender and ethnicity are now being given a greater place in policy measures, but this is not being immediately reflected in increased representation at local level.

In all three of our case studies, women, in both rural and urban environments, are being particularly affected by poverty and social exclusion. Women tend to participate in partnerships as individuals and/or representatives of project teams or small groups rather than as representatives of larger institutions. The nature of their involvement in partnerships particularly reflects their communication and dialogue skills, as well as their commitment and coordination abilities. Their customary contact with day-to-day community life means that they can have the power to take coordinated action on local issues and solve problems which need resources and skills to be brought together. It is not chance that women's involvement tends to be more associated with the horizontal approach of 'parceria' and that they tend not to participate in the vertical relationships of 'partenariado'. Despite the fact that women are slowly assuming a greater role, they are however still more visible in the implementation of activities than in management roles.

Conclusion

On the basis of these three case studies, we have argued in this chapter that partnership, both as a concept and as practice, may be important to enhance processes of local development in Portugal, particularly in the struggle against poverty and social exclusion. Further, we have argued that the success of this enhancement will depend largely upon the capacity of local development agents to take advantage of partnership both as a process of relatively informal collaboration and cooperation emerging from and structured by the local level (parceria) and as a process of formal collaboration and cooperation, capable of mobilizing a coalition of interests and of committing a range of partners to a common agenda, that rethinks the local situation on the basis of very wide-ranging inputs, providing support, facilitating planning and the capacity to voice demands at regional, national and supranational levels (partenariado).

The challenge to refocus partnership from its dominant role as a means of improving the efficacy of the 'system', at a time of major change in this system, to a new form of collective action at the local level, with potential to promote greater participation by all citizens in the conduct of their daily lives and to stimulate an integrated development that tries to combine criteria of economic viability with social, environmental and cultural concerns, depends upon the successful articulation of 'parceria' with 'partenariado'. The distinction we have drawn here between these two partnership forms leads us to conclude that, in the Portuguese context, there is a need to combine the special features of cooperation that have developed over time in Portugal as a means of dealing with problems and meeting needs, with the experiences and learning that have developed elsewhere and have, due to globalization, become the context for local partnership.

References

Almeida J, Capucha L, Costa A, Machado F, Nicolau I and Reis E (1992) *Exclusão Social: factores e tipos de pobreza em Portugal*, Oeiras: Celta Editora.

Amaro R, Henriques M and Vaz M (1992) *Iniciativas de Desenvolvimento Local (caracterização de alguns exemplos)*, Instituto Superior de Ciências do Trabalho e da Empresa/Instituto de Emprego e Formação Profissional.

Beck U, Giddens A and Lash S (1994) *Reflexive Modernization*, Cambridge: Polity Press.

Chanan G (1992) *Out of the Shadows: Local Community Action and the European Community*, Dublin: European Foundation for the Improvement of Living and Working Conditions.

Craig S (1994) *Progress Through Partnership*, Dublin: Combat Poverty Agency.

Dale R (1996) 'Towards an Analysis of the Effects of Globalisation on Education', paper presented at the Faculdade de Psicologia e de Ciências da Educação, University of Oporto.

Ferreira A (1994) O Estado e a resolução dos conflitos de trabalho, *Revista Crítica de Ciências Sociais*, 39, 89–118.

Geddes M (1997) *Partnership Against Poverty and Exclusion? Local Regeneration Strategies and Excluded Communities in the UK*, Bristol: The Policy Press.

Geddes M (1998) *Local Partnership: A Successful Strategy for Social Cohesion?*, Dublin: European Foundation for the Improvement of Living and Working Conditions.

Giddens, A. (1990) *The Consequences of Modernity*, Cambridge: Polity Press.

Gould A (1993) *Capitalist Welfare Systems – A Comparison of Japan, Britain and Sweden*, London: Longman.

Melo A and Benavente, A (1978) *Experiments in Popular Education in Portugal 1974–76* (Educational Studies and Documents, 29), Paris: UNESCO.

Mozzicafreddo J (1994) 'Concertação social e exclusão social', *Organizações e Trabalho*, 97–119.

Mozzicafreddo J (1997) *Estado Providência e Cidadania em Portugal*, Lisboa: Celta Editora.

Rodrigues F and Henriques J (1994) *Final Report on the European Programme for the Integration of Less Advantaged Groups*, Lisbon: UED/Brussels: European Commission.

Rodrigues F and Stoer S (1993) *Acção Local e Mudança Social em Portugal*, Lisbon: Edições Escher.

Rodrigues F and Stoer S (1997) 'The role of partnerships in promoting social cohesion – Portugal', Final Report, Dublin: European Foundation for the Improvement of Living and Working Conditions.

Samoff J (1996) 'Which Priorities and Strategies for Education?', *Journal of Educational Development*, 16, 3, 249–71.

Santos B S (1990) *O Estado e a Sociedade em Portugal 1974–88*, Oporto: Edições Afrontamento.

Santos B S (1993) O Estado, as relações salariais e o bem-estar social na semiperiferia: o caso português, in Santos B S (ed.) *Portugal: um Retrato Singular*, Oporto: Edições Afrontamento.

Santos B S (1994) *Pela Mão de Alice, o Social e o Político na Pós-modernidade*, Oporto: Edições Afrontamento.

Santos B S (1995) *Toward a New Common Sense, Law, Science and Politics in the Paradigmatic Transition*, London: Routledge.

Silva M (1964) Oportunidade do desenvolvimento comunitário em Portugal, *Análise Social*, 7–8, 498–510.

8 A new approach to partnership

The Spanish case

Jordi Estivill

A review of partnership

As far as Europe is concerned, the word partnership is no longer a novelty in social policy. In spite of this, we must recall that it has several meanings and usages in different countries and languages. It has come a long way from its Latin ('particeps') and Greek ('hetairea') roots, from fourteenth-century England ('partaker') and the French Revolution ('partenaire') until its present definition and use (Estivill 1993a). Today it is a key concept in Irish social policy (Sabel 1996; Walsh, Craig and McCafferty 1997; Department of the Taisoeach 1997; and Walsh, this volume) referring to the increasingly complex interplay between the public administration, employers' organisations, trade unions and voluntary agencies. In Portugal (Chambel 1997) it is featured in the legal texts defining the requirements that anti-poverty projects must fulfil. In France (Rocard 1989) and Belgium (Hiernaux 1998) the spirit of partnership is not only present in common language but is also a tool of the decentralisation process and urban policies in the former country and of the ongoing federalisation of the latter. It is even starting to be used in the relationships between town councils and voluntary organisations in cold Finland (Heikkilä and Kautto 1997), where the Scandinavian welfare state model had previously meant the hegemony of public provision; and in warm Greece where until very recently local authorities had few resources and limited opportunities to work in concert with other actors.

The recent research sponsored by the European Foundation for the Improvement of Living and Working Conditions (Geddes 1998) has highlighted this increasing popularity of partnership even beyond Europe (OECD and European Foundation for the Improvement of Living and Working Conditions 1998).[1] Whereas a decade ago partnership was a novel feature of a small experimental EU Community Programme, Poverty 3, now it is present in many of the programmes and initiatives launched by the European institutions and has become one of the key concepts underpinning

---

1 As far as Canada is concerned, see Comeau and Favreau (1998).

the Commission's proposal for the reform of the Structural Funds, which will inform the development of the European Union in the 2000–2006 period.

It is within this context that we need to review our experience of partnership – first, in order to identify the economic, social and political conditions which either favour or hamper its progress and, second, to highlight the contributions that the Spanish situation and experiences can provide. These are the two aims of this chapter. The following sections discuss important dimensions of the Spanish experience: the economic context of partnership; the changing structure of the state, its role in social welfare and relations between the three spheres of state, market and civil society; local power relations; and the character and distribution of poverty and social exclusion.

The chapter concludes by emphasising the continuing influence of sociocultural identities and informal social networks, and the need for more formal partnerships to connect with these if they are to be broadly based and sustainable.

Concentration of economic activities and corporative partnership

There are few Spanish studies that highlight the material bases of partnership dynamics – most research has been primarily concerned with the institutional role of the actors involved or with the local character of partnerships. Although such factors are not to be neglected, the Spanish evidence suggests that the economic context can be crucial to the development and sustainability of partnership.

In the first place, it is very difficult for partnerships to materialise in a given area if there is not a certain level of concentration of economic activities. When there is a geographical concentration of an industrial sector (e.g. iron and steel, chemistry, textile, etc.), a specific product (e.g. shoes, pottery, seasonal agricultural articles, etc.), or a specific economic function (e.g. communications, commerce, industrial services etc.), it certainly seems easier to organise and defend corporative interests (e.g. trade unions, enterprises, guilds, etc.) around partnership schemes than when the economic structure is more diffuse. The corporative defence of mutual interests that leads the traditional socioeconomic actors to act in concert together usually coincides with three circumstances. The first is an economic crisis, a recession or an industrial or commercial restructuring. Asturias, a region polarised around mining and the iron and steel industry, is an example of such corporatist negotiation among national and regional authorities and trade unions in order to reach an agreement when faced with the production limits imposed by the EU. A recent example is milk production in Galicia, where most producers have joined efforts to oppose the quotas fixed from Brussels. Such negotiated restructuring is not always successful of course: other similar cases (Sagunto and the Basque Country in the 1980s) ended with street riots between workers and the authorities.

The second form of material basis for partnership lies in sectional attempts (either on a territorial basis or by a particular social group) to redress its material disadvantage or increase its competitive advantage, for example by attracting public investment in urban services or communication infrastructures. In recent years, local authorities have frequently set up more or less informal partnership mechanisms for lobbying purposes and offered facilities for private investments and multinationals. Large retail developments and the consumption and leisure sectors are a good example of this tendency. In recent years, employment creation and local development – promoted, for example, through the EU's Territorial Employment Pacts – have been becoming generators of this type of partnership.

The third material basis for partnership arises when an economic sectoral expansion galvanises an area. A case in point is the island of Majorca, where massive tourism is the major economic resource and brings together the interests of tour operators, owners of urbanisations, hotel investors and the government, in alignment with political and institutional structures. In such cases, partnership frameworks often act as an arena for negotiation between conflicting interests, such as small traders against supermarkets, consumers' associations against large companies, environment-friendly movements against builders of recreational ports, etc. Economic growth is not always associated with partnership between public and private interests though, especially when the organisation of economic interests does not coincide with territorial administrative structures. This is true of both the 'Patronato de la Costa Brava' or the 'Consorcio de la Costa del Sol', both of whose fields of influence do not coincide with administrative boundaries.

We must not forget, however, that in Spain as elsewhere economic development can also generate forces working against territorial economic concentration. Phenomena such as industrial deconcentration, productive decentralisation, the 'fabrica difusa', the dislocation of local economies brought about by the underground economy and financial, service and consumption mobility, are not unknown in the Spanish space-economy. Economic globalisation is another cause of delocalisation. The small comparative advantages of a locality disappear when faced with international investment strategies and although the Spanish economy has not been as attractive to multinationals as have countries such as Ireland in recent years, it is also quite sensitive to the oscillation of such strategies. One of the questions arising from these considerations is precisely: how can it be possible to build up a partnership process that is effective in relation to economic globalisation? While this issue cannot be fully explored here, an important part of the answer must surely lie in supranational collaboration and partnership between localities.

Decentralisation of the state and the changing relations between state, market and civil society

If the question above leads to supranational partnerships, we now turn to the structure and role of the nation state. Important factors in relation to partnership are its level of decentralisation and the degree of flexibility or rigidity of state structures, as well as factors such as the degree of central-isation of employers' organisations, trade unions and non-profit-making bodies, which affect the nature of their relationship with the State.

As is clear from other chapters in this book, in those countries where the State has historically been the main provider of social protection and occupies a hegemonic position in relation to the distributive mechanisms and the whole of the services aimed at the population, the germination of partnership initiatives is very difficult indeed as they require the existence of actors of quite a different logic and nature and a good level of internal flexibility.

From this point of view, the example of Spain is quite interesting in that it combines a centralist tradition with the recent creation of strong regional institutions. In effect, in the last 20 years the despotic, centralist and Jacobin model of the State has overlapped with a process of negotiation between the territorial levels (national, regional, local) by which the latter, and the regions in particular, have achieved high degrees of political and institu-tional representation and power, which are the grounds for their legitimacy. The result is a quasi-federal configuration – the so-called 'Autonomous Communities' or regions.

This process underlies many of the peculiarities and complexities of a system that is under regular renegotiation, since the Constitution itself as well as the Statutes that rule regional powers have more than one reading according to the political majorities and the alliances in the different govern-ments. Moreover, the level of decentralisation is not homogeneous. The Basque Country and Navarra collect their own taxes directly and it is only later that the central administration receives its share, while in the other regions the mechanism is exactly the opposite: citizens pay a number of their taxes to the central administration, which transfers a share of the money collected to regional governments with which they must supply the services for which they are responsible. In the social field, the funding and management of Social Security is the responsibility of the State, but a number of benefits have been devolved to regional administrations. This explains, for instance, why the Basque Government was the first to introduce minimum income schemes in 1989 (Estivill 1993b). Its pioneer example was followed by the remaining Autonomous Communities, which have set up their own funds, conditions of elegibility and integration projects. The central administration partly counter-attacked with the 'Plan Concertado', through which budgets are negotiated with the Autonomous Communities on a yearly basis for them to supply certain services (e.g. home help, information and guidance, accommodation and integration, etc.), which are managed at the local level. Another example in the social field is the anti-poverty policy, where regional governments have also been the first in launching and developing comprehensive plans in pursuing such an end (e.g. the Basque Country, Catalonia, Galicia, Castilla-León, etc.).

In the fields of culture, health and education there has also been a process of decentralisation, to the extent that in some areas all powers have been transferred to lower levels. This complex and contested decentralisation process has its advantages: it ensures a greater adaptability to each particular situation, the formulation of regional models with a learning and emulating effect and sometimes a degree of rationalisation of resources, but it also results in contradictions and overlapping responsibilities. A characteristic of the system, therefore, is the need for vertical and horizontal partnership and co-ordination.

There are, however, a number of obstacles to this. First, within the State each link of the territorial chain defends its own interests by trying to monopolise resources and be the principal managerial actor, and second, because the dominant tradition of the public sector in Spain has been opposed to co-operation with the private sector (Estivill 1992). This tendency reasserted itself under the socialist government of the 1980s. Although all the Social Services laws enacted by the Regional Parliaments (CEBS 1987; Vila and Montraveta 1995) mentioned collaboration with private non-profit-making organisations, the extent of such co-operation and the role of these organisations has not been homogeneous, differing widely between subordination (Aragon), 'concertation' (Catalonia) and a range of other possibilities such as subsidisation or service-level agreements. As for profit-making organisations, 'concertation' with them was ruled out in most of these laws and therefore only occurred in exceptional cases (e.g. Galicia, Navarra).

However, this situation changed significantly during the 1990s. The economic crisis had a restrictive effect on the growth of public expenditure, which also faced an increase in needs and demands, providing a major reason for public administrations to transfer the management of services to the private sector. The experience of public management during the 1980s had also revealed its routinisation and bureaucratisation, compelling the government to seek more flexible and effective formulas which were closer to private management. This was not something altogether new, as from the 1980s market logic had been gaining ground in society as a whole. The prototypes of the employer, of the emergent yuppie, of the ambitious bank manager, were praised in the framework of Spanish versions of neo-liberal thought. Criteria of productivity, competitiveness and efficiency have been gradually introduced, weakening the old model of public hegemony and leading to the emergence of a diversity of management formulas. Even profit-making provision has appeared where there is a solid demand (e.g. services for the disabled, old age homes, etc.).

At the same time, the number of voluntary and not-for-profit associations has increased considerably (Casado 1992). Organisations linked to the Catholic Church have achieved a higher level of professionalisation, and thousands of initiatives have appeared which are managed by each target population itself, their families or professionals. A diversified voluntary sector is increasingly present side by side with major organisations such as Caritas, the Red Cross, ONCE, etc., and national federations have been built up from local or regional bases in such a way that the latter retain a high level of decision-making power. At the same time that organisations have formed around common target populations (e.g. gypsies, handicapped, migrants, etc.), there has also been an increased transverse interplay around a given subject (e.g. integration, local development, training, rehabilitation, etc.) and an exuberant flowering of small but active local organisations, which cater for aspects such as self-help, information, support and welfare claiming. Last but not least, since the end of the 1970s, a diversity of social economy organisations (e.g. co-operatives, social enterprises, labour societies, foundations, etc.) have grown and matured (Estivill, Bernier and Valadou 1998).

Debate around the welfare state and its prospects has also contributed to this diversification of actors and a lessening of their internal rigidity. Some have argued that Spain should reach the levels of social protection of the most developed European countries; others pursue the modernisation of the State; while a third position stresses the need for building up the 'welfare society'. There has been a gradual rise in awareness that neither the public sector's hegemony nor privatisation at any price are feasible or even desirable. It is precisely in this framework that partnerships have emerged as mixed, intermediate formulas in which responsibilities are shared.

A good example to illustrate this mixture and multiplicity of actors is a project that was financed by the national Ministry of Social Affairs through a fund which is allocated 0.5 per cent of the taxes paid by citizens, who must choose between the Catholic Church or lay organisations as the recipients of such funds. The project, which was carried out by a private non-profit-making association, 'Asociación para la Promoción e Inserción Profesional', undertook the renewal of dwellings inhabited by low income older people in Barcelona, Valencia and Zaragoza. The project ensured the financial and technical co-operation of the three town councils as well as the collaboration of the primary social network of neighbours and some of their community groups. It had also to negotiate with the private profit sector, with the dwellings' owners and with building enterprises for them to supply the necessary materials and the labour force, who in some cases were young unemployed. The involvement of a diversity of actors in this process of housing renewal has resulted in an improvement in the old people's living conditions at a cost below that of their institutionalisation (GES and APIP 1991).

There are also some signs of greater flexibility in the previously centralist and rigid employers' organisations and trade unions. Collective bargaining and the dynamics of social pacts have favoured the signature of agreements between the top ranks of both parties. At the same time, in certain sectors there is also a tendency towards company agreements, while the territorial structures of trade unions, which in Spain have a considerable weight, are increasingly concerned about wider issues of citizen welfare and not only those of the workforce. Though not their main strategy, Spanish trade unions have certainly reinforced their social role since the beginnings of the 1990s and after the general strike of 1988, when they set up common unionist platforms and negotiated the implementation of minimum income schemes in every region. They also started to show their concern, as in other countries (Nicaise and Henriques 1995), for a number of excluded populations such as jobless women, foreign migrants, pensioners, seasonal or casual workers, etc., and have obtained public support, mostly from European funds, to help them. Employers' organisations also benefit from these aids, particularly for training purposes, and are structured as well into local and regional federations with a certain level of decision-making powers. The Chambers of Commerce and Industry, the federations of small and medium-sized firms, saving banks and guilds complete the list of actors involved in local partnerships. In recent years, there has been a gradual advance in the notion of social responsibility for economic decisions, which is resulting in the creation of schemes such as foundations and sponsorships and in an increasing participation of the entrepreneurial and financial world in the promotion of cultural and social activities at the local level.

Local partnerships, local power and 'caciquism'

In Spain, therefore, the 'unravelling' of the centralist, authoritarian state, the expansion of the not-for-profit sector, and a relaxation of the rigid postures of the social partners, are combining to promote partnership. At the local level, however, the emergence of horizontal partnership between different actors depends on the structures of local power and the way it is exercised.

The first question in this respect concerns the degree of autonomy and initiative of local authorities. In Spain, the municipalities have broad powers for social services, which are detailed in the 'Ley de Régimen Local' and in the regional laws of Social Services, although these are still under discussion. Their resources, however, are rather limited since their power of taxation is restricted and central and regional administrations continue to keep the lion's share in national budgets. On the other hand, social needs and demands have grown and many of these have distinctively local dimensions. Therefore, the situation is very heterogeneous and diverse across Spain. There are a number of towns, mostly medium-sized, which are able to provide good services and a broad base of social assistance, while some quarters of big cities or some rural municipalities have very few resources. But the abundance or shortage of local resources is not only related to their formal amount, but also to factors such as local political leadership and will, the extent of citizens' involvement and the campaigning capacities of their representative organisations.

This is precisely the second element with an influence on local partnership dynamics, which demands a political leadership and involvement including an agenda of negotiated priorities with the citizens' participation. It would be too complex to explain here the oscillations in this level of participation, which was very high in the 1970s, immediately before and after Franco's death, decreased in the 1980s and has been looking for new modes of expression in the 1990s.

Spanish experience suggests that the number and quality of the actors involved, and above all the balanced or unbalanced capacities between them, is another key element for partnership development. Partnerships can be a form of theatre where only the main actors have a part and the others are mere spectators who clap at the end; or, on the contrary, they can establish the rules of the game in such a way that the diverse talents of the whole company can make their contribution. As there is no perfect equality, it is of the utmost importance that at the end of the 'game' everyone has made a gain, small though it may be, and that the common project has an added value beyond particular benefits. However, this is a difficult game to play in Spain, where everyone wishes to be the protagonist and individualism and competition often outweigh collective interests. One result of this is that each locality seeks its own way and organises partnership schemes accordingly: some have taken advantage of special events such as Barcelona with the 1992 Olympic Games, and Seville with the World Expo, also in 1992.

Local partnerships are also rendered fragile by the changes brought about by regular elections and the turnover of technical advisers, as the maturation of partnerships is time-demanding. This has been proved true by many Spanish projects funded by EU initiatives with tight and very restricted terms of execution and financing.[2] Another source of weakness is the formulation of such ambitious, global and unattainable aims that the actors involved are constantly working against the clock. In this context, the EU's demand for partnership often becomes reduced to an administrative exigency of drawing up long initial lists of potential 'partners' to satisfy the formal requirements.

But much more problematic than the invention of more or less phantom 'partners' (as the real actors will eventually surface), is the reproduction of the local 'caciquismo' or clientilism – that old plague of some Mediterranean countries – for which partnership is sometimes a front. We cannot forget that although partnership is a different system of power division, local

2 This has been the case, for instance, of many Horizon and Integra projects, which have only been in operation for two years.

'caciquismo' and 'clientelismo' are still alive in Spain, and even on the increase through the ability of traditional elites to use and pervert partnership frameworks. If this happens, co-operation may degenerate into complicity and an opaque distribution of resources towards a securing of consent through patronage, the neutralisation of critical voices and the legitimation of the establishment. Fortunately, this has not been the path followed by most of the Spanish partnership experiences, but it is a real risk in some southern and northern rural areas and in all places where power is particularly concentrated and opaque.

The localisation of social problems: exclusion, urban inequality and rural poverty

The higher or lesser level of concentration of social problems is an important factor in whether partnership is likely to be a successful strategy in combating poverty and exclusion. Both poverty and social exclusion can be spatially diffused, when they affect low income individuals living in different quarters (old women), or when the recipients of social benefits are not territorially visible (single parent families), or moving targets (travellers), but in general terms in Spain nearly all poverty surveys[3] have stressed its unequal territorial distribution. The diversity of living standards among regions and towns and within each one of them; the differences in unemployment rates and in the performance of local labour markets; the bad living conditions in terms of housing, collective services, environment, etc., of one locality in comparison with those nearby; the access to and the use of health services; a higher or lesser availability of the different educational levels; the concentration of certain ethnic or migrant minorities, etc., are some of the factors that explain why local partnerships are increasingly seen as a vehicle for the expression of comparative grievance, or demands, or for achieving co-operation and solidarity between those directly or indirectly involved.

In Spain the qualitative differences between rural and urban poverty and the need to adopt differentiated approaches is an important issue. To what extent are partnership schemes useful to cope with the problems of depopulated and marginalised areas and their scattered populations, characterised by ageing and isolation, with great distances between people and services and above all by fatalism, passivity and the lack of collective organisations? A number of attempts have proved this to be difficult but not impossible. To succeed in such areas, partnerships require an effective diagnosis which analyses the deep roots of problems; if they are external to a given territory, these will also have to be tackled, as correcting 'internal' problems is not enough. For instance, the standard of living of old people in rural areas will be improved more by a rise in retirement pensions within the system of

---

3 The latest has been published by Cáritas Española.

generic social protection than by the renewal of village sewerage systems. The importance of partnership is that such a diagnosis must be the result of a consensus that reflects a common understanding of problems and of the consequent priorities, while recognising that the integration of the most excluded is not a necessary by-product of general economic development. In rural areas this diagnosis will need to consider, alongside the formal economy, the economic circuits for domestic production and consumption, mutual help among neighbours, prevailing social values, etc. Thus, in this context, partnership is above all a formal or informal opportunity to take stock of needs and to encourage the confluence of internal and external efforts.

A further added difficulty concerns the human and technical resources that will promote partnership development, as external teams are at great risk of acting as parachutists who, in not knowing the ground where they are landing, will make erroneous decisions from their urban and professional background.[4] On the other hand, is it possible to find on-the-spot activists who are not voluntary or defeated accomplices of exclusion?

In urban areas social problems (e.g. drug addiction, crime, school absenteeism and drop-out, housing decay, etc.) are often easier to detect because they tend to be concentrated in specific areas, such as 'historical' quarters and slums. Such problems are frequently associated with high unemployment. A recent survey (Arias 1998) of towns with over 50,000 inhabitants identified 374 neighbourhoods with an average unemployment rate of over 30 per cent of the working population, including urban areas in Andalusia, the Canary Islands and Extremadura, as well as large metropolitan areas and industrial towns; a juvenile unemployment rate close to 50 per cent in regions in industrial decline such as Asturias and the Basque Country, and associated problems of illiteracy, precarious work and decaying dwellings over the average. As the European Poverty 3 programme, which has been very influential in Spain, had already stressed through its three principles of partnership, participation and multidimensionality, local partnership can be an important part of a comprehensive response to the concentration and pluridimensionality of such urban problems.

In Spain, anti-poverty partnership has developed at both the regional and more local level. Within the first category, a well-known example is that of the Basque Country. Here, the initial impetus towards partnership was the launch of the minimum income schemes in 1989. This brought together the public administration at the different levels (Autonomous Community, 'Diputaciones' and municipalities) through a number of departments such as Labour, Education and Health. In Catalonia, after early initiatives such as a Poverty Audit, a Comprehensive Plan to Combat Poverty was adopted in May 1995 following a consultative process involving a wide range of

4 This is the case of El Ribeiro county (Galicia), documented in Estivill and Martinez 1996.

socioeconomic actors. This Plan included multidimensionality and partnership among its principles. In Castilla-León, a number of initiatives aimed at particular target populations (e.g. the disabled, women, ethnic minorities, the elderly) have been undertaken, together with one that was specifically designed to combat poverty (1995–8), and which included co-operation between private and public organisations. Other Autonomous Communities such as Galicia have produced their own plans and all 17 have adopted minimum income schemes, which include integration measures jointly carried out by public actors (town councils) and non-governmental organisations (Aguilar, Gaviria and Laparra 1995).

An important conclusion from the Spanish experience is that local partnerships against exclusion achieve maximum results when they are able to combine European funds (from Community Initiatives and Social Action programmes), national programmes (supporting local employment initiatives, programmes of 'Escuelas Taller y Casas de Oficios', and integrated urban renewal ('Áreas de Rehabilitación Integrada', etc.), and regional ones (in Andalusia the Action Programme in Priority Quarters; in Catalonia, the Community Development Plan; in Madrid, the Programme for Priority Action, etc.). Not all recent experiences, however, have the same dynamic or achieve positive outcomes. European funds are sometimes used for purposes other than those for which they are intended, or for public administrations to carry out what they should be doing through other resources.[5] Some national programmes have not resulted in the horizontal co-ordination of action at the local level, while some of those at the regional level have been abandoned (The Comprehensive Plan for Social Development in the Community of Madrid) or have only achieved patchy results (the Action Programme in Priority Quarters in Andalusia). There has also been success when partnership platforms against exclusion are a part of broader strategies of urban and socioeconomic development in which an entire town is involved. A good example is the Strategic Plan of Gijón, where a number of employment, commercial, environmental, and communication plans have been implemented, starting from the local agency for economic promotion and employment, which gathered an enterprise consortium, a 'mixed society' for tourism, training services, a scientific and technological park, etc. In the quarter of Las Moreras (Córdoba) it has been citizen initiative which, stemming from concern about drug addiction, has widened its field of action towards socioeconomic development and thereby launched a remarkable number of projects aimed at young people, women, school absenteeism, socio-cultural revitalisation, etc. However, the most representative example of them all is in Girona, one of three case studies which illustrate both the potential and the problems of partnership in Spain.

---

5 The URBAN programme has stressed urban issues instead of the environment and the social dimension.

A negotiated dynamic: Partnership in Girona

Girona is a small city in the north east of Catalonia with a population of 70,000, and the capital of one of the country's most affluent provinces. The economy is remarkable for the high proportion of people employed in the tertiary sector, but manufacturing is also diversified. There is a high employment rate and unemployment is below both the Catalan and Spanish averages. However, the layout of the city tends to make physical integration difficult, producing pockets of social marginalisation and, in some cases, extreme inequality. The Onyar Est project was located in such a marginalised area.

When Spain joined the EU in 1986, certain projects, including Girona Council's Family Care Programme, were taken into the EU Poverty 2 programme. This experimental scheme was used and expanded in the Onyar Est project, which became one of the three Spanish 'model actions' in the Poverty 3 programme, 1989–94. Consistent with the Poverty 3 objective of integrated, medium-term geographically concentrated projects, Onyar Est provided integrated action in an area including the old city centre and suburbs. Whereas previously (under the period of socialist control of local government) the public sector tried to be the leader and 'sole operator' in combating poverty, the Poverty 3 project required joint financing, which meant the involvement of all levels of public administration, including the European Commission, the Spanish Ministry of Social Affairs, the Department of Social Welfare, and the Girona local authority. These public agencies were brought together in a broadly-based Executive Committee, to which were also invited the trade unions, Chamber of Commerce, National Employment Institute, and a financial institution, in addition to Caritas, the Red Cross, and the local Federacion del Voluntario.

This new initiative was initially met with surprise and caution by many of those invited to participate, and initial involvement tended to fall into one of three categories. Active partners (including Caritas, the Department of Labour and the Employers' Federation, along with the local authority) were those who took positions on problems, made proposals and offered solutions. At the other extreme were passive partners who did not try or want an active role: these included the Ministry of Social Affairs and the Unión General de Trabajadores. In the middle were a group who tended to play an active role only when invited, including the Chamber of Commerce. The key moment for the partnership came when the limitations of purely social interventions to combat social exclusion were recognised. This led to new efforts to work on employment integration and to the involvement of two new partners: the local delegate of the Department of Labour and the president of the Federation of Employer Associations of Girona. Key partners in the Onyar Est partnership are also present in the town's Economic and Social Committee, which is concerned with the development of the town as a whole, ensuring that social inclusion is part of the wider economic strategy and can benefit from the active labour market in what is, overall, a prosperous town (Mora 1998).

Thus, the Onyar Est partnership succeeded in mobilising a large number of the city's players and sectors, which had not previously been involved in issues of poverty and social exclusion. It produced a far greater common understanding of problems and a broader based and more effective approach. Local activists within the poor areas spoke highly of the initiative, and although at the end of the Poverty 3 programme some problems seemed to be re-emerging, the lessons of Onyar Est were being copied in six other districts. The lessons from this partnership included, first, the strong leadership offered within the partnership, especially by young, active local politicians, along with the technical leadership of the project team. These two forms of leadership succeeded in ensuring that the project reflected the interests of most of the partners, while the local dimension of the action was vital in giving a clear focus. Finally, the impetus given by participation in the Poverty 3 programme was a considerable stimulus, demonstrated by the difficulties which re-emerged after the end of the programme in 1994.

Difficulties in rural areas: Partnership in El Ribeiro

The second case study, of an initiative in El Ribeiro, Galicia, provides an instructive contrast with the Poverty 3 partnership in Girona.

The El Ribeiro District is situated in the centre-south of Galicia, bordering on Portugal. It is characteristic of many inland rural areas in Galicia, with a dispersed and ageing population with low education levels, a predominance of agriculture and high unemployment, emigration, and a lack of social and cultural dynamism in local communities.

In 1991 the Galician government produced a plan to combat poverty, which included provision for integrated community development initiatives. In 1995 a model action was initiated in El Ribeiro, concerned with economic integration, employment insertion and health promotion. The action was to be led by an institutional partnership comprising the Directorate General of Social Services, the General Directorate of the Family, a consortium of local authorities in the El Ribeiro District, the local Society for District Development, and the IDC, a private sector body given the task of managing the project. El Ribeiro was chosen for this initiative because a number of factors seemed to be in its favour. First, the district has obvious economic potential for tourism and a well-established business and economic structure in wine production, with a number of private businesses which might be involved in economic integration activities. Second, the consortium of local authorities constituted a supra-municipal structure for collaboration. Third, the Society for District Development was already involved in integrated projects to combat poverty. Finally, the presence locally of initiatives funded by other European programmes (INTERREG and LEADER) suggested possible synergistic effects.

In practice, however, the El Ribeiro initiative failed to take off as anti-cipated. A short time before the end of the project period the partnership structure was not yet operational. Many local interests, especially local politicians, regarded the initiative with distrust, as an external intervention and moreover one which did not bring with it any new resources. The roles of the public agencies were not well defined. Underlying these difficulties were the problematic social relations of remote rural areas like El Ribeiro, where communal co-operation goes hand in hand with disagreements and feuds, where public authorities are seen as alien, and local politicians as paternalist and clientilist. El Ribeiro thus lacked a robust associative structure and the kind of collaborative culture between political, social and economic bodies necessary for partnership.

Minimum Income and a Global Plan Against Poverty: Vertical and horizontal partnership in the Basque Country

As was noted above, the Basque Country has been the location for an ambitious, partnership-based initiative to establish a minimum income and a comprehensive anti-poverty strategy. There were a number of reasons why this initiative was undertaken here. The restructuring of the industrial base of the Basque region was, by the late 1980s, having a negative effect on a growing number of the population, and a change of government to a Nationalist/Socialist coalition was determined to make an impact on this. There was also a political will to respond to European initiatives on poverty and minimum income, and, in the Alava area, an administrative and organ-isational framework that had been the base for earlier experiments. A Mini-mum Income scheme was introduced, therefore, in 1993, as one part of a Global Plan Against Poverty, which aimed to intervene in all dimensions of poverty, involving all institutional (regional and local) and departmental (Employment, Education, Health) public structures. The initiative was to run for four years, and was to design and implement specific initiatives, distri-bute funds, and monitor and evaluate the impact of the Plan. Intervention focused on three groups: people with no income; those in need of emergency help; and sectoral interventions.

Given its wide scope, the initiative has had considerable success via the impact of the benefits on some of the most excluded groups in society. How-ever, in terms of partnership, the Basque experience shows the difficulty of establishing – in a relatively short space of time – 'vertical' and 'horizontal' partnership relationships across such a large geographical area, even when confined largely to the public sector, and these difficulties were exacerbated by a loss of political impulse due to subsequent swings in political control. As a result, the three parts of the Basque country tended to take different directions. In the Alava area, the larger local authorities played an active role, but in the smaller ones the higher level authorities retained respons-ibility. Moreover, the wide-ranging powers of the public sector, and the weakness of the association sector, seriously limited broadly-based partnership, although more progress was made where personal relationships were good, objectives were clear, and where concrete interventions provided a basis. In practice, therefore, partnership often flourished most effectively at the micro-level. One example concerns the gypsy community, where a dynamic association, the Gao Lacho Drom Gypsy Association, which operates in the fields of training and social integration through education, housing and employment, has developed an effective partnership with the Basque Government, the local authority and the Autonomous Authority, in which the public authorities provide funding, advice and supervision but the intervention is managed by the Association.

The strength of sociocultural networks and identities

Thus in Spain, the recent period has witnessed both the emergence of positive local partnership experiences and the premature demise of some less successful ones, although the ultimate balance has been positive. The success of local partnership in Girona, and its failure in some other locations, raises the question of whether sustainable partnerships are only feasible in developed, strong, societies with employers' and non-governmental networks? Put another way: does the lack of socioeconomic cohesion always produce fragile and discontinuous partnerships? If partnership is only a formal forum of negotiation among powerful actors, the answers to both questions have to be affirmative. But, without neglecting the merits of formalisation, this conception overlooks other possibilities present in Spain, which will now be discussed in conclusion.

A first interpretative key to the issues in question is the classic distinction between community (Gemeinschaft) and association (Gesellschaft) (Tonnies 1979). These two models often mix, although in the former relationships are characterised as affective, emotional, and linked to human nature, and are regarded as an end by themselves, while in the latter, attitudes are rational, calculated and instrumental, and deep beliefs and values only play a small role. Spanish society is richer in examples of the first model, which creates another type of partnership, than of the second one.

In the first place, the weight and vitality of the primary social network (family, 'paisanaje', friendship, etc.), which has always been a basic element in Spanish society, has increased with the economic difficulties of recent years (e.g. young people do not leave their families as they are not able to find a job and a house of their own, budgets are more familial than individual, etc.). These primary social networks provide access to more than 60 per cent of jobs (Requena 1991). The underground economy, which represents between 15 per cent and 20 per cent of the Spanish GDP, also reinforces these networks. Second, both individual inclusion and local social cohesion are linked to processes of survival (e.g. health, labour, housing, etc.), reproduction and self-protection. In this regard, 'partnership' is part of an ongoing process through which the community as a whole organises itself,[6] rather than the result of the formalised collaboration of different stakeholders. The struggle against poverty and exclusion is above all a moral obligation, perhaps a proof of pride and dignity, of the members of a village, a neighbourhood, or a family. 'I have to join with others with whom I have close interests so as to help my people' could be the phrase summarising this position.

It is partly in this sense that the social role of individuals and social groups is multidimensional in Spain. A sport or leisure event may be easily used for political purposes or to raise funds for social aims. A festive committee of a village or a neighbourhood with the more or less formal participation of young people, women, craftsmen, restaurateurs, artists, etc., may organise recreational and sporting activities; collect money from different sources (public funds and their own, the sale of products and tickets, etc.); contribute its own activity; and after the conclusion of its work and a good meal, reserve any surpluses to help the most underprivileged or to build up a collective service. The following year, the committee's membership as well as the activities may change and any surplus be earmarked, for instance, for third-world development aid.

The second key, which is closely linked to the first, is the strength and diversity of socio-cultural identities all over Spain. There are many frameworks of identity which may be accumulative, contradictory or complementary. Where do you come from? What are your roots? are frequent enquiries into a person's origins and sense of belonging, which reveal a certain world view. Nearly every locality, quarter, village, town, county, province, region or nation, has its own calendar, historical and cultural heritage, gastronomy, idioms, particular signs, symbols and sometimes values, which are typical of them and distinguishable from others. In Spain partnerships are unlikely to make much progress if they do not connect with these identities. Since partnership is the equidistant point where consensus and conflict meet – there is no partnership without both aspects – and where power emerges and is disseminated, internal consistency and shared values play a very significant role.

Thus, the Montes de Oca anti-poverty project in rural northern Spain, which was funded by the EU Poverty 3 programme, for instance, achieved meagre outcomes due to the artificiality of the territorial field of action selected, as nearly no one felt identified with it and it lacked any city that was clearly recognised as its capital, as well as having to confront acute and tense polarisation of local social and political positions. The project's Steering Committee, which included members from all the municipalities involved, trade unions, employers, the civil society and the different levels of the public administration, drew up a written framework for partnership,

---

6 This is quite different from British experiences, where community groups tend to be the basis of organisation (see Chanan 1992).

but this hampered rather than eased the activity of the project. Consequently, the evaluation of the initiative concluded that it achieved little more than the distribution of resources from 'Europe', rather than being able to use these resources as an impulse towards self-sustained local development.

Conclusion

In Spain the history of formal partnership is relatively short, but from its initial importation as an exotic term from 'Europe' it has achieved considerable national currency in the context of local development and as a result of decentralising tendencies within the state, and a new fluidity in the social policy roles of the public, private, and voluntary and community sectors. Partnership can be linked, problematically, to traditions of clientilism, but much more positively to the contribution of informal social networks to social solidarity and inclusion in the face of unemployment and the multifaceted urban and rural crisis that affected many parts of Spain in the 1990s. If these conditions are fulfilled, what started with the importation of an exotic word (partnership) can end as a tool and strategy for the participative development of civil society.

References

Aguilar M, Gaviria M and Laparra M (1995) *La caña y el pez*. Madrid: Fundación Foessa.
Arias F (1998) *La desigualdad urbana en España*. Madrid: Ministerio de Fomento.
Casado D (ed.) (1992) *Las organizaciones voluntarias en España*. Barcelona: Editorial Hacer.
CEBS (1987) *Aplicación de las leyes de Servicios Sociales*. Madrid: Editorial Mansierga.
Chambel E (1997) 'Prefacio', in Estivill J (ed.) *O partenariado social na Europa*. Lisboa: Editorial Utopia.
Chanan G (1992) *Out of the Shadows*. Dublin: European Foundation for the Improvement of Living and Working Conditions.
Comeau Y and Favreau L (1998) 'Le développement économique communautaire en milieu urbain au Quebec', *Politiques Sociales*, Special Issue, 'Entreprendre autrement'.
Department of the Taisoeach (1997) *Partnership 2000 for Inclusion, Employment and Competitiveness (1997–2000)*. Dublin: Stationery Office.
EDIS et al (1998) *Las condiciones de vida de la población pobre en España. Informe general*. Madrid: Fundación Foessa.
Estivill J (1992) 'Le débat public-privé dans la protection sociale en Espagne', *Politiques Sociales*, 3/4, 55–66.
Estivill J (1993a) 'Partnership and exclusion', unpublished paper presented at the EU Poverty 3 Seminar, Huelva, 24–27 March.

Estivill J (1993b) 'The origins of the minimum income in Spain and in Euskadi', in Moreno L (ed.) *Social Exchange and Welfare Development*. Madrid: Consejo Superior de Investigaciones Científicas, 251–75.

Estivill J and Martínez R (1996) *The Role of Partnerships in Promoting Social Cohesion. National Report for Spain*. Dublin: European Foundation for the Improvement of Living and Working Conditions.

Estivill J, Bernier A and Valadou C (1998) *Les entreprises sociales en Europe*. Paris: Comité National des Entreprises d'Insertion.

Geddes M (1998) *Local Partnership: A Successful Strategy for Social Cohesion?* Dublin: European Foundation for the Improvement of Living and Working Conditions.

GES and APIP (1991) *Evaluación del Programa de Reparación de Viviendas de Gente Mayor sin Recursos Económicos*. Barcelona: Editorial Hacer.

Heikkilä M and Kautto M (1997) *Local Partnership and Social Cohesion in Finland*. Helsinki: National Research and Development Centre for Welfare and Health.

Hiernaux J-P (1998) 'Le partenariat, une perspective de développement du travail social', *Action Sociale*, 5, 91–7.

Mora A (1998) 'Onyar-Est, un proyecto de lucha contra la pobreza', *Políticas Sociales en Europa*. 3, February, 51–72.

Nicaise I and Henriques J M (1995) *Trade Unions, Unemployment and Social Exclusion*. Leuven: Hoger Instituut voor de Arbeid.

OECD and European Foundation for the Improvement of Living and Working Conditions (1998) *Partnerships, Participation, Investment, Innovation*, paper presented at the Joint Conference, Meeting the Needs of Distressed Urban Areas, Dublin, 17–19 June.

Requena F (1991) 'Redes sociales y mecanismos de acceso al mercado de trabajo, *Sociología del Trabajo*, 11, 117–40.

Rocard M (1989) 'Pour une solidarité renouvélé, pour un partenariat actif', in Kouchner B (ed.) *Les nouvelles solidarités*. Paris: PUF.

Sabel C (1996) *Ireland. Local Partnership and Social Innovation*. Paris: OECD.

Tonnies F (1979) *Comunidad y asociación*. Barcelona: Ediciones Península.

Vila L and Montraveta I (1985) 'La legislación autonómica de Servicios Sociales', *Revista de Política Social y Servicios Sociales*, 4/5, 6–9.

Walsh J, Craig S and McCafferty D (1998) *Local Partnerships for Social Inclusion?* Dublin: Oak Tree Press.

9 Local partnerships and social exclusion in the United Kingdom[1]

A stake in the market?

Mike Geddes

Introduction

The United Kingdom has experienced a more rapid increase in social inequality and poverty than most other EU member states, both as a result of exclusion from employment and growing differentials in income from paid employment. The growth of poverty and exclusion is now widely recognised to be damaging to both social cohesion and economic competitiveness. The geographical concentration of poverty has also increased in recent years, confirming the need for spatially targeted, multidimensional and multi-agency responses. The recent establishment of a new Social Exclusion Unit (SEU) by the Labour government elected in 1997, with a focus on well-publicised aspects of social exclusion such as school truancy and problem public housing estates, reflects both a new recognition of the discourse of social exclusion and the need for government to be seen to be addressing it.

At the same time, partnership has become one of the vogue words of the 1990s in the UK policy community. Government, business, local government, community organisations and the voluntary sector increasingly subscribe to the value and virtues of partnership. Local partnerships have been supported by key government programmes of the 1990s for urban and rural regeneration such as City Challenge and the Single Regeneration Budget, and have been endorsed across the political spectrum. The emergence of partnership as a perceived solution to a wide range of complex and intractable public policy problems and to public expenditure constraints reflects a number of factors, including the increasing role in public policy of business, market models and managerial methods; the development of a mixed market in the provision of local services; and an emphasis on localised responsibility for policy implementation; as well as the growth of poverty and exclusion.

1 This chapter draws on Geddes (1996) The role of partnerships in promoting social cohesion: Research Report for the United Kingdom, Working Paper WP/96/29/EN, European Foundation for the Improvement of Living and Working Conditions, Dublin.

However, although partnership is more strongly established in the UK than in nearly any other EU country, it remains a subject of considerable debate and ambiguity. This ambiguity concerns the 'politics' of partnership in terms of interest representation, and its impact on the patterns and processes of governance; the depth and extent of the commitment of key actors; the outcomes of partnership and its effectiveness in comparison with other ways of making and implementing policy. This chapter will focus on such issues, beginning by locating the emergence of partnership in its historical context.

The post-war consensus

The period after the end of the Second World War saw the emergence of a broad political consensus in Britain which produced a welfare state operating on universalist principles and in the context of historically high levels of employment and government commitment to the principle of full employment and Keynesian macroeconomic management to rebuild the British economy. Employment disparities, principally between regions, were addressed by a regional policy administered by central government, which was also responsible for key components of the welfare state (e.g. benefits, health) while local government also played a significant role in social provision, particularly in education and housing. A major programme of urban renewal through the building of new towns was implemented by executive government agencies. The combination of high levels of employment, rising wages and the expansion of the social wage reduced poverty to the perceived status of a marginal phenomenon. State responsibility for social provision and redistributive policies frequently embodied a major role for the private sector (e.g. in the construction of public housing), but any notion of 'partnership' was significantly absent, although in the 1960s bodies such as the Regional Economic Planning Councils began to introduce a form of interest representation that we would probably now describe in terms of partnership.[2]

During the 1970s, however, the faltering of economic growth, especially following the oil price 'shock' of 1973, introduced a new era of rising and more structural unemployment, initiated an incipient crisis of the welfare state, and provoked a so-called 'urban crisis' (Rees and Lambert 1985). During the 1980s successive recessions were associated with large-scale industrial restructuring and decline and the emergence of a 'new poverty' much greater in extent and depth, dispelling the comfortable notion that poverty had been largely eliminated during the Fordist boom.

---

2 Interest representation on the Regional Economic Planning Councils was chiefly, but not exclusively, drawn in corporatist manner from the state, industry and trade unions.

New poverty and social exclusion

The UK has been distinguished in recent decades by a larger growth of poverty than any other member state of the EU, and a faster rate of growth of inequality than any other industrialised country with the exception of New Zealand (Gaffikin and Morrissey 1994b). A number of commentators see more in common between the UK and US experiences than between the UK and most other European countries, pointing to the way in which similar economic policies in the 1980s were associated with a polarisation of the labour market.

While some of the facts and issues remain strongly contested (see, for example, Dennis 1997), there is much evidence showing that the UK has been experiencing a widening of social inequality and a serious growth of poverty and deprivation. There are different measures of poverty in use in the UK, but they all show growing poverty and inequality in the 1980s and the early 1990s. Between 1979 and the beginning of the 1990s, the number of those living on or below 50 per cent of average income grew from 9 per cent to 24 per cent of the population, and has remained at about that level throughout the 1990s. The share of national income of the poorest 20 per cent of the population fell from 10 per cent in 1979 to 6 per cent at the beginning of the 1990s (Oppenheim 1993; Townsend 1994), and this group appear to have failed to benefit from economic growth, in contrast to the rest of the post-war period (Joseph Rowntree Foundation 1995).

The growth in inequality in the UK can be attributed to a number of factors. On the one hand, the proportion of the population which has benefited from recent economic trends has experienced rapidly rising incomes that have fuelled conspicuous levels of 'yuppie' and 'fat cat' consumption. Consequently, the income gap between those with earnings and those dependent on benefits has widened and differences in income from work have also grown rapidly.[3] More people are dependent on benefits, as a result of both higher unemployment and social and demographic factors. Social change has increased the numbers of single parent, largely female households that are particularly at risk of poverty and are likely to have very limited capital in addition to low incomes. Members of ethnic minorities are nearly twice as likely as other social groups to suffer poverty as a result of unemployment, both because of differentials in education and qualifications and as a result of employer discrimination (Amin and Oppenheim 1992). Over 60 per cent of adults receiving income support are women, as are 65 per cent of those on low wages below the Council of Europe's decency threshold (Oppenheim 1993).

3 In principle, a rise in inequality can be consistent with rising living standards for the poor along with others. In practice, such a 'trickle down' effect is not evident and the growing gap between rich and poor is seen to be damaging the social fabric and weakening social cohesion, with a substantial minority of the population having no stake in the prosperity of the country.

These widening disparities are rooted in sweeping processes of economic, industrial and employment restructuring and change. In the second half of the 1970s and the first half of the 1980s unemployment rose consistently and sharply. A major cause was the crisis of overcapacity in traditional industries (coal, steel, shipbuilding), producing very high and long-term unemployment and growing poverty, in mining villages and regions for example. This process tended to intensify differentials between North and South (poor North, prosperous South), but growing overcapacity and restructuring in industries such as motor vehicles and aerospace also began to bring 'new poverty' to southern and midland England. For the Conservative government, the emergence of high and persistent unemployment was not a signal for new employment-creating initiatives, but an opportunity to test the dictum of reliance on market processes to promote structural adjustment. The inability of the National Union of Mineworkers (NUM) to reverse this policy over pit closures became a significant marker of the defeat of traditional Labour movement responses to unemployment and industrial change.

In the later 1980s and the first half of the 1990s alternating periods of expansion and recession have brought new economic growth to some areas and social groups (if we define growth in terms of GDP or profit), but this has been marked by a number of features: expansion of the service, consumption and financial sectors; part-time, temporary and casual employment, increased labour market flexibility and insecurity, and expansion of female more than male employment. This economic flux has eroded the previous pattern of inter-regional disparity (Martin 1998), while introducing a much more localised pattern of poverty and affluence, in which very affluent neighbourhoods sit cheek-by-jowl with local areas of intense and entrenched poverty and deprivation (Green, Gregg and Wadsworth 1998). Areas such as the latter now bear all the hallmarks of cumulative marginalisation, in which exclusion from employment (production) or low wages within employment create exclusion from the norms of consumption enjoyed by the majority of the population (Bauman 1998); tendencies that are reinforced by the low and declining quality of public and private services (the closure of bank branches and rural shops for example, in addition to poor schools and public transport) and marginalisation from decision-making processes (Power 1997). In areas such as these – which may be seaside towns or rural areas as well as inner city or urban periphery housing estates – exclusion from the economic and social mainstream is inevitably associated with crime and fear of crime (Lea 1997), informal and illegal economic activity, poor health, and with marginalised social groups from ethnic minorities to single parent families and the homeless. In some of the areas of most concentrated deprivation, poverty overwhelms new investments made in the physical fabric and in social facilities.[4] A number of alienated young people are out of control in such areas, terrorising the old in particular (Danziger 1995). In the words of the new government Social Exclusion Unit (1998), 'they have become no-go areas for some and no exit zones for others'. Exclusion, in this sense, remains rooted in the fact that such populations are surplus to the current and foreseeable requirements of the capitalist economy (Byrne 1997); but is experienced equally through exclusion from consumption norms and from social and political citizenship. Ironically, such areas are frequently discussed in terms of a rhetoric of 'community', which is frequently conspicuous only by its absence, despite the continuing attachment of some residents to such areas. In a period when previous class formations have been shattered, the excluded are often invisible (in rural areas, for example) or appear defined by categories such as those of identity and generation (young black males, for example).

The debate on poverty and socio-economic polarisation has drawn on two related concepts: the 'new poverty' (Funken and Cooper 1995) and, more recently, that of social exclusion (Room 1995). Both signify not only the quantitative growth of poverty, but also its structural association with fundamental processes of industrial change, the restructuring of the welfare state and changing patterns of social and political allegiance, and its 'multi-dimensional' nature. The continuing relevance of the 'new poverty' analysis, now tending to be submerged under the idea of exclusion, lies in its insistence on the structural nature of deprivation in the contemporary 'advanced' economy. Alongside this, the notion of social exclusion is intended to recognise not only material deprivation, but also the inability of the excluded to fully exercise their social and political rights as citizens. Further, it suggests that where the material living standards and citizen rights of significant numbers of people are restricted by persistent, multiple and concentrated deprivation, social cohesion is threatened (Room 1995). Social exclusion remains a contested concept in the UK. Critics argue that it implies a potentially inclusive and cohesive society which is at odds with the realities of class and other divisions, leading to an over-simplistic polarisation between the 'included' and the 'excluded', and that it presumes the reinsertion of the excluded into the labour market as the basis for policy (Levitas 1996). These are valuable warnings. But can exclusion also be a concept which focuses attention on active social processes of exclusion, not simply on their symptoms and consequences, and which opens up possibilities of building bridges between those disadvantaged to different degrees and by a wide variety of social, economic and political processes? To the extent that this is the case, it need not imply any less concern with the essential economics of poverty, and with distributional policies, but may help to link these to related questions of social and political participation and power.

4 A recent and influential report by a Commission of Inquiry into Income and Wealth, established by the Joseph Rowntree Foundation and with membership drawn from a wide range of stakeholders including major industrial and financial interests, the trade unions and the voluntary sector, concluded that the social costs of poverty are substantial, but also that increasing inequality can be damaging to economic competitiveness, if the latter depends on systematic investment in human and physical capital.

In this context, the emergence of partnership at the local level may be seen as a significant reflection of the 'new' agenda of social exclusion: in the focus of policy on localised concentrations of 'extreme poverty'; in the emphasis on a concerted and integrated approach to the multidimensionality of exclusion; and in the 'partnership' model of a concerted, multi-agency response involving private as well as public actors and empowering the disadvantaged themselves. The success or failure of local partnerships may be one important test of the value of the concept of social exclusion as a tool for changing as well as understanding contemporary patterns of inequality.

The emergence of local partnership

The emergence of local partnership in the UK as an increasingly important element of urban policy can be traced to the 1970s. This period was one of the new constraints placed by government on public expenditure – symbolised by the resort to IMF support in 1976 – and the abandonment of the full employment commitment. Partnership began to emerge as a means by which other actors might be induced to share responsibility for, and find new solutions to urban problems, alongside an increasingly constrained public sector, initially through the creation of Inner City Partnerships in major cities in the 1970s. However, these early partnerships were primarily concerned to integrate the efforts of national and local government departments – 'community' interests were involved only at the margin and the private sector was a relatively minor player.

During the 1980s however, successive Conservative governments, inspired by neo-liberal and new Right ideology (Gamble 1981; Levitas 1986) instituted a far-reaching revolution in public policy. A primary intention was the 'rolling back of the state' through processes of deregulation and privatisation, the reduction of public expenditure (Doogan 1995), and a thoroughgoing challenge to the universalist welfare state on grounds of cost, efficiency and in terms of the alleged dependency it is held to create among its 'clients' (Green 1993). One outcome of this was fragmentation and organisational proliferation within the public sector, with the break-up of 'monolithic' public organisational structures at both central and local level and the creation of many new state and quasi-state agencies, including local-level agencies, such as the Training and Enterprise Councils (TECs) in England and Wales, as well as newly-privatised sectors such as the utilities. The result has been a much greater need for inter-organisational collaboration and partnership within the public sector itself, as well as between the public and private sectors. Successive Thatcher governments also attempted to institute a general shift to 'market'-led as opposed to public sector-led governance. A more 'business-like' state was encouraged, with the extension of 'quasi-markets' and contractual relationships, and a stronger role for the private sector in both setting and implementing the public policy agenda (Clarke and Newman 1997). In relation to local governance and urban policy, this was reflected in the view that lasting economic, social and environmental regeneration required the active involvement of the private sector; that making urban areas attractive to the business community would bring wider benefits including 'trickle down' effects such as job creation; and that the role of elected local government (increasingly in Labour hands, and regarded as part of the problem, not as part of the answer) should be reduced in favour of agencies involving business leaders and government officials (see Harding and Garside 1994).

In the 1980s therefore, local partnership predominantly meant putting pressure on the public sector to provide mechanisms and incentives that would encourage the private sector to take the lead in local regeneration. The emphasis of the previous model of public-private partnership was reversed to one of private-public partnership, with the private sector presumed to play the leading role through a range of new policy initiatives of which the Urban Development Corporations and Enterprise Zones were leading examples.

The deficiencies of this approach – including the limited willingness and capacity of business to take up its envisaged role, as well as the narrow political base created by the non-involvement or marginalisation of other actors – have now been widely documented (Bassett 1996; Hastings, MacArthur and McGregor 1996). The evolution of Conservative policies in the 1990s embodied a recognition of this to some degree and introduced a rather more inclusive conception of partnership. In the sphere of urban regeneration, the focus shifted from a narrow preoccupation with physical regeneration to a wider concern with the economic and social regeneration of communities. Social as well as physical investment became an important element in partnership programmes and this brought with it the involvement of 'community' interests alongside the public and private sectors, in local partnerships funded by programmes such as City Challenge, New Life for Urban

5 City Challenge was launched in 1991 with the aim of providing greater coherence in urban regeneration policy. Resources were allocated for up to five years to local partnerships of local authorities, the private sector and local communities, on the basis of competing bids presented to the Department of the Environment. In 1993 a further radical shake-up of urban policy, involving the merging of 20 previously separate programmes administered by five different government departments, led to the introduction of the SRB. SRB funds are allocated by competitive bidding and negotiation with government Regional Offices, involving bids from local partnerships comprising public, private and voluntary sector organisations, usually but not necessarily led by local authorities and/or Training and Enterprise Councils (TECs). Bids are expected to meet some of the following objectives:

- enhancement of local employment, education and skills, especially among disadvantaged groups;
- lever in further resources, from the private sector and European funding;
- encourage economic development and local economic competitiveness;
- environmental and housing improvement, including tackling crime;
- enhancing health and quality of life;
- increasing community participation.

Scotland, and the (still current) Single Regeneration Budget (SRB) (Oatley 1998).[5] Competition between localities remained the government's preferred method of allocating the limited resources made available, but these programmes had wider remits than their predecessors, and they offered a more important role to local government, local communities and the voluntary sector. The Single Regeneration Budget has particularly emphasised strong local partnership as the basis for a successful bid for funding. Regional Challenge and Rural Challenge schemes were also developed on a partnership format.

The more broadly-based 1990s' version of local partnership gained broad political support from the main opposition parties. The Liberal Democrats sponsored a Commission on Wealth Creation and Social Cohesion, which argued in its report for a stakeholder economy and a social framework of inclusion (Dahrendorf et al 1995). Similar ideas were promoted by the Labour Party, which gave strong backing to local public-private partnerships, while emphasising the role played by Labour-controlled local authorities. While there remain important differences between the positions of the main parties and the roles they would envisage in partnerships for different partners, there is nonetheless a broad political consensus about a partnership approach in the UK, reflecting the move towards a new centre of gravity in electoral politics, focused on a centrist coalition based on middle-class interests.

Partnership thus became a central feature of a new model of local governance in the 1990s, both creating and reflecting changing relationships between the public and private sectors. The implementation of national policy programmes through local partnerships has been dubbed a 'new localism' in public policy, combining elements of urban managerialism, competitive mechanisms of resource allocation, and the involvement of a variety of local interests in a distinctive manner (Stewart 1994). A feature of the partnership approach in the UK is that strong central direction of policy by government has been combined with some decentralisation of policy delivery at the local level. But although government is not usually a partner in local regeneration projects, it remains a dominant influence. Central government sets the framework of policy and funding for local partnerships, allocates resources between competitive locally-generated bids according to bidding criteria which it specifies, and monitors and evaluates the performance of local partnerships. Moreover, although government departments are not directly involved in local partnerships, stronger government Regional Offices were established in the early 1990s to enhance the capacity of government to manage locally-administered programmes, along with a new Ministerial Committee for Regeneration – changes which represented a measure of response by government to criticisms of inadequate policy coordination and the fragmented and limited nature of the outcomes of urban policy (Robson et al 1994). The Labour government elected in 1997 has pressed forward strongly on this front, introducing regional assemblies in

Scotland and Wales and setting up Regional Development Agencies (RDAs) in the English regions, moves which are likely to lead to a more coherent regional framework for local regeneration partnerships in the future (Wilks-Heeg 1998).

In contrast to the role of government, EU programmes have been less influential in shaping the development of local partnership than in a number of other European countries.[6] The limited scale and relatively restricted funding of European programmes compared with nationally funded ones has limited their impact in the UK. Nonetheless, the EU's Poverty 3 programme was of relevance because it generated a debate on poverty and social exclusion, and the LEADER programme has had a significant impact in rural areas in the peripheral regions of England, Wales and Scotland.

The local partnership approach to regeneration in geographically concentrated areas of deprivation and poverty in the UK thus exhibits specific features within a European context.

Urban regeneration partnerships

The dominant model of local partnership in the UK derives from the influence of recent government programmes, especially City Challenge and the Single Regeneration Budget Challenge Fund. These urban regeneration local partnerships are formal, multi-sectoral partnerships combining local public, private, voluntary and community interests, implementing multi-dimensional policy programmes which may include physical regeneration, business support, employment and local labour market interventions, environmental improvement and crime prevention and community safety programmes. Such partnerships are often formally constituted as trusts or limited companies. The partnership structure will typically include a partnership management board on which a wide range of partner interests are represented, a tighter executive committee of core partners, and a full-time partnership team. Partnerships such as those described below are responsible for large budgets, and often for major 'flagship' redevelopment projects in town centres and on industrial and housing estates, as well as training programmes, community facilities and a range of smaller projects.

The Castlemilk Partnership, Glasgow

The city of Glasgow in central Scotland hosts several local urban regeneration partnerships on large peripheral housing estates, which have become major concentrations of poverty and social exclusion, with different experiences of economic and social regeneration initiatives. In the Drumchapel

---

6 Although the European Social Fund (ESF) and European Regional Development Fund (ERDF) have had more of an influence at regional level.

area, the local authority set up Drumchapel Opportunities, an employment, training and neighbourhood regeneration initiative, which emphasises the economic empowerment of local residents. In the Easterhouse and East End areas there have been similar, though less prominent, initiatives.

A further initiative has been located in Castlemilk, a large peripheral estate on the southern edge of the city. The Castlemilk Partnership was established in 1988 by the Scottish Office as an Urban Partnership Area, on the base of an earlier small-scale local initiative with a strong community network. At the outset of the partnership the estate was characterised by low average household incomes, high unemployment, low educational and skill levels, poor and unpopular housing, a degraded environment, poor private services and high demand for public services, and a poor image. Population had halved from a high point of 37,000 in 1971.

The main issue facing the partnership was to arrest population decline and to create in Castlemilk a well functioning suburb, better integrated with the Glasgow conurbation but with more local jobs and services. Large-scale housing and environmental renovation and diversification has been accompanied by training and employment projects and social and community initiatives. Anti-poverty initiatives have been one element of this strategy, especially to improve public services and reduce their cost to poor people. Approximately £150 million in public capital expenditure was invested over an initial five-year period, 75 per cent of it on housing. The £110 million public housing spend has been accompanied by £20 million private investment.

The partnership has membership drawn from the public, non-statutory and private sectors. Public partners include the representatives nominated by the Scottish Office, Strathclyde Regional and Glasgow District Councils, the Employment Service, the Greater Glasgow Health Board and Glasgow Development Agency. The private sector is involved through the Castlemilk Business Support Group. The partnership is not a legally constituted body, but a committee of independent organisations that seeks to influence the policies of its members.

An evaluation of the first phase of the partnership (O'Toole, Snape and Stewart 1995) suggested that there were significant achievements in housing and in raising skill levels, and in collaboration between professionals and with the community in education, health and community care. Resources expended elsewhere would be unlikely to have produced equivalent results without the catalytic effects of partnership. However, the impact on jobs was limited. Consequently, while some of the consequences of poverty have been alleviated, it was beyond the power of the Castlemilk local partnership to significantly reduce poverty. Local community businesses have been supported by a Local Development Agency, but the community withdrew from participation in this because of its perceived lack of accountability to local people (Stewart and Taylor 1995).

Partnership working in Castlemilk was seen as an important learning experience in multi-agency co-operation between government and community and between departments and professions within government, due to high-level political commitment by leading stakeholders, and resource support. However, the role of the private sector in partnership activity has been more limited to objectives close to its direct interests, such as training, rather than the broader strategy. There was also little sign of long-term community empowerment, partly because of the tension between allowing time for community involvement and the rapid delivery of major investment programmes. Achievement of the objectives of the partnership was therefore seen to be a long-term process, with a continuing need for levels of public and private investment at least as large as those of the first five years, and greater emphasis on smaller projects with community involvement as well as large-scale investment programmes (O'Toole, Snape and Stewart 1995).

North Tyneside City Challenge Partnership

In common with the Castlemilk Partnership, North Tyneside City Challenge was a major urban regeneration project, with a five-year strategy and action plan that involves integrated physical, economic and social regeneration, in which tackling poverty, unemployment and exclusion are seen as priorities.

North Tyneside lies at the mouth of the River Tyne in north-east England, in an area of high and long-term unemployment caused by the decline of traditional industries such as coal mining and shipbuilding. Within the area are several large and run-down housing estates, including the Meadowell estate which was the scene of serious rioting in 1991. There is a long history of regeneration projects and programmes in northeast England and on Tyneside. In the 1970s Community Development Projects in both Newcastle and Tyneside were part of an experimental UK government programme of localised anti-poverty initiatives. In the 1980s an Urban Development Corporation was set up to redevelop the run-down waterfront area of North Tyneside, and the City Challenge area lay adjacent to this. The City Challenge proposal was led by the local authority, North Tyneside Metropolitan Borough Council, but the successful bid also included community initiatives on the Meadowell estate, where community leaders had developed plans for renewal in the wake of the 1991 disturbances.

The strategy of the partnership sought to encourage the entrepreneurial activity of local people and their participation in community life. The action plan included both a number of large 'flagship' projects concerned with the renewal of industrial, commercial and residential areas, and many other projects and initiatives to increase employment, develop industry and commerce, raise skill levels, improve the environment, reduce crime and improve community facilities. Over the five years of its operation from 1993 to 1998, North Tyneside City Challenge partnership drew on £37.5 million of City Challenge funds, largely channelled through the local authority. The majority of projects that the partnership undertook were co-funded by other partners and the programme therefore accessed substantial further public money and private investment.

The partnership was a limited company run by a Board of Directors with 20 members grouped into five 'Forums', representing business, housing, an 'economic assembly' including the TEC, English Partnerships, the Development Corporation and the police, a community forum and local government interests. Community representation was organised on an area basis from each of the main housing estates, increasingly by election from local community forums which the partnership supported to help represent the views of local people, together with Community Development Trusts to implement some of the community projects.

In North Tyneside, the City Challenge partnership encouraged a wider partnership approach to local regeneration than earlier government programmes. While the intention of government was that City Challenge should be business-led, in North Tyneside it offered a more prominent role to the local authority in particular. NTCC developed effective partnership working among public agencies and with private sector interests also represented. Active community involvement remained relatively restricted however.

The investment and projects undertaken by the partnership have had a major effect in modernising important elements of the industrial, commercial and housing infrastructure, but partners remained cautious about the ability of the partnership to tackle poverty, partly due to contributory factors beyond the control of local actors. Thus, while the partnership was responsible for a very considerable investment programme, its experience indicates that in areas of severe deprivation, even strong local partnerships with significant resources may only be able to have a limited impact on employment and hence on poverty and exclusion.

Coventry and Warwickshire Partnerships Ltd

While the City Challenge programme developed this type of approach in a limited number of large cities and towns in the early 1990s, the more recent Single Regeneration Budget Challenge Fund has extended this model more widely. In Coventry and Warwickshire, for example, a new partnership framework established in the mid-1990s was successful in obtaining substantial resources (£22.5 million) from the SRB. Coventry is a major manufacturing city in the English Midlands, whose traditional industries have been a microcosm of the broader West Midlands regional economy based on the car industry and other manufacturing and basic industries. The economy of the surrounding county of Warwickshire is closely linked to that of Coventry by travel to work patterns and inter-firm linkages. The decline of traditional industries has impacted particularly on certain social groups and neighbourhoods.

The overall aim of the new partnership framework – again taking the form of a limited company – was to develop an economic regeneration strategy to 'improve the quality of life, prosperity and wealth of the people of Coventry and Warwickshire'. Ten strategic objectives were identified, grouped into four action programmes concerned with physical regeneration, business development, human and social development and advocacy on behalf of the area. Action to tackle poverty and exclusion constitutes one part of this broad economic and social regeneration agenda.

The partnership brought together public, private, voluntary and community partners. The founding members were Coventry City Council, Warwickshire County Council, the Training and Enterprise Council (TEC) and Coventry and Warwickshire Chambers of Commerce and Industry. Further members include the second tier district councils in Warwickshire, the two local universities and other higher education institutions, manufacturing and service sector businesses, voluntary and community organisations, and trade unions. The partnership has a two-tier structure with a main board (on which the main stakeholders are represented) and executive committee responsible for overall strategy. Beneath the main decision-making level, specific areas of activity are the responsibility of either subsidiary companies/partnerships or of partner organisations themselves.

Anti-poverty partnerships

Contrasting with the broad urban regeneration policy remit of local partnerships associated with recent government funding programmes are the local partnerships supported by the EU Poverty 3 programme, 1989–94. These initiatives also established formal multi-partner local partnership structures (although employer representation tended to be less and community representation greater) and developed multidimensional strategies and action programmes. However, the Poverty 3 local partnerships focused their strategies and activities much more directly on problems of deprivation, poverty and exclusion, and regarded the facilitation of processes of community development and empowerment as central to their agenda. Poverty 3 partnerships are also of interest in focusing on the needs of specific social groups. The Brownlow partnership identified three key 'target' groups: women, children and young people, and the unemployed, while the Granby-Toxteth partnership focused on the needs of the black and ethnic minority communities in the area.

Brownlow Community Trust

Brownlow is a housing estate of approximately 9000 people in a predominantly rural area of Northern Ireland not far from the border with the

Republic. Twenty-five miles from Belfast, the estate was built in the 1960s as part of a proposed New Town, the product of a major plan for the redevelopment of Belfast and economic expansion within Northern Ireland. However, recession in the 1970s and 1980s meant that the plans were abandoned after the Brownlow estate was built, leaving it in a physically, economically, and socially isolated position.

Brownlow Community Trust (BCT) had its roots in active community organisation that dates back to the late 1960s and the development of the town itself (Bailey et al 1995; Gaffikin and Morrissey 1995). With the closure of a major employer and a failure to attract further investment, Brownlow suffered from high and long-term unemployment, leading to population decline and an increase in crime and vandalism. In 1988, Brownlow community groups published a Greater Brownlow Review, leading to a co-ordinated effort by community representatives and statutory agencies to develop a common strategy to regenerate Brownlow. This led in due course to a successful funding application to the EC's Poverty 3 programme. As one of the Model Actions of the Poverty 3 programme, the remit and objectives of BCT reflected the programme's principles of partnership, participation and multidimensionality. The strategy and activity plan developed by the Trust focused on the needs of three main social groups: women, children, and the unemployed. BCT supported and resourced activity and projects for all these groups. Initiatives included a Brownlow Women's Forum, a Children's Policy Forum and a health project. The Trust attempted to build community infrastructure within Brownlow, to focus the policies of public agencies, and to promote more effective working between agencies and the community.

Funding of approximately £2.2 million was obtained for a five-year period from 1989–94 from the Poverty 3 programme. A separate economic development fund was set up with funding from the Department of the Environment and the Investment Fund for Ireland to promote business investment. The BCT Management Board was made up primarily of representatives from statutory agencies and community interests. Agency representation included the health, education, housing and economic development agencies and the local authority. The Trust invested considerable resources in ensuring that different elements of the community were represented, although this continued to be a source of some tension. Representation was both from community organisations and by election from different parts of the estate. Due to the limited number of significant local employers and the existence of a separate economic development agency, the private sector was under-represented. There was strong representation of women on the management board on the 'community side' and in the project team.

Although Poverty 3 funding lasted only five years, BCT helped create a new culture in the area, with greater inter-agency collaboration and consultation with local people, and an innovative and multidimensional approach to social policy issues in a highly marginalised and excluded area. However, the level of resources available to the Trust, although significant, did not enable it to have a major effect on the material conditions in the lines of Brownlow's inhabitants.

Granby-Toxteth Community Project

The Granby-Toxteth Community Project was another of the UK model actions funded by the EU's Poverty 3 programme, in an inner city district of Liverpool with a large and long established ethnic minority population. Granby-Toxteth remains one of the poorest areas of the city with a history of antagonism between and within black, ethnic and white local communities, with class, gender and racial dimensions, despite 20 years of programmes and initiatives to combat deprivation and poverty.

The strategy of the Granby-Toxteth partnership focused on enabling local people to benefit from urban regeneration schemes being undertaken by central and local government, both by helping to enable the local community to participate in decision-making, and by local labour and training schemes. The partnership also aimed to provide a community development resource for the locality, for example through a project to encourage local people to claim state benefits due to them, and a community newspaper. GTCP brought together a range of partners including central and local government, community organisations, the University, religious organisations and, less centrally, the private sector. The central and local government representatives saw themselves as lead partners and the involvement of other public and voluntary organisations was less consistent. Community representation existed through three Black and Afro-Asian Caribbean organisations.

However, the partnership encountered continual problems in delivering a coherent work programme and making good use of its funding. Liverpool has been the scene of long-standing conflicts between central and local government, between local public authorities and sections of the community, especially some black and ethnic groups, and within the diverse ethnic community. The Granby-Toxteth partnership offers a graphic example of the barriers that such conflicts can present to effective local partnership against social exclusion (Moore 1997).

Partnership in rural areas

In general, the partnership approach developed more slowly in many rural areas, partly reflecting the lesser status of rural questions in the UK. However, as noted above, EU programmes, particularly LEADER, have provided a recent stimulus to partnership in rural areas, in particular in Scotland and Wales.

The Western Isles, Skye and Lochalsh LEADER Partnership

The Western Isles, Skye and Lochalsh are situated in the remote northwest of Scotland's Highlands and Islands. The area has remained largely peripheral to the major processes of urban industrial growth that have transformed other regions, and has suffered a long history of depopulation and out-migration as a result of the marginal nature of the local economy. The philosophy of the EU's LEADER I programme was that local people are the principal assets of rural areas, due to their ability to identify what forms of development are best suited to their environment, culture, working traditions and skills. The WISL LEADER partnership adapted this philosophy to the local area, through an emphasis on the restoration of confidence in the area's unique cultural heritage, and the use of this as a springboard for development based on the area's identity. This was associated with encouragement to local people to come forward with their own ideas, and assisting in turning them into projects. The activities and projects assisted covered a wide spectrum, including tourism, crafts and agricultural marketing (Black and Conway 1995).

The core of the partnership consisted of the two local enterprise companies (Western Isles Enterprise and Skye and Lochalsh Enterprise), the two local authorities (Western Isles Islands Council and Highland Region Council), and two NGOs, Comunn na Gaidhlig and the Scottish Crofters Union, each of whom nominated two representatives to the partnership. LEADER groups were then developed in the two main areas including a number of other organisations, especially higher education, tourism and environmental agencies.

The partnership received an allocation of £1.4 million from the EU over about two years between 1992 and 1994. Together with matching public and private funding, global expenditure amounted to over £4.9 million. In all, over 220 projects were funded, with many individual projects developed and implemented on a partnership basis. As a result, the LEADER partnership achieved considerable success in stimulating local 'bottom-up' development initiatives and initiating a shift away from a local 'dependency culture'. The LEADER I programme has now terminated but its success encouraged the agencies involved in the partnership to remain together and develop a successful follow-up LEADER II project.

Partnership and the restructuring of local governance

In recent years, the growing pervasiveness of the practice of local partnership, and the increasing requirement for funding programmes to require evidence of a partnership framework as a condition of funding, has led to the very widespread development of less formalised local partnership arrangements, and the emergence in some localities of 'nested tiers of partnership' at different geographical scales (Peck and Tickell 1994).

A local partnership within a deprived neighbourhood may coexist with a regeneration partnership for the wider urban area concerned, which in turn may relate to partnership relationships at the regional level. Thus, partnership seems to be becoming a feature of the wider sub-national pattern of governance. The wide application and diffusion of the partnership approach in the UK, both as a means of generating and implementing new solutions to policy problems and, frequently, as a condition for accessing funding, means that 'partnership' has been associated with a far-reaching restructuring of local governance.

In the first place, this restructuring has involved a shift from local government to local governance – from a situation where local authorities and other localised public agencies (responsible for health and policing, for example) were primarily and often exclusively responsible for the provision of local public services, to one where that responsibility has become far more widely spread across the public, private and not-for-profit sectors, and where the boundaries between these sectors have become more blurred as the so-called 'mixed market' of service provision has become the hegemonic model. While the extent of this shift and the balance of benefits and costs associated with it remain highly contentious, it has had major implications for all interests and agencies concerned.

In many instances, local authorities are dominant or leading actors in local partnerships. Local authorities in the UK have become used to a framework of 'partnership'. Many authorities have accordingly sought to reposition themselves in the new context of the mixed market and constraints on local government spending by emphasising their wider role of local community or civic leadership in partnership with other agencies and community interests, claiming legitimacy through the democratic process and their responsibility to represent the interests of the whole of local society, not 'merely' sectional interests (Benington 1997). The new Labour government has encouraged such a role in its proposals for the modernisation of local government, arguing that 'councils are in a unique position to take the lead in developing a vision for their locality'. Indeed, local authorities are to be required, not merely exhorted, to promote the economic, social and environmental well-being of their areas, through a new mandatory duty to be imposed. At the same time, the government argues that local government cannot exercise its leadership role alone, but must do so in partnership with other agencies, the local community, business and the voluntary sector (Department of the Environment, Transport and the Regions 1998: 35–7). This stance is reflected in the Local Government Association's New Commitment to Regeneration programme, which is sponsoring partnership-based local regeneration initiatives by leading local authorities. The New Commitment differs significantly from other programmes such as the SRB in that the spatial focus is to be the whole local authority area, not specific neighbourhoods; the aim will be to involve all mainstream spending programmes and functions, not only specific regeneration funds; and to involve national government as a partner (Local Government Association 1999a).

Partnership thus marks a shift of emphasis from a conception of local government as an arena in which conflicting (party) political agendas are shaped and worked out, to one which foregrounds a relationship between the local authority and a citizen body presumed to have a common interest.

At the same time, local authority opposition to partnership with business, while still evident especially among traditional Labourist authorities, has given way over the past decade to a more pragmatic approach:

> Listening to business, finding out what local businesses want and need from local government, is a priority for the LGA. And the reason is simple – neither businesses nor local government can effectively deliver what their communities need without the other. Partnership is the key to establishing thriving communities which encourage fresh thinking about old problems and a straightforward 'joined up' approach to providing services and local governance.
>
> (Local Government Association 1999b)

The leading role that local government still plays in many partnerships means that the impact of the latter in restructuring the public-private divide, while very significant, should not be over-exaggerated. Partnership has, perhaps, had at least as much impact within local government itself, both in relation to a shift in the balance between representative and participatory forms of local democracy, and on the relative influence of politicians and officials. One feature of many partnerships is the direct representation in partnership decision-making and implementational structures of 'community' interests, including those of marginalised and excluded social groups. While the limits to this are discussed below, partnership thus often introduces forms of participatory and pluralist (interest group) democratic representation alongside the traditional structures of local representative democracy. Indeed, it is fairly clear that one of government's intentions in promoting partnership has been as a challenge to the role and legitimacy of local politicians.

Partnership has also tended to challenge the role of local elected (party) politicians for two other reasons. The consensual principles of partnership working are very dissimilar to traditional local party politics, which serves to emphasise the different agendas of party politics. First, partnership requires local politicians to refocus their party allegiances within a wider 'civic leadership' context. Second, local partnerships frequently include a range of non-elected state and quasi-state agencies alongside 'democratic' local government. The advantages of a partnership approach are often quite evident to such agencies, such as health and hospital authorities and TECs, which frequently play an important role in local partnerships. A public-private partnership framework at local level is, for example, particularly important for the TECs, whose government contracts for the delivery of training and business support programmes require a partnership approach (Local Government Management Board 1995). The TECs (LECs in Scotland), which were established by government in the late 1980s to implement local training policies and to involve local business in the development of training and business development programmes and wider local economic strategies, make important contributions to the local labour market dimensions of local partnership strategies. Other public bodies such as police authorities and health authorities recognise that partnership working enables them to share the difficulties that they encounter in responding to problems of poverty and exclusion.

Successive Conservative governments made major efforts to install business within the policy process, and business representation in local partnerships has been one aspect of this agenda, leading to claims of the emergence of a business-led agenda of local governance (Peck and Tickell 1995; Imrie and Thomas 1993). Others, however, question the degree of commitment and capacity on the part of business to involvement in partnerships (Bassett 1996). Business has undoubtedly responded to government's advocacy of partnership both through employer organisations and through the involvement of individual employers, but the nature and extent of business involvement varies widely, from the largely symbolic to a substantial commitment of resources. Organisations such as Business in the Community, formed to encourage corporate responsibility among business interests, has been an influential catalyst in stimulating business involvement in local partnerships in numerous localities (Roberts, Russell, Harding and Parkinson 1995), and it is not difficult to quote many examples of participation by individual

7 These range from construction and development companies (especially in partnerships such as City Challenge with substantial resources for physical regeneration and commercial and housing property development, as in North Tyneside or Castlemilk, for example) to manufacturing and service sector firms (as in Coventry and Warwickshire where the chairman of the partnership board was the chief executive of Jaguar Cars, one of the leading local employers). The interests of employers in local involvement – including participation in partnerships – can include both advantages to the company itself and a more general commitment (and the need to demonstrate a commitment) to the economic and social prospects of their locality:

> No business exists in a vacuum. If a community as a whole flourishes, the individual members of that community tend to flourish too. The more prosperous a community is, the more it will buy our goods and services. This is mutually beneficial, since the more we can improve our financial performance, the more we can give back to the community.
>
> (Thorn-EMI in Employment Department Group 1995)

8 Chambers of Commerce are the main umbrella bodies for business (especially small and medium-sized firms) at a local level. There are a number of instances where Chambers have developed an outward-looking and proactive role in the local economy and in local partnerships (e.g. the London Enterprise Agency, LENTA, and in Birmingham), but in other locations Chambers are less active, and there can be 'turf wars' between local Chambers, TECs, and the new Business Link organisations providing local business support.

companies in local regeneration partnerships.[7] On the other hand, many partnerships (in the Poverty 3 programme, for example) have experienced difficulty in finding and keeping business 'partners', and especially in involving the SME sector. The weaknesses of many local Chambers of Commerce[8] are often cited as reasons for difficulties in involving local employers in partnership agendas (Martin and Oztel 1996), especially when these do not offer direct rewards to firms.

However, if the question about business involvement in partnership has been about the extent of its significance and extent, that about trade union involvement is much more straightforward – trade unions are generally absent from local partnerships. The declining power and influence of the labour movement nationally, with the rejection by Conservative governments of corporatist arrangements, is thus reflected at local level, where the previously powerful position of public sector trade unions over public services has been eroded by the rise of the 'mixed market' and partnership modes of local governance. The absence of trade unions from partnerships appears to reflect a combination of at least three factors: the pressures on trade unions to concentrate their energies on basic threats to their membership and rights; their exclusion by government from partnerships established by Conservative administrations; in addition to the tradition of centralism within trade unions themselves, and a suspicion of local organisations (such as local Centres for the Unemployed established in a few areas),[9] which have often adopted more radical positions than national union hierarchies. Undoubtedly, therefore, partnership is currently associated with a shift in the relative influence of capital and labour over important local policy issues, and the potentially important contribution of the labour movement on questions of local development and social exclusion largely goes by default.

Some of the tensions over the politics of local organisation and activity within the trade union movement date from the experiences of the late 1970s and early 1980s, when a widespread response to the crisis of inner urban areas and rising unemployment was the emergence of the so-called 'new social movements' (Pickvance 1995) and attempts, such as those promoted by some of the Community Development Projects (established by, but soon highly critical of, government) to build local alliances between local groups and organisations such as those of residents and tenants and local trade unions, linking workplace and community-based struggles against the restructuring of capital and, not infrequently, against the local state (Community Development Project 1977). This tradition was also influential within some of the local economic strategies developed by 'new left'

---

9 Centres for the Unemployed provide a focus for support and organisation by unemployed workers, and for links with other local activity. On Merseyside, for example, an area of high long-term unemployment, the Centre houses a library, sports centre, children's centre, printing press and recording studio.

local administrations in the early 1980s in areas such as London and Sheffield (Geddes 1998). While the local influence of the labour movement has declined steadily since then, there has been an opposite movement to incorporate local voluntary and 'community' interests in the new structures of local governance such as partnerships.

Major voluntary sector agencies have traditionally had an important role to play in social policy, especially in relation to the needs of specific social groups, such as elderly people and children. Increasingly, such agencies have entered into much closer partnership relationships with local government and the public sector in the provision of a range of services, and are often involved in local partnerships, although not necessarily as formal partners. Church-based organisations and smaller local voluntary organisations may also be partners in, or have a close involvement with, local partnerships concerned with poverty and exclusion. The voluntary sector in the UK argues that non-statutory and not-for-profit organisations can make an important contribution in bringing additional resources and expertise to local partnerships because of their extensive knowledge and experience in identifying and meeting needs in the community (NCVO and LGMB 1993), and their sensitivity to issues such as those of race and gender. The National Council for Voluntary Organisations (NCVO), the umbrella organisation for the voluntary sector, welcomed the fact that the changing direction of government policy in the 1990s, especially the Single Regeneration Budget (SRB), encouraged greater voluntary sector participation as partners in local regeneration partnerships, but noted that the participation of voluntary agencies was still patchy and frequently marginal, and suggested that government should continue to press for greater voluntary (and community) involvement (NCVO 1995).

To a greater extent than the voluntary sector however, the direct involvement of community interests (of place, but also of identity and interest) is now a central element of a partnership approach. At the local level, community involvement in partnerships can be through local community organisations (e.g. tenants and residents associations, welfare rights or community groups), through local forums representing local community interests in various ways (such as Community Development Trusts), or through the involvement of individual activists. Although local government often claims to be the legitimate voice of the local community as a whole, community organisations bring to partnerships a more intimate knowledge and experience of the needs of specific local constituencies and communities, which are vital in informing strategy and policy processes if local people are to benefit directly from partnership activities. The Community Development Foundation, the government-supported body promoting community development in the UK, argues that the community can play a number of important roles in local regeneration partnerships and projects. The community is one of the beneficiaries of partnership activity; community partners are representatives of local opinion; community organisations can help to deliver parts of partnership programmes; and the community can be a long-term partner in the regeneration process (Community Development Foundation 1995; Wilcox 1994).

However, the extent to which community interests are included in partnership decision-making processes, and the degree to which the agendas of partnerships are constructed around community interests or merely seek to involve 'the community' as a junior partner in other agendas, still varies considerably. While the capacity of local community organisations to play a leading role in the development of strategies for their areas has been amply demonstrated, community involvement is frequently hampered by a number of factors, from disagreements and tensions within communities and community organisations to the under-resourcing of community organisations, the lack of familiarity of community partners with the rules, procedures and skills of formal partnership projects, and the unwillingness of other partners to operate in ways more accessible to community interests. National organisations such as the Community Development Foundation, the Neighbourhood Initiatives Foundation and the Development Trusts Association, while welcoming the greater opportunities for community involvement offered in more recent government programmes, want further steps to strengthen this, including better targeting of projects to specific groups including ethnic minorities, women, young people, people with disabilities, and the unemployed; procedures to enhance community consultation during the progress of local schemes; more role for community organisations as deliverers of projects; and attention to the capacity of community groups and organisations to continue after the end of fixed-term initiatives.

However, the view that voluntary and community organisations should seek a deeper involvement in local partnerships is not universally shared. Some hold that this is leading to a dilution of the essential purpose and nature of the voluntary and community sectors, making voluntary organisations much more like local state agencies, with enhanced service delivery functions coming to dominate their representational and advocacy roles. There are fears about the incorporation and submergence of community organisations in the implementation of regeneration programmes, and concern at the implications of increasingly influential communitarian perspectives that might threaten to dilute state commitment to its role in promoting social justice (Osborne 1998; Henderson and Salmon 1998).

By the middle of the 1990s, local partnership had become firmly established in the UK and seemed set to be an important element of the policy response to problems of poverty and social exclusion for the foreseeable future. Despite this, many policy-makers still suspect that partnership is frequently only skin-deep, especially where it reflects an element of compulsion as a condition for access to resources rather than a willing commitment by some partners, and there is increasing recognition of the difficulties and costs of partnership working, especially for less powerful and well resourced partners (Stewart and Taylor 1995). The priority that local regeneration partnerships give to problems of poverty and exclusion (compared, for example, to the promotion of local economic competitiveness) is of course linked to the degree to which the voices of the poor and excluded are heard in partnerships.

It remains very difficult, however, to demonstrate the outcomes of the partnership approach. This is partly a methodological problem – it is not easy to identify the specific benefits, or costs, which may result from partnership working, as opposed to the impact of project funding for which partnerships are responsible (Mackintosh 1992; Geddes 2000). A number of factors also limit the willingness and ability of local partnerships to collect evidence and make it available – the 'lean' management of many partnerships, their short-term nature, and their concern to advertise positive outcomes rather than investigate more complex realities. The case for partnership as a means of tackling social exclusion and poverty remains not proven. We also need to remember that the era of partnership is one during which socio-economic disparities in the UK have widened decisively.

Partnership and New Labour

The Labour government elected in 1997 has already demonstrated its continuing commitment to local partnership as a means of tackling social exclusion. The major existing partnership-based programme from the Conservative era, the Single Regeneration Budget (SRB), has been retained, with an announcement that funding will be allocated more in accordance with needs-based criteria than in the past. In addition, the Social Exclusion Unit (SEU) has initiated a further programme, New Deal for Communities, which is intended to form the centrepiece of a more strategic approach to poverty and exclusion in the worst housing estates, the National Strategy for Neighbourhood Renewal. Recognising that Britain has become much more socially divided, that problems have become entrenched in certain areas, and that previous policies, and the expenditure of very large sums, have often not worked, the New Deal programme will allocate further funding, over a five-/ten-year time horizon where early outcomes are good, to the implementation of community-based and led plans, initially in 17 'pathfinder' areas intended to become 'showcases' for other areas. It is emphasised that these may be led by 'social entrepreneurs' from the private or voluntary/community sectors, not necessarily by local government. Perhaps just as significantly, 18 Policy Action Teams were established in central government to promote better co-ordination between government departments, and interchanges between central and local government officials are being actively promoted (Social Exclusion Unit 1998). Finally, alongside the New Deal pathfinder projects are a range of further locally-based initiatives including Health, Employment and Education Action Zones, while the New Deal programme to tackle youth unemployment is also being implemented locally within a partnership framework.

The commitment of the Blair government to local partnership is, however, only one way in which it has adopted a policy approach close to that of its predecessor. Labour has committed itself to maintaining the highly restrictive public expenditure plans of the Conservatives, and promotes itself forcefully as the party of business (on European integration, for example), while frequently distancing itself from previous Labour governments' closeness to the trade unions. Labour has made it clear that it has little or no appetite for intervening in what is seen as the rightful preserve of business, a position exemplified most clearly by the decision to pass responsibility for interest rates to the Bank of England. While a minimum wage has been introduced, this is set at a low level, and those under 21 are excluded from its provisions. While announcing its decision to end the previous system of compulsory competitive tendering (CCT) for locally-provided public services, the new system of Best Value continues to emphasise exposure of public services to the market, if under a rhetoric of public-private partnership rather than externalisation *per se*, and the 'build now, pay later' Private Finance Initiative for public sector capital projects has been extended. In the wider field of welfare, Labour again remains strongly committed to a pluralism of provision, and shares with the Conservatives a concern for 'affordable welfare' and for a movement towards a so-called active welfare system or social investment state (Giddens 1998) in which labour market reintegration is a central plank, headed by the workfare ethos of the New Deal for the young unemployed (Powell and Hewitt 1998). This signifies a clear break from an emphasis on redistribution as the primary solution to economic polarisation and poverty, an approach criticised as ineffective and dependency-inducing (Gregg 1998), and from a commitment to full employment to one of 'employability'. Labour has followed recent Conservative governments in advancing neo-liberal, supply-side policies, which are principally focused on enhancing the international competitiveness of the British economy, increasing productive efficiency and reducing costs by improving the supply and utilisation of factor inputs:

> The best way to cut unemployment and create jobs that last is to modernise our economy and build competitive industries that can succeed all around the world.
>
> (Gordon Brown)

> To achieve (economic modernisation) in the new global marketplace, the job of government is neither to suppress markets nor surrender to them but to equip people, companies and countries to succeed within them.
>
> (Labour Party, A New Economic Future for Britain, quoted in Thompson 1996)

The new Labour administration is therefore downplaying the role of public ownership and provision, looking primarily to private enterprise operating in the context of a regulated market to achieve its objectives. Social welfare and infrastructure provision is increasingly seen to require private investment to improve efficiency, while citizen interests in public services are increasingly cast in terms of freedom and choice rather than equity and equality.

Partnership has an important ideological and practical role at the heart of this New Labour project:

> We are sure that only through partnership, with government playing its proper role alongside shareholders, managers and workers, can success be achieved.
>
> (Labour Party, ibid)

Partnership is the banner under which society is invited to join in the neoliberal project, as 'stakeholders' in its outcomes. The concern must be, however, that this is not, when the chips are down, primarily a model in which business makes a substantive commitment to a more just society, but one in which society is a stakeholder in 'UK plc'. The communitarian impulse of New Labour to 'empower' local communities may hand them greater responsibility for their own futures, but without real power, either over the market or indeed over the more crucial decisions of government. While some businesses may play a role in local partnerships, their commitment to them, or to tackling social exclusion, is strictly limited. Indeed, the intensified problems of poverty and exclusion which local partnerships confront are, in large part, the consequences of the labour market and profit strategies pursued by business, and these strategies are not offered by business as part of the partnership agenda. Local partnership therefore offers the excluded a stake in the market, but, as is the case for small shareholders generally, this may not be a stake that carries much clout.

References

Amin K with Oppenheim C (1992) *Poverty in Black and White*, London: Child Poverty Action Group.
Bailey N et al (1995) Brownlow Community Trust, Ch 5 in *Partnerships in Urban Policy*, London: UCL Press.
Bassett K (1996) Partnerships, business elites and urban politics: New forms of governance in an English city. *Urban Studies*, 33, 3, 539–55.
Bauman Z (1998) *Work, Consumerism and the New Poor*, Buckingham: Open University Press.
Benington J (1997) New paradigms and practices for local government: Capacity building within civil society, in Kraemer S and Roberts J (eds.) *The Politics of Attachment: Towards a Secure Society*, London: Free Association Books.

Black J S and Conway E (1995) Community-led rural development policies – an evaluation of the EU LEADER Programme in the Highlands and Islands. *Local Economy*, 10, 3, 229–45.

Business in the Community (1994) *Regenerating Britain: Common Purpose, Uncommon Energy*, London: BIC.

Byrne D (1997) Social exclusion and capitalism:the reserve army across space and time, *Critical Social Policy* 17, 27–51.

Clarke J and Newman J (1997) *The Managerial State*, London: Sage.

Cochrane A (1993) *Whatever Happened to Local Government?* Buckingham: Open University Press.

Coe T (1995) *Giving Something Back: A Survey of Managers' Involvement in the Local Community*, Luton: Institute of Management/Local Government Management Board.

Community Development Foundation (1995) *Regeneration and the Community: Guidelines to the Community Involvement Aspect of the SRB Challenge Fund*, London: CDF.

Community Development Project (1977) *Gilding the Ghetto: The State and the Poverty Experiments*, London: CDP Inter-Project Editorial Team.

Dahrendorf R *et al.* (1995) *Report on Wealth Creation and Social Cohesion in a Free Society*, London: Commission on Wealth Creation and Social Cohesion.

Danziger N (1995) *Danziger's Britain: A Journey to the Edge*, London: HarperCollins.

Dennis N (1997) *The Invention of Permanent Poverty*, London: IEA.

Department of the Environment, Transport and the Regions (1998) *Modernising Local Government: Local Democracy and Community Leadership*, London: DETR.

Doogan K (1995) *Market Forces and Local Public Service Jobs*. Employment Policy Institute Economic Report, Vol 9 No 10.

Employment Department Group (1995) *Who Cares Wins: An Employers Guide to Involvement in the Community*, London: EDG.

Erskine A and Breitenbach E (1994) The Pilton Partnership: Bringing together the social and the economic to combat poverty, *Local Economy* 9, 2, 117–33.

Funken K and Cooper P (1995) *Old and New Poverty: The Challenge for Reform*, London: Rivers Oram.

Gaffikin F and Morrissey M (1995) *The Brownlow Poverty Project Evaluation Report*, BCT: Brownlow.

Gaffikin F and Morrissey M (1994a) In Pursuit of the Holy Grail? Combating Local Poverty in an Unequal Society. *Local Economy* 9, 2, 100–16.

Gaffikin F and Morrissey M (1994b) Poverty in the 1980s: a Comparison of the United States and the United Kingdom. *Policy and Politics*, 22, 1, 43–58.

Gamble A (1988) *The Free Economy and the Strong State*, London: Macmillan.

Geddes M (1988) The capitalist state and the local economy: Restructuring for labour and beyond. *Capital and Class* 35, 85–120.

Geddes M (1997) *Partnership Against Poverty and Exclusion? Local Regeneration Strategies and Excluded Communities*, Bristol: Policy Press.

Geddes M (2000) Tackling social exclusion in the European Union? The limits to the new orthodoxy of local partnership, *International Journal of Urban and Regional Research* 24, 4, 782–800.

Giddens A (1998) *The Third Way: The Renewal of Social Democracy*, Cambridge: Polity Press.

Green A E, Gregg P and Wadsworth J (1998) Regional Unemployment Changes in Britain, in Lawless P, Martin R and Hardy S (eds.) *Unemployment and Social Exclusion: Landscapes of Labour Inequality*, London: Jessica Kingsley, 69–94.

Green D G (1993) *Reinventing Civil Society: The Rediscovery of Welfare Without Politics*, London: IEA.

Gregg P (1998) Comment: Employment, taxes and benefits, in Oppenheim C (ed.) *An Inclusive Society: Strategies for Tackling Poverty*, London: IPPR.

Harding A and Garside P (1994) Urban and Economic Development, in Stewart J and Stoker G (eds.) *The Future of Local Government*, London: Macmillan.

Hastings A (1996) Unravelling the process of partnership in urban regeneration policy. *Urban Studies* 33, 2, 253–68.

Hastings A, MacArthur A and McGregor A (1996) *Less Than Equal? Community Organisations and Estate Regeneration Partnerships*, Bristol: Policy Press.

Henderson P and Salmon H (1998) *Signposts to Local Democracy: Local Governance, Communitarianism and Community Development*, London: Community Development Foundation.

Imrie R and Thomas H (1993) *British Urban Policy and the Urban Development Corporations*, London: Paul Chapman.

Jessop B (1994) The transition to postfordism and the Schumpeterian welfare state, in Burrows R and Loader B (eds.) *Towards a Post-Fordist Welfare State?* London: Routledge.

Joseph Rowntree Foundation (1995) *Inquiry into Income and Wealth*, York: JRF.

Labour Party (1997) A New Economic Future for Britain, London: Labour Party.

Lea J (1997) Postfordism and criminality, in Jewson N and MacGregor S (eds.) *Transforming Cities*, London: Routledge, 42–55.

Levitas R (1986) *The Ideology of the New Right*, Cambridge: Polity Press.

Levitas R (1996) The concept of social exclusion and the new Durkheimian hegemony, *Critical Social Policy* 16, 1, 5–20.

Local Government Association (1999a) *New Commitment to Regeneration*, London: LGA.

Local Government Association (1999b) *Listening to Business: Building Stronger Partnerships Between Local Government and Business*, London: LGA.

Local Government Management Board (1995) *Partnership in Action: Case Studies of Collaboration Between TECs and Local Authorities*.

Mackintosh M (1992) Partnership: Issues of policy and negotiation, *Local Economy* 7, 3, 210–24.

Martin R (1998) Regional dimensions of Europe's unemployment crisis, in Lawless P, Martin R and Hardy S (eds.) *Unemployment and Social Exclusion: Landscapes of Labour Inequality*, London: Jessica Kingsley.

Martin S and Oztel H (1996) The business of partnership: Collaborative-competitive partnerships in the development of Business Links. *Local Economy* 11, 2, 131–42.

Moore R (1997) Poverty and partnership in the Third European Poverty Programme: The Liverpool case, in Jewson N and MacGregor S (eds.) *Transforming Cities*, London: Routledge.

NCVO and LGMB (1993) *Building Effective Local Partnerships*, London: NCVO/LGMB.

NCVO (1995) *The Single Regeneration Budget Handbook*, London: NCVO.

Oatley N (ed.) (1998) *Cities, Economic Competition and Urban Policy*, London: Paul Chapman.

O'Toole M, Snape D and Stewart M (1995) *Interim Evaluation of the Castlemilk Partnership*, Scottish Office Central Research Unit, Environment Research Programme, Research Findings No 12.

Osborne S P (1998) Partnerships in local economic development: A bridge too far for the voluntary sector? *Local Economy* 12, 4, 290–5.

Oppenheim C (1993) *Poverty: The Facts*, London: Child Poverty Action Group.

Peck J A and Tickell A (1995) Business goes local: dissecting the 'business agenda' in Manchester. *International Journal of Urban and Regional Research*, 19, 1, 55–78.

Peck J and Tickell A (1994) Too many partnerships...the future for regeneration partnerships, *Local Economy* 9, 3, 251–65.

Pickvance C (1995) Where have urban movements gone? in Hadjimichalis C and Sadler D (eds.) *Europe at the Margins: New Mosaics of Inequality*, Chichester: Wiley.

Powell M and Hewitt M (1998) The end of the welfare state? *Social Policy and Administration* 32, 1, 1–13.

Power A (1997) *Estates on the Edge*, London: Macmillan.

Rees G and Lambert J (1985) *Cities in Crisis: The Political Economy of Urban Development in Postwar Britain*, London: Arnold.

Roberts V, Russell H, Harding A and Parkinson M (1995) *Public/Private/Voluntary Partnership in Local Government*, Luton: Local Government Management Board.

Robson B T et al (1994a) *Assessing the Impact of Urban Policy*, London: HMSO.

Robson B T (1994b) Urban policy at the cross-roads, *Local Economy* 9, 3, 216–23.

Room G (ed.) (1995) *Beyond the Threshold: The Measurement and Analysis of Social Exclusion*, Bristol: Policy Press.

Social Exclusion Unit (1998) *Bringing Britain Together: A National Strategy for Neighbourhood Renewal*, London: HMSO.

Stewart M and Taylor M (1995) *Empowerment and Estate Regeneration*, Bristol: Policy Press.

Stewart M (1994) Between Whitehall and Town Hall: the realignment of urban regeneration policy in England. *Policy and Politics* 22, 2, 133–45.

Thompson N (1996) Supply side socialism: The political economy of New Labour. *New Left Review* 216, 37–54.

Townsend P (1994) Think globally, act locally, *European Labour Forum* 13, 2–9.

Wilcox D (1994) *The Guide to Effective Participation*, York: Joseph Rowntree Foundation.

Wilks-Heeg S (1998) The implications of RDAs for urban policy and sub-regional partnerships, in Dungey J and Newman I (eds.) *The New Regional Agenda*, London and Harlow: LGIU and SEEDS.

10 Partnerships as networked governance?

Legitimation, innovation, problem-solving and co-ordination

John Benington

Introduction

This chapter reflects on the concept and practice of partnership as a key component in the strategies for tackling social exclusion that are being developed within the EU and in several of its member states. It draws both on theory and on the empirical evidence presented in previous chapters, in order to analyse and explain the phenomenon of partnership.

The argument is based on the notion of a networked society and networked governance, which are associated with the development of new information technologies and communication systems (Castells 1996). Partnerships are conceptualised as a particular manifestation of new patterns of networked governance, which are emerging in response to the contradictions faced by the two other main alternative models of governance, based upon hierarchies and markets (Thompson, Frances, Levacic and Mitchell 1991).

The chapter is divided into two main sections. Section 1 reviews the changes in the political economic and social context of Europe, which we began to discuss in Chapter 2, and discusses in particular the implications of the information and communications revolution for governance and organisation. Section 2 conceptualises partnerships as a form of networked governance, which may help the nascent European state to respond to dilemmas in relation to legitimation, innovation, problem-solving and co-ordination, under conditions of organisational complexity and uncertainty.

Section 1: The information and communications revolution and the network society

The European Union has been undergoing a long and profound process of political, economic, and social restructuring (see Chapter 2). The European market and state are subject to both centrifugal and centripetal pressures, some leading towards further integration and others towards fragmentation. These competing forces at the European supranational level are linked to wider processes of globalisation and a restructuring of the relative roles of the nation state, regions and localities (Higgott 2000). In addition, techno-logical changes associated with the revolution in information and com-munications systems are leading to the further restructuring of political, economic and social processes, and the emergence of a new networked society. The traditional patterns of governance based around fixed hier-archies of territory and place (local, regional, national, supranational) are being overlaid by a new kaleidoscope of shifting and cross-cutting relation-ships and inter-organisational networks, which link the different levels of governance, from the local to the global, in much more direct and interactive ways (Castells 1996).

These twin, countervailing, forces of globalisation and localisation are leading to new patterns and paradigms of multi-level, multi-nodal and multinational, networked governance, which cut across both the tiers of the polity (European, national and local) and the spheres and sectors of the economy (public, private, voluntary and grass roots) (Benington and Harvey 1999).

The patterns and forms of organisation of governance in Europe are being revolutionised in at least three different ways:

- Shifts in the interrelationships between supranational, national, regional and local tiers of the State, including increases in the scale and balance of EU membership; extensions in the EU's reach, competence and influence (although this varies markedly between policy areas); the establishment of new institutions of regional governance and administration (e.g. the Committee of the Regions (COR) and strengthened relationships with networks of local authorities (Benington and Harvey 1994).
- Shifts in the interrelationships between actors and institutions from the spheres of the State, the market and civil society, and the crossing or blurring of boundaries between these spheres, as a result of processes such as the privatisation and contracting out of public services, the develop-ment of a mixed economy of welfare provision, pressures from user groups and interest groups, and the popularisation of ideas about social capital, citizen-centred government and a Citizens' Europe (Benington 1998).
- The development of new cross-cutting inter-organisational forms (public/private partnerships, cross-national policy communities, transnational networks and European-wide associations) as an increasingly important part of an emerging system of pluralistic, networked governance (Rhodes, Bache and George 1996; Benington and Harvey 1998; Geddes 1998).

One of the characteristic forms of the networked governance which is emerging is that of partnership – both horizontal partnerships between public, private, voluntary and community organisations, and vertical partnerships between local, national and supranational levels of government.

Europe's specific histories and current conjunctures make this an important arena and an ideal moment in which to explore and test some of the above ideas, to trace the shifting patterns of interests and issues, and to conceptualise and analyse these changing institutional forms of governance (Wallace and Wallace 1996).

These changes in the forms of governance are linked to wider changes in the political economic and social context, and particularly the revolution in information and communication technologies and systems.

The information and communications revolution and the networked society

The major technological revolution that is taking place globally means that new core technologies based upon computing and micro-electronics are becoming as significant and widespread in their impact as previous technological revolutions such as steam and electricity, for example. Some observers have seen this as leading to the displacement of the Fordist system of mass production of standardised (often metal-based) commodities for mass markets, by a post-Fordist system of small-batch production of customised products for niche markets. Others argue that the emergence of new micro-electronic and computer-based information technologies and systems is having a major impact not only on the processes and relations of production, but also upon social processes and spatial patterns. According to Castells, the information revolution is resulting in the re-organisation of most of the major social institutions in network form (Castells 1996). He sees the new spatial order as a 'space of flows' quite different from our traditional 'space of places'. People still cluster in specific localities but their clusterings take their shape from involvement in global as well as local networks. Such changes in the patterns of production, consumption, association and everyday life challenge existing organisational forms and boundaries, and lead to a process of organisational innovation and inter-organisational relationships.

This type of technological restructuring is having particularly sharp and wide-ranging implications for the processes of production and distribution in the public service sector. The traditional form of organisation in government has been the large hierarchical pyramid in which information is passed up and down many vertical tiers of the bureaucracy. The main medium of communication has been paper – the memo, the letter, the circular, and the written report. The main tools and technologies have been typewriters, word processors and filing cabinets.

Governmental organisations are now in the throes of an information and communications revolution. External and internal pressures are combining to transform the nature and shape of the organisation. Vertical hierarchies are being overlaid by horizontal networks; centralised systems are being counterbalanced by devolved and decentralised patterns of working. Paper is rapidly being complemented by electronics as the main medium for information storage and communication; main frame computers are being displaced by personal computers and distributed systems. Mobile telephones, pagers, portable computers and e-mail mean that the technology and information systems follow the individual person in all their movements, and that information and communications need no longer be centralised in an office within a bureaucracy, but can be decentralised to an infinite number of access points. The Internet and the World Wide Web are not simply a vast interactive global communications system, but a metaphor for the new forms of organisation emerging within and between the State, the market and civil society.

The state in particular is facing the challenge of moving beyond the mechanistic forms of organisation and activity which emerged to respond to the problems of the previous industrial and technological revolution (based upon mass production of standardised goods and services for a mass market assumed to be homogeneous in its needs). The UK government, for example, in its programme of modernisation and improvement, is concerned to develop new more flexible and adaptive forms of governmental organisation, which are capable of responding more flexibly to the diversity and changes of needs among different groups within the population, and to the cross-cutting problems (e.g. unemployment, crime and community safety, ageing, poverty and social exclusion) that now face citizens and communities, and that do not fit easily within the traditional frameworks and forms of organisation of government, which have been based upon separate departments, disciplines and professions.

These changes in patterns of technologies, organisation and communication inevitably carry enormous implications for governance at all levels, for civic leadership, political parties, policy-making processes and public sector managers. For example, the UK White Paper on Modernising Government (Cabinet Office 1999) commits public authorities at all levels to providing holistic, citizen-centred services that respond to the cross-cutting problems facing people in their everyday lives, on a seven-days-a-week, 24-hours-a-day basis. Information systems and technologies are seen as helping to achieve the 'joined-up' government that the Prime Minister wants to achieve, and the White Paper makes a commitment that 100 per cent of government transactions will be supported by modern communications technologies by 2008. In several of its policy documents and action programmes, the EU also recognises a similar imperative to modernise the forms of organisation of government and public service, including the use of the new information and communication technologies.

Inter-organisational networks and partnerships between different levels of government (European, national, regional and local) and between different spheres of society (public, private, voluntary and community), are clearly seen as part of the EU's repertory of more flexible adaptive forms of governance for a complex and fast-changing society (including its response to social exclusion, as discussed in Chapter 2).

The implications of political restructuring in the European Union

The movement towards integration within the core of the EU is counter-poised by the disintegration of the surrounding political structures (in the former USSR and Soviet bloc) and continuing conflicts over boundaries and identities along national, religious and ethnic lines (e.g. in the former Yugoslavia). The simple post-war division of Europe into a capitalist West and a communist East has broken down into a far more complex and volatile set of cross-cutting definitions and divisions.

A number of analysts have suggested that this is leading to the collapse of the previous dominant form of European politics based upon conflict between polarised opposites (communism/capitalism; left/right; friend/enemy, etc.), and its replacement by a new form of European politics, a third way beyond left and right (Giddens 1994; 1998; 2000), based less upon antagonistic conflict and more upon 'agonistic' pluralism (Mouffe 1993). 'Agonistic' politics (derived from the Greek word 'agon' – a gathering, a public celebration of games, a contest for the prize) is concerned with wrestling with issues, contesting differences and diversities, resolving conflicts through pluralistic democratic debate in public arenas, rather than through bi-partisan political or industrial conflict or war. The argument is that the old politics of opposition is having to be replaced by a politics of proposition, in which 'western' Europe has to define its identity not by what it is against ('eastern' Communism) but by what it stands for. This new form of developmental politics is seen as complementing the vertical tiers of representative democracy with horizontal and overlapping spheres of participative and associative democracy (Benington and Taylor 1994; Hirst 1994).

In addition, there is concern throughout Europe over the decline in participation in formal representative politics (e.g. low turnouts in European, national and local elections), and the high degree of political alienation, scepticism and disengagement especially among the current generation of young adults. European citizenship is seen as a project in need of completion (Pinder 1995) The practical expression of this is seen as lying in a more open and participative and public process of policy formulation through policy forums, town meetings, citizens' panels and juries, electronic democracy, and through the active involvement of popular movements, voluntary associations, and networks within civil society (Benington 1996).

Recent EU documents have been at pains to argue the need to search for a distinctive European model of 'sustainable development which combines economic dynamism with social progress...[and which] can only be made if the issues are openly debated and a consensus arrived at'. The rich diversity of cultural and social systems within the European Union is seen as 'a competitive advantage in a fast changing world...but diversity may deteriorate into disorder if the common goals which embody the distinctive values of

European society...are not defended by the efforts of the member states and by people themselves' (Commission of the European Communities 1994). This linkage between a dynamic knowledge-based economy and social inclusion was re-affirmed at the European summit in Lisbon in March 2000.

This is the political context within which social cohesion is seen as an important goal, and partnerships as a means of achieving that goal. The search for a common European purpose and identity is taking place against a wider background of fragmentation and atomisation in society, in which the traditional political divisions and definitions based primarily around class are breaking down into a much more complex and diverse set of post-modern identities based on gender, race, culture, lifestyle and so forth (Beck 1994, Castells 1996, Harvey 1989, Leonard 1997).

Partnership is therefore seen by the EU partly in terms of broadening and deepening the opportunities for citizenship and participation, and partly as helping to legitimate its increasingly active role in fields that now go well beyond its formal legal competencies; by co-opting and involving a wider range of groups and interests into the policy-making process.

Section 2: Partnerships as a form of networked governance: legitimation, innovation, problem-solving and co-ordination

The previous section highlights a number of the challenges facing governments in this period of political, economic and social restructuring, and the context within which partnerships are being promoted as part of the State's response.

It is clear, however, that the concept and practice of partnership contain a number of tensions, contradictions and potentialities. These can be summarised analytically as dilemmas surrounding (political) legitimation, (economic) innovation, (social) problem-solving and (organisational) complexity and co-ordination.

This section offers a critical appraisal of the role of partnerships as a specific form of networked governance, in terms of the greater capacity of networks to respond effectively to these four dilemmas, compared to the two other main competing forms of governance, through hierarchies and through markets. This argument will be developed with reference to the examples of partnerships in different nation states presented in Chapters 3 through 9.

Partnerships and networks as responses to the legitimation crisis of the state

The first explanation for the emergence of partnerships and inter-organisational networks within the EU lies in the crisis of legitimation affecting the traditional forms of the State. Partnerships between public, private and voluntary organisations may provide an opportunity to co-opt a wider range of potentially competing or conflicting interests into responsibility for governance and management of the increasingly complex, cross-cutting problems facing society, and an alternative form of legitimation for the actions and the interventions of the State, given the erosion of confidence in elected representation.

In practical terms, the legitimation crisis of the State finds expression in increasingly low turnouts by voters in elections, in widespread distrust of politicians, and in growing alienation or by-passing of the formal political processes by many sections of the population (e.g. younger people). There have been increasing debates and doubts about the democratic legitimacy of the political processes in the EU. The European integration project is seen as suffering from a democratic deficit, driven by a Commission which is un-elected and only weakly accountable to a Parliament that has too few real powers, and lapses into being a 'talking shop'. At national level, representatives are elected on low electoral turnouts, and governments are formed through procedures that rarely correspond with the actual distribution of votes, and which leave many interests and opinions severely under-represented. The territorial basis of elections (with representation based on geographical constituencies and wards) also tends to reduce different cross-cutting interests to two relatively crude categories – the political party and the spatial community. There is growing recognition that these traditional categorisations are increasingly inadequate for the task of reflecting and representing the complex diversity of competing and sometimes conflicting interests within today's society, and that new forms of more proportional representation must be found. An electoral system based wholly upon geographical constituencies is also vulnerable to gerrymandering (as shown by the Westminster City Council case where council housing was allegedly sold to middle-class tenants in order to change the voting composition and political control of the neighbourhood).

The whole concept and practice of representative democracy is increasingly being challenged in terms of its legitimacy, accountability and responsiveness. From the Right, the challenge has been in terms of the rigidities and inefficiencies of bureaucratic government hierarchies dominated by the producer interests of politicians, professionals and trades unions, rather than by customers and the commercial discipline of the private competitive market. From the Left, the challenge is in terms of the need for greater democratisation of government structures and processes, more decentralisation to allow participation by a wider and more diverse range of stakeholders, and greater accountability by quangos and other non-elected bodies. At supranational level this has led to criticism of the democratic deficit in the EU, to calls for greater powers for the elected European Parliament over the non-elected European Commission, and to arguments for a principle of subsidiarity in the devolution of decision-making to the lowest possible levels.

However, beyond all this concern with the democratisation and decentralisation of constitutions, structures and procedures, there is an even more fundamental challenge to the whole conception of representative government and competitive party democracy.

A number of political theorists have argued that representative democracy and competitive party democracy are both part of a particular historical conjuncture and may not survive current structural changes. Claus Offe has pointed out that the two main components of 'democratic capitalism' in Europe have taken shape in the aftermath of two world wars – democracy through party competition beginning after the First World War and the Keynesian welfare state coming after the Second World War. Offe suggests that introducing the notion of competition into politics, and the idea of authoritative allocation of values into the economy (e.g. by demand management, transfers and regulations) resulted in both the marketisation of politics, and the politicisation of the private economy, and that this inter-locking helped to mediate the incompatibilities between mass democracy and the market economy (Offe 1984).

Offe and other commentators suggest that this 'politically instituted class compromise' between the interests of capital and labour (which offered liberal democratic rights, trade union rights, and protection of jobs and wages, in exchange for acceptance of the logic of the private competitive market economy in relation to the development of both the national, regional and local economies) has broken down irrevocably. Several reasons are suggested. Offe argues that the Keynesian welfare state has largely been able to solve the problems of macroeconomic demand stabilisation, but in doing so has also 'interfered with the ability of the capitalist economy to adapt to the production/exploitation problem. To the extent the demand problem is solved, the supply problem is considerably widened'. He also quotes Taylor-Gooby's comment on the contradiction between the economic and the social, which is embedded within the social democratic settlement: 'What the Right has recognised much better than the Left is that the principles of the welfare state are directly incompatible with a capitalist market system...The welfare state eats the very hand that feeds it. The main contradiction of the welfare state is the...tension between the market and social policy' (Offe 1984: 196–7).

Others set the crisis of liberal democracy within a longer-term historical analysis and question not only the social democratic Keynesian welfare state, but also the whole notion of the State as the primary site and focus for political activity. Magnusson and Walker argue that globalisation of the economy is now leading to a breakdown in the State's capacity to mediate between global capital and local communities, and that nation states are having to admit that 'they cannot plan their domestic economies and still secure protected spaces for social welfare within them. As a result, citizenship in an advanced capitalist country no longer ensures inclusion in the benefits of capital...capital itself has been de-centred...No State can control capital in its money form...What we have to recognise is that there is a new reality taking shape, and that its political form is unlikely to be a global State or a State system. This has profound implications for political practice' (Magnusson and Walker 1988).

The ways in which the State came to be placed at the centre of political discourse and practice and seen as the main focus and site for democratic activity is explored by several post-structural theorists. Foucault argues that political discourse has been dominated by a reductionist view of the State (reduced to its productive and reproductive functions) and that what is really important is 'not so much the étatisation of society, as the 'governmentalisation' of the State'. He describes governmentality as a particular form of power that comes to take pre-eminence over both 'the State of justice' characteristic of the Middle Ages (based on the sovereignty of the prince, and the feudal type of territorial regime which corresponds to a society of laws and reciprocal obligations) and 'the administrative State' that developed during the fifteenth and sixteenth centuries ('born in the territoriality of national boundaries, and corresponding to a society of regulation and discipline'). He contrasts both of these earlier forms of power with 'the governmental State' that emerged from the eighteenth century onwards, and which is defined not so much in terms of control over territory, as control over the mass of its population. Foucault sees 'governmentality' as a very specific form of power, which has population as its target, political economy as its principal form of knowledge, statistics (state-istics) as its science, and apparatuses of security as its main mechanisms of control. He argues that the governmentalisation of the State has made possible the continual definition and redefinition of what is within the competence of the State and what is not, what is the public and what is the private and so forth; and that this is why and how the techniques of government have become the only political issue, the central arena for political struggle and contestation (Foucault 1978).

The changing relationships between the State and the public and the private are also explored by several critical theorists, notably by Habermas in *The Structural Transformation of the Public Sphere* (Habermas 1962). In an essay entitled *Rethinking the Public Sphere*, Fraser reviews the strengths and the limitations of Habermas's contribution to the critique of actually existing democracy. She sees the strength of Habermas's conception of the public sphere or public space as 'a theatre in modern societies in which political participation is enacted through the medium of talk. It is the space in which citizens deliberate about their common affairs, hence, an institutionalised arena of discursive interaction. This arena is conceptually distinct from the State; it is a site for the production and circulation of discourses that can in principle be critical of the State. The public sphere in Habermas's sense is also conceptually distinct from the official economy; it is not an arena of market relations but rather one of discursive relations, a theatre for debating and deliberating rather than for buying and selling. Thus this concept of the public sphere permits us to keep in view the distinction between State apparatuses, economic markets, and democratic associations; distinctions that are essential to democratic theory' (Fraser 1993). Habermas sees this democratic public sphere as being gained by the liberal bourgeoisie of the nineteenth century, and then lost through the growth of consumerism, mass media, and the displacement of 'the public', by publicity and public relations.

Fraser and other critical social theorists argue that Habermas idealises the liberal public sphere as a democratic space, by ignoring the extent to which it reflected and reinforced economic and social divisions and inequalities in the wider society, and was 'a masculinist ideological notion that functioned to legitimate an emergent form of class rule'. A further limitation is that Habermas fails to examine other, non-liberal, non-bourgeois, competing public spheres, such as women's organisations, pressure groups and protest organisations, that lay outside the network of philanthropic, professional and cultural societies that acted as the power base of the bourgeois male elite, who were then coming to see themselves as a universal class, and preparing to assert their fitness to govern. Fraser concludes that the bourgeois conception of the public sphere is not adequate for contemporary critical theory, and that what is needed is 'a post-bourgeois conception that can permit us to envision a greater role for (at least some) public spheres than mere autonomous opinion formation removed from authoritative decision making...any conception of the public sphere that requires a sharp separation between (associational) civil society and the State will be unable to imagine the forms of self-management, interpublic coordination, and political accountability that are essential to a democratic and egalitarian society' (Fraser 1993: 26).

Fraser is not alone in advocating a stronger focus on associational civil society as an arena for democratic activity. Paul Hirst, for example, argues that 'the exhaustion of the great competing intellectual systems of social organisation, liberal democratic capitalism and collectivistic State socialism, that came to fruition in the nineteenth century' is opening up new political spaces for a new type of associative democracy (Hirst 1994). Hirst suggests that centralisation and bureaucracy have been common features of these two conflicting social systems, and that the growth in their scope and scale has been based upon notions of omni-competence and comprehensive intervention ('administrative agencies capable of influencing by their actions the fate of their societies and virtually every person in them'). He argues that the supposed legitimation of these large-scale State bureaucracies (through one political party and the proletariat in the communist East, and through competing political parties and representative government in the capitalist West), has broken down irrevocably, both in terms of democracy and also effectiveness: 'The main threats to the stability of Western societies are no longer class war within or enemy states without; they are diffuse social problems and sources of unrest. Centralised bureaucratic and repressive structures cope so badly with these more amorphous threats, of crime and drug addiction, for example, that these problems can hardly provide the old state structures with a convincing raison d'être' (Hirst 1994: 9). Instead, he proposes a return to an alternative tradition of democratic associationalism which started in the nineteenth century with Robert Owen's co-operative self-regulating communities and enterprises, and continued through to the guild socialism of GDH Cole and Harold Laski in the 1920s. Associationalism is seen as having two main characteristics: a decentralised economy based on principles of co-operation and mutuality; and radical federalist and political pluralist ideas as an alternative to the centralised and sovereign state.

Hirst's conception of associative democracy is attractive as a more localised and rooted alternative to the prevailing centralised and bureau-cratised State-centred versions. However, it runs the risk of utopianism. Like Etzioni's communitarianism (Etzioni 1993), it is high on the ethics of reciprocal rights and responsibilities, but not so clear on how conflicting interests between community groups and associations are to be mediated or resolved. Chantal Mouffe shares Hirst's analysis that liberal democracy has been characterised by an over simple binary split between conflicting opposites (e.g. communism and capitalism, East and West, government and opposition); but instead of dissolving the dichotomy into a romanticised, earthly paradise, she recognises the centrality of the friend/enemy relation in politics, and the constitutive role of antagonism in social life (Mouffe 1993). Her argument for an 'agonistic pluralism' is designed to treat the opponent 'not as an enemy to be destroyed, but as an adversary whose existence is legitimate and must be tolerated. We will fight against his ideas but we will not question his right to defend them'. Unlike Habermas's public sphere, however, Mouffe's public arena is characterised by contest rather than rational discussion.

Partnerships as a new form of legitimation ?

The implications of the above ideas for our thesis about partnerships as a new form of legitimation is that neither the State, nor representative government, nor political parties, can be seen as the exclusive, or even the primary, focus for democratic thought or action. Each have now to be seen rather as one among many sites of political struggle, and as arenas where the terms of debate, contest and engagement have to a large degree been shaped and structured by a particular set of dominant interests and ideas (associated by many of the above authors with the hegemony of bourgeois liberal democracy). There is also a growing sense of the erosion of that hegemony, the stultification of its particular preferred forms of political activity (com-petitive party politics and representative government), and the re-focusing of democratic discourse and attention less exclusively on the State and more on civil society and the informal third sector. This critique of State-centred politics is closely linked to the debate about the challenges to the nation state on the grounds that it is now too small and too powerless to handle the macro issues (e.g. globalisation and Europeanisation of the economy) and too big and inflexible to respond to the micro issues (e.g. changing and diverse needs in the local community).

In this context, partnerships may be seen as a mixed and more flexible form of governance capable of resolving some of the above problems of legitimation faced by the State. Horizontal partnerships may help to bind public, private and voluntary organisations into sharing the responsibility (and the political and economic risks and costs) for responding to the complex, cross-cutting problems (e.g. social exclusion, unemployment, crime and community safety) that now face citizens and community organisations, and which confront governments, acting on their own, with intractable problems and additional political pressures. Vertical partnerships between local, regional, national and supranational/European levels of government may help to perform a similar legitimation function, by co-opting different tiers of the State into sharing responsibility for forms of intervention and action that lie outside the remit or the capacity of any one level of government acting on its own. This is especially necessary for the EU, which has only very limited formal or constitutional competence in the field of social policy, but which increasingly recognises the need to compensate disadvantaged groups and communities for some of the costs of industrial restructuring, and to counterbalance increased economic competition with greater social cohesion.

However, there is a limitation to partnerships and networks as new forms of legitimation. They are more complex than traditional forms of representative government in terms of democratic accountability. Partnerships between different organisations are notoriously hard to hold to account by and to their parent organisations, and tend towards autonomy rather than accountability. Multiple lines of accountability can result in reporting to many, but final accountability to none.

These tensions are illustrated in evidence from our empirical research. The role of local partnerships in legitimation is evident in the case studies in Chapters 3 through 9 of many partnerships in many countries, but especially where interest representation in a partnership is on a wide, cross-sectoral basis. This is typical of many partnerships in the United Kingdom or Ireland, and in partnerships in countries which are funded by EU programmes, such as Poverty 3. In Ireland, local partnerships have had a particularly important function in legitimating successive governments' commitment to tackling poverty and social exclusion because, as Walsh discusses in Chapter 6, representative local government in Ireland is relatively weak and acutely lacks legitimacy. The local partnership in Girona in Catalonia, discussed by Estivill in Chapter 8, offers a classic example of a partnership (supported by the EU Poverty 3 programme) that was able to draw legitimacy from two sources in particular: the inclusion of market-based actors and institutions alongside those from the public and voluntary and community sectors; and the emergence of 'new' local politicians not tied to traditional perspectives.

However, the research also shows clearly some of the tensions and limits of the capacity of local partnerships for legitimation. A number of our case studies – ranging from those in Granby-Toxteth, Liverpool in the United Kingdom to El Ribeiro in Spain – illustrate the difficulties of both building and (even more difficult?) holding together a cross-sectoral partnership. Local partnerships do not, therefore, universally perform or sustain the legitimatory functions expected of them. Moreover, the cross-sectoral representation of interests in partnerships may bring contradictions in terms of accountability. Partnerships can obscure questions of wider accountability beyond the specific interests and individuals actually represented within a partnership. Case examples analysed in the research, such as that in Mantes in France discussed by Le Galès and Loncle-Moriceau in Chapter 4, show that partnerships may function as arenas for the contest of more traditional confrontational party and representative politics, to the detriment of their legitimacy in the eyes of diverse stakeholders. The descriptions of the partnerships in El Ribeiro and the Basque country in Spain prompt similar conclusions. In Ireland, the diffusion and dominance of 'local partnership governance' is now prompting concerns about democratic accountability. In the United Kingdom, concerns about the limited accountability of quangos point in a similar direction.

Before they can stand securely at the core of the new forms of networked governance, partnerships still have to demonstrate that they can deal with the issue of accountability as well as that of legitimation.

Partnerships and networks as a method of pooling the risks and the costs of innovation

A second element in our analysis of the emergence of partnerships as one of the new forms of networked governance lies in their potential capacity to spread the risks and the costs of innovation between a number of partners. There is a growing body of literature which argues that the European economy needs rapid modernization and restructuring if it is to be able to compete in an increasingly competitive and fast-changing global economy, particularly against the USA (Cecchini 1988). Innovation based upon the new information and communication technologies is seen as potentially one of the most effective forms of modernization (Borja and Castells 1996). Innovation in these fields carries extremely high costs and risks, and these are prohibitive for individual organizations investing in isolation.

The hierarchies of the State have been criticised for being too rigid and too inflexible to act as catalysts for rapid sustainable innovation. By itself, the private competitive market is rarely able to provide the context of trust and collaboration necessary for high-risk innovation. Joint ventures and strategic alliances are therefore seen by many private sector firms as sensible ways of funding 'blue skies' research, development and innovation. Similarly, in situations where problems cross the boundaries between the sectors, inter-organisational partnerships between a range of private and public organizations may help to spread the risks and rewards of innovation, in ways that no individual organization can carry on its own.

Organisations may choose, therefore, to combine in partnerships and networks in order to collaborate in the search for solutions to the complex problems of modernisation which confront each of them, and to generate new concepts, new ideas, new strategies and new innovative projects.

As it is not easy to put a price on leading-edge knowledge, imaginative ideas or innovative experience before they are produced and tested, they are not easily susceptible to trading or exchange in traditional markets. It may be in the interests of individual actors and organisations to pool their experimental efforts and their resources in order to share in the search for solutions, both in order to spread the costs and the risks involved, and in order to gain the most rapid access to the experimental results. Collaborations of this kind may depend heavily upon negotiated trust.

Partnerships and networks can be seen as part of the research and development process in the production of the knowledge and innovation necessary for the governance of a global, complex and uncertain environment. This requires a conceptualisation of the political economy of partnerships and networking in terms of the relationships of production (of knowledge and innovation) as well as the relationships of distribution and exchange (of resources of power and money) (Benington and Harvey 1999).

The evidence from the case studies in this book suggests that the contribution of local partnerships to innovation is not a straightforward issue. There are, of course, a number of inspiring examples. Partnerships such as those in Wulkow and Wedding in Germany, discussed by Birkholzer and Lorenz in Chapter 5, and the ARCIL partnership in central Portugal analysed by Rodrigues and Stoer in Chapter 7, indicate how, in certain circumstances, local partnerships can both promote and implement innovative local economic strategies for excluded social groups and communities. It is interesting that in all three cases innovation stemmed from the interplay between grass roots local communities and organisations, and sympathetic external actors. A second example is provided by partnerships supported by the EU's LEADER programme, of which examples from Scotland and Brittany are discussed in the chapters by Geddes and Le Galès and Loncle-Moriceau. These offer some evidence that the particular framework of the LEADER programme, in which funds were available to stimulate and support local initiative and entrepreneurship, rather than being used in pursuit of a defined programme agreed at the outset of the project, promoted innovation in the local economy. More generally, it might be suggested that the ability of local partnerships to bring together social and economic interests within a multidimensional strategy is consistent (where this is realised) with contemporary notions of a 'social investment state' (Giddens

1998) in which social policy is integrated closely with the economic policy objectives of growth and competitiveness.

One of the strongest arguments for the role of local partnerships in economic innovation has been made by Sabel in a study of local partnerships in Ireland (Sabel 1996). He argues that some Irish local partnerships are promoting innovative approaches to local economic development which can shake up the traditionalist and ineffective approach of mainstream state agencies to local economic development. He claims that some local partnerships are adopting the organisational model of the 'work-team' characteristic of many leading-edge private sector organisations, and that networking, learning and emulation between local partnership 'work-teams' can transfer the benefits of economic advance to vulnerable groups and communities. However, the Irish research study reported in Chapter 6 found little evidence to support Sabel's argument, showing indeed that even 'successful' Irish partnerships, such as the Paul Partnership in Limerick and that in Tallaght on the edge of Dublin, acknowledged that they had little leverage in the local labour market. Our research shows that many local partnerships find it difficult to encourage key local employers – who often have few local roots – to commit themselves to partnership strategies to tackle poverty and social exclusion. It may be relevant that even in examples such as Girona, where some success was achieved with local employers, this was not sustained after the Poverty 3 funding came to an end. Some larger partnerships – such as that in North Tyneside discussed in Chapter 9 – are substantial actors in local economic regeneration, but there is little evidence that this activity is linked meaningfully to a wider concern with economic innovation, and indeed even the substantial local investment and associated job creation undertaken by such partnerships may still not be enough to replace the results of private sector dis-investment in such localities.

The conclusion from the cases we have researched seems to be that local partnerships can make a valuable contribution to micro-level innovations in the social and political sphere (e.g. in social policy, service delivery and the relationship of the State to its citizens, users and local grass roots communities), but that it is much harder for local partnerships to have any significant impact on innovation in the economic sphere (e.g. on jobs and economic development).

Partnerships as part of the problem-solving capacity of the State under conditions of complexity and uncertainty

The third element in our analysis of the role of partnerships within the new patterns of networked governance is in terms of their presumed greater capacity for 'problem-solving' than either State hierarchies or competitive markets (Borzel 1998). While, within the current context of continuous change and complexity, one of the primary challenges for the market is innovation, a similar challenge for the State is how to respond to the complex, cross-cutting problems that face governments, citizens and communities.

Governments all over the world are grappling to find effective solutions to the apparently intractable problems that affect their citizens and local communities in a complex, globalised and fast-changing world: economic instability; spatial inequalities; social exclusion; unemployment and poverty; crime, drugs, disorder and threats to personal safety; racial and ethnic tensions; environmental degradation; abuses of human and civil rights; ageing of the population; and changes in family values and household patterns. For many people, in many countries, daily life is experienced as full of risk and uncertainty, with deep fears not only about how to meet basic human needs, but also about a loss of moral values, direction and control over their futures.

Competitive markets proliferate commodities to satisfy individual desires, but are increasingly seen as unable to cater for more profound and longer-term social and human needs – for example, care for an ageing population (Benington and Taylor 1994). Markets are also seen as externalising many of the costs and uncertainties of production, dumping the 'bads' arising from their production of goods and services (e.g. environmental pollution), and failing to take responsibility for the social consequences of unregulated competition (e.g. the chaos of an unco-ordinated transport system).

Equally, governments and public services, which traditionally have been expected to deal with social needs and issues, are often now seen as part of the problem rather than as part of the solution (Benington 1996). The combination of party political bargaining and policy analysis by public bureaucrats (which were developed as a primary means of State decision-making in a period of mass production of standardised services for a population whose needs were assumed to be more or less homogeneous), are often too crude a response to the much more variegated needs of a diverse multicultural population. The State's traditional methods of problem-solving through legislation and public spending may be less effective in those situations where problems cut across the responsibilities of several different departments and professions and levels of government; where past programmes have patently failed to make a lasting impact (as is the case with social exclusion, after 30 years of anti-poverty pilot programmes); and where problems are too complex, fluid and fast-changing for policy and legislation to be framed without far fuller knowledge.

Part of our explanation for the proliferation of partnerships and networks is their potentially greater capacity than either hierarchies or markets to function as complex adaptive systems, with capabilities for co-ordination between many different actors and organisations, and the organisational flexibility to respond to the flux and flow of continuous change.

The traditional hierarchical structures and bureaucratic procedures of government, organised as they have been around professional disciplines and functional departments, are increasingly found to be too rigid and too inflexible to respond adequately to the complex problems and policy issues that cut across the boundaries and divisions between the vertical organisational skyscrapers of most public services. Equally, competitive markets are found to be too atomised to provide the degree of inter-organisational co-ordination necessary to respond to cross-cutting problems, or to respond to social needs which are not easily commodified (e.g. the need for a safe, unpolluted environment) (Peters 1998).

The hierarchical structures of public bureaucracies are often too rigid to respond to fast-changing and increasingly diverse patterns of need in the community, and too remote and too disconnected from the front line where needs and problems are first identified, and where solutions have to be developed and tested.

In this context, vertical partnerships between different levels of government can sometimes provide a means of short-circuiting the hierarchical tiers of bureaucratic decision-making, and speeding up the flow of information and intelligence from the front line where problems are identified and defined, directly and rapidly to the centre, where policy and legislation is framed. Governments are increasingly using local partnerships and networks as flexible antennae, probing and scanning the continuously changing environment, gathering in data about diverse patterns of need, and prospecting for possible solutions, prior to committing themselves to legislation or mainstream funding.

Horizontal partnerships between actors and organisations in the public, private, voluntary and informal community sectors may help governments to tap into additional knowledge, ideas, staff capability and financial resources to help identify and conceptualise complex problems, and to develop and test pilot programmes.

There is thus a growing recognition that fundamentally different kinds of governance, public policy making and intervention are now required to respond to the structural changes and social problems facing societies in this period of complexity, change and uncertainty. Under these conditions, partnerships and networks can be interpreted as providing more effective and flexible means of problem identification and problem definition than either the hierarchical state or the competitive market.

However, while partnerships and networks can demonstrate their capacity for problem identification and policy formulation, it is less clear whether they are as effective in problem-solving and policy implementation, because the State continues to retain most legislative and financial powers to intervene, and the market has an unmatched capacity to mass produce solutions (Benington and Harvey 1998).

In addition, while the strength of partnerships and networks is their flexibility and adaptability, their limitation is their instability and volatility. They are better adapted to change than to continuity.

The evidence from our research in the foregoing chapters provides interesting examples of the capacity of local partnerships in terms of problem-solving and resolving dilemmas of complexity and co-ordination. In Finland, for example, as Chapter 3 demonstrates, some of the more interesting experiments in partnership were responding to the manifest difficulties of traditional State institutions in reacting to 'cross-cutting' social policy issues. Partnership between public agencies and tiers of the State, and between the State and the not-for-profit sector, seemed to be becoming an effective way of breaking free from traditional straitjackets. The same argument is made in relation to the role of local partnerships in France. In Germany, the local initiative in Wulkow offers an inspiring example of the capacity of a cross-sectoral initiative to respond to the challenge of a local community faced with extinction. The ARCIL partnership in Portugal, discussed by Rodrigues and Stoer in Chapter 7, indicates how local level partnership between the public and voluntary/community sectors can find new and 'joined-up' ways of responding to the problems of social groups such as those with disabilities.

The question is, how far can we draw general conclusions from such examples? First, we confront the difficulties in finding hard evidence of the results achieved by local partnerships, which we recognised in Chapter 1. Few of the partnerships analysed in our research were able to offer systematic evidence of outcomes, and even less were able to show convincingly how far outcomes were the result of partnership structures and working practices and relationships. This is a crucial issue given that many partnerships, including many of those discussed in this book, are small-scale and avowedly experimental. If the objective is to disseminate the achievements of pilot programmes and partnerships such as Poverty 3, and to mainstream their findings within government policies and spending programmes, then this requires more substantial evidence of 'what works' than is often available. Second, however, our research shows that the ability of local partnerships to solve social problems and resolve dilemmas of complexity and co-ordination is often offset by the way in which partnership working is itself often problematic, volatile and consuming of both time and resources. A particular aspect of this problem, encountered in a number of the partnerships analysed, appears to be the unwillingness or inability of higher tier (national and supranational) State agencies and their personnel to make the transition from 'command and control' modes of working to the more equal, flexible and open relationships necessary for local partnership to be effective. However, the 'opportunity costs' of partnership working are a generic issue: cross-sectoral, cross-institutional and sometimes cross-national collaboration inevitably involves new and difficult processes of learning, negotiation and co-ordination, and of organisational and cultural change. Examples of success by partnerships in finding new solutions to complex problems of co-ordination are paralleled in our research by the pressures and difficulties experienced in making local partnership work effectively.

Conclusion

There is a growing recognition, in both the academic and the policy litera-
tures, that neither a hierarchical bureaucratic State nor a competitive
private market provide adequate models for governance or public service
in a complex, fast-moving, fluctuating and increasingly globalised world.
In order to grapple with such issues, government has to be active and innovative, and rooted not only in the State or in the market, but also in civil
society – the world of everyday life, including households, informal associations, voluntary agencies, and grass roots community organisations. Governance can no longer be located within the State alone, but must now include
leadership and management of the interrelationships between State, market
and civil society.

The law of requisite variety (Ashby 1956) suggests that in order to be effective, organisations have to develop structures and processes that match the
complexity and the diversity of the environments in which they operate.
Complexity theory suggests that for organisations to survive and thrive in
high velocity unpredictable environments, they need to change and reinvent
themselves constantly over time, through a relentless flow of improvisation,
co-adaptation, regeneration, experimentation and time pacing (Brown and
Eisenhardt 1998).

Partnerships and inter-organisational networks can be seen as one of the
responses to these changes in the environment, with the potential to provide
a more flexible form of citizen-centred governance and more integrated
services to groups of citizens and local communities – a more complex
adaptive system that can cut across the previous boundaries and divisions of
responsibility between:

- different levels of government (local, regional, and national)
- different spheres of society (public, private, voluntary and the informal
  community)
- different localities, regions and countries.

Our research raises as many questions as it answers about the capacity of
local partnerships to tackle the crises of legitimation, innovation, problem-
solving and co-ordination that faced the previous State-centric forms of
governance.

In part, the different messages from the research reflect the different conditions and contexts of partnership across the EU – in different countries,
associated with different programmes, and with different 'mixes' of partners.
This issue will be pursued in the next and final chapter.

However, our findings also reflect some of the fundamental tensions and
contradictions surrounding the notion of partnership. Can the State develop
closer relationships simultaneously with both the private market and
civil society? Can the very different sources and patterns of legitimation,

innovation, problem-solving and co-ordination that prevail within the State and the market be reconciled (let alone integrated) either in theory or in practice? Can substantial organisational and cultural change be generated within the public service sector without the external catalyst provided by the private market? Can class and political party divisions really be dissolved within the consensual framework of partnerships? How far do local partnerships represent a pre-figurative model for new patterns of networked governance, and how far are they little more than sticking plasters concealing a deeper wound facing the State? Is the undoubted trend towards local partnership part of a new, long-term settlement between historically competing interests, leading to new forms of governance as part of a more flexible and adaptive system within a complex fast-changing society, or merely a temporary and unstable compromise?

We may be forced to conclude, as we suggested in Chapter 1, that partnership reformulates, rather than resolves, the key contemporary governance issues that it claims to address.

References

Ashby W R (1956) *An Introduction to Cybernetics*, London: Methuen.

Beck U (1992) *Risk Society: Towards a New Modernity*, London: Sage.

Beck U (1994) The reinvention of politics: towards a theory of reflexive modernization, in Beck U, Giddens A, Lash S (1994), *Reflexive Modernization*, Cambridge: Polity Press.

Benington J (1996) New paradigms and new practices for local government: capacity building within civil society, in Kraemer S and Roberts J *The Politics of Attachment: Towards A Secure Society*, London: Free Association Books.

Benington J (1998) Risk, reciprocity and civil society, in Coulson A (1998) *Trust in the Public Domain*, Bristol: Polity Press.

Benington J and Harvey J (1994) Spheres or tiers? The significance of local authority transnational networks, *Contemporary Political Studies*, Vol 2, Political Studies Association, 943–61.

Benington J and Harvey J (1998) European networking: passing fashion or new paradigm, in Marsh D (ed.) *Policy Networks in Europe*, Buckingham: Open University Press, 149–66.

Benington J and Harvey J (1999) Networking in Europe, in Stoker G (ed.), *The New Management of Local Governance*, Basingstoke: Macmillan.

Benington J and Taylor M (1994) Changes and challenges facing the UK welfare state in the Europe of the 1990s, in Ferris J and Page R (eds.) *Social Policy in Transition*, Aldershot: Avebury.

Borja J and Castells M (1996) *Local and Global: The Management of Cities in the Information Age*, London: Earthscan Publications.

Borzel T (1998) Organising Babylon – on the different conceptions of policy networks, *Public Administration* Vol 76 Summer 1998, 253–73.

Brown S L and Eisenhardt K M (1998) *Competing on the Edge: Strategy as Structured Chaos*, Boston: Harvard Business School Press.

Cabinet Office (1999) *Modernising Government*, Cm 4310, London: HMSO.

Castells M (1996) *The Information Age; Economy, Society and Culture.* Volume 1: *The Rise of the Network Society*; Volume 2: *The Power of Identity*; Volume 3: *End of Millenium*, Oxford: Blackwell.

Cecchini P (1988) *The European Challenge. 1992 – The Benefits of a Single Market*, London: Wildwood House.

Commission of the European Communities (1994) *European Social Policy – The Way Forward for the Union* (White Paper) COM (94) 333, Brussels.

Commission of the European Communities (1995) *Medium-Term Social Action Programme 1995–1997*, Social Europe 1/95, Brussels: European Commission, DGV.

Etzioni A (1993) *The Spirit of Community: The Reinvention of American Society*, New York: Simon and Schuster.

Foucault M (1978) Governmentality, reprinted in Burchell G, Gordon C and Miller P (1991) (eds.) *The Foucault Effect, Studies in Governmentality*, Brighton: Harvester Wheatsheaf.

Fraser N (1993) Rethinking the public sphere, in Robbins B (ed.) *The Phantom Public Sphere*, University of Minnesota Press: Minneapolis.

Geddes M (1998) *Local Partnership: A Successful Strategy for Social Cohesion?* European Foundation for the Improvement of Living and Working Conditions: Dublin.

Giddens A (1994) *Beyond Left and Right: The Future of Radical Politics*, Cambridge: Polity Press.

Giddens A (1998) *The Third Way: The Renewal of Social Democracy*. Cambridge: Polity Press.

Giddens A (2000) *The Third Way and its Critics*, Cambridge: Polity Press.

Habermas J (1962) *The Structural Transformation of the Public Sphere* (translated Thomas Burger with Frederick Lawrence), Cambridge, Mass: MIT Press 1989.

Hartley J and Benington J (1999) *The Connected Council: Leading the Community in the Information Age*, Bristol: Foundation for Information Technology in Local Government (FITLOG).

Harvey D (1989) *The Condition of Postmodernity*, Oxford: Blackwell.

Higgott R (ed.) (2000) *Non State Actors and Authority in the Global System*, London: Routledge.

Hirst P (1994) *Associative Democracy*, Cambridge: Polity Press.

Leonard P (1997) *Postmodern Welfare: Reconstructing an Emancipatory Project*, London: Sage.

Magnusson W and Walker R (1988) De-Centring the State, *Studies in Political Economy*, 26 Summer.

Marks G, Scharpf F, Schmitter P and Streeck W (1996) *Governance in the European Union*, London: Sage.

Mouffe C (1993) *The Return of the Political*, London: Verso.

Offe C (1984) *Contradictions of the Welfare State*, London: Hutchinson.

Peters G (1998) Managing horizontal government: the politics of co-ordination. *Public Administration*, Vol 76 Summer 1998, 295–311.

Pinder J (1995) European citizenship: a project in need of completion, in Reinventing Collective Action, *The Political Quarterly*, (ed.) Crouch C and Marquand D, Oxford: Blackwell, 112–22.

Rhodes R A W, Bache I and George S (1996) Policy networks and policy making in the European Union: a critical appraisal in Hooghe L (ed.) *Cohesion Policy and European Integration*, Oxford: Clarendon Press.

Sabel C (1996) *Ireland: Local Partnerships and Social Innovation*, Paris: OECD.

Thompson G, Frances J, Levacic R and Mitchell J (eds.) (1991) *Markets, Hierarchies and Networks: The Co-ordination of Social Life*, London: Sage.

Wallace H and Wallace W (1996) *Policy-Making in the European Union*, Oxford: Oxford University Press.

11 Local partnerships, welfare regimes and local governance

A process of regime restructuring?

Mike Geddes and Patrick Le Galès

Introduction

We have tried in this book to examine the processes and outcomes of local partnerships to combat poverty and social exclusion as specific new forms of governance, or problem-managing devices, and/or policy discourse. In so doing, we have tried to avoid several pitfalls in dealing with partnership: first and foremost, to avoid normative and naive visions, sometimes heavily embedded in various documents from the European Commission; second, to avoid thinking about local partnership in isolation from its wider political and economic context, and by contrast to situate local partnership within national and European frameworks, to better identify opportunities and constraints; and third, to avoid a deterministic view. Although it may be only a temporary respite, European welfare states have mostly not yet been reshaped solely to fulfil the needs of national competitive economic regimes. There are dangers, risks, possibilities of this becoming true, but we are reluctant to consider this trend as pre-determined. We therefore see the situation as one in which there is scope for a variety of actors to have some influence on the course of events.

What is undoubtedly true is that European societies are having to cope with several worsening trends which are by now well established:

- Various forms of poverty and social exclusion have been on the increase all over Europe, as a result of structural economic, social and political transformations, in particular changing labour market conditions.
- Problems of social and spatial segregation and disintegration have to be confronted not only in most European cities (Musterd and Ostendorf 1998), but also in what we have traditionally called rural areas.
- National welfare states have reacted in diverse ways all over Europe. Beyond simple retrenchment, pressures to construct more competitive welfare states are being felt (and resisted) at different levels in Europe. Beyond the pressures of competition, a number of reorganisations are taking place for autonomous political and policy reasons.

- Whatever their merits, and in contrast to the expectations of the 1960s, national welfare policies have neither managed to eradicate poverty, nor prevent its increase. In other words, the majority of welfare systems have to cope with some 'impuissance publique', a lack of capacity to tackle, or at least be seen to be tackling, poverty and social exclusion.

There are various ways to interpret the challenges facing European societies and the emergence of local partnership in this context. Three approaches in particular inform the arguments in this chapter. First, a stimulating – if slightly deterministic – interpretation relies upon the predicated emergence of the post-national Schumpeterian Workfare State (Jessop 1993). One key purpose of the 'hollowing out' of the state which he describes is to reinforce countries' competitiveness through the subordination of social policies to the flexibility requirement of the labour market. One might therefore expect various forms of territorial decentralisation of the welfare state (as in the USA) and restructuring of welfare in order to cut costs and increase efficiency (by concentrating expenditure in specific localities, for example). New forms of urban governance such as local partnership and various new policies to combat poverty can be interpreted as evidence of the hollowing out of the state and the trend towards the progressive 'reinvention' of social policies – for instance in order to foster 'welfare to work' policy to discipline the work-force (Peck 1998).

Second, a number of obvious links can be made between notions of a 'hollowed out' national state and a tendential restructuring of historically diversified welfare regimes within (and beyond) the European Union. The debate stimulated by the identification of welfare 'regimes' with reference to differentiated social and political traditions and forces across various groups of countries, has several points of relevance to us: first, whether notions of distinctively supranational 'Scandinavian', 'Anglo-Saxon' and 'Bismarckian' regimes are consistent with continuing national specificities; but, second, whether both national and supranational regime specificities are subject to erosion and convergence.

Third, are there distinctive sub-national (local and regional) dimensions to different welfare regimes? At the time of what some European integration specialists have called 'the Delors moment' in the EU, there was a vision of a 'Europe of the regions'. The idea of partnership was partly associated with this social and political dynamic (Hooghe 1996; Heinelt and Smith 1997). As previous chapters and case studies demonstrate, the EU emphasis on partnership which partly derived from this 'moment' may represent a very interesting case of policy export. In this chapter, partnerships and their dynamic are examined from the point of view of territorial social and political mobilisations that go beyond the issue of combating poverty. Questions surrounding the making of coalitions in cities and localities are usually examined from the point of view of economic development (Stoker 1999; Harding 1997; Keating 1991). It is suggested here that in some places, institution-building for social issues, such as partnerships to combat poverty and social exclusion, have an important contribution to make to the governance of European territories. Bagnasco and Le Galès (1999) for instance analyse European cities both as political and social actors and as local societies. This approach is reluctant to see the city (or other localities) as passive space. One key dimension of cities/localities, therefore, is the extent to which various types of actors, social movements, and more or less organised interests are brought together in processes of governance. The organisation of cities as actors could also be interpreted as a collective response to the threats associated with a deregulated capitalist market. In this context, local actors may try to forge coalitions not simply to 'play the markets' in economic competition between cities, but also to pursue social (or environmental) goals.

This concluding chapter thus attempts to understand local partnership in terms of the articulation between various 'tiers and spheres' (local, national and supranational, state, market and civil society) in Europe. We consider first the impact of the restructuring of national welfare states in the making (or not) of local partnership, but then turn to the supranational considerations suggested by the conception of welfare regimes, before returning to the sphere of local governance.

Making sense of national specificity: local partnership, national policies and cross-national welfare regimes

In Chapters 3 through 9 of this book we have explored the different national contexts of local partnership in a number of member states of the EU. These chapters have demonstrated the existence of diverse patterns and frameworks of social policy and governmental attitudes to public provision; relationships between national, regional and local government and between public authorities and local communities; and different traditions of involvement in social policies on the part of employers, trade unions and voluntary organisations. These differences mean that local partnership initiatives to combat social exclusion have developed very strongly in some countries but very weakly in others. As Rhodes and Meny have recently suggested, the politics of social policy is still to a very considerable extent a national affair. While welfare states may be everywhere under threat, this threat has partly resulted in the 'freezing' of the institutional framework rather than root and branch restructuring (Rhodes and Meny 1998: 2–3). In the larger and stronger nation states particularly, policy formulation and debate continues to be conducted mostly within a national perspective, while it is mostly in the smaller and weaker countries that such debates have been more heavily influenced by European perspectives and EU policies. While the nation state may be subject to a hollowing out, there is life in the old hulk yet. The persistence of the national framework, moreover, continues to structure patterns and perceptions of poverty and social exclusion to a considerable degree.

We will first supplement the experience of those countries to which chapters of the book have been devoted by considering briefly other countries within the EU, before moving on to draw some comparative conclusions.

Local partnership in the other member states

In *Austria* until the mid-1980s, economic growth and full employment were seen as the base for social welfare, but since the decline in economic growth priorities have changed. The emphasis is now on reducing public expenditure. The 'crisis of the welfare state' is associated with pressures for privatisation and decentralisation, although in practice a pragmatic political compromise tends to favour the development of 'welfare pluralism' – the inclusion of a wider range of bodies in the development and delivery of services and programmes (Kain and Rosian 1996).

In Austria labour market policy is the responsibility of the Federal government, but the social welfare system is primarily the responsibility of the nine federal provinces. In addition, local authorities have certain social welfare responsibilities, and the relative roles of provincial and local authorities, and of public, private and voluntary sectors, varies from province to province. In the social welfare field, growing demands associated with demographic change and the absence of an integrated approach led in the mid-1970s to the establishment of 'Social Services and Healthcare Districts' intended to develop, expand and network social welfare and health provision, and in doing so to include 'partners' such as the provincial and local authorities, public and private providers and the local community. A new emphasis on active labour market policies has included the establishment of 'labour foundations'. These initiatives by the social partners have been established in companies, in industrial sectors, and in regions and localities in response to job losses, and offer a locally-tailored package of measures from career guidance and training to support for new business start-ups. By the end of 1995 there were 43 such foundations, involving the regional social partners, provincial and local governments and the (federal) Employment Service.

However, the development of local partnerships in Austria remains extremely limited and mostly involves collaboration among public agencies and with the social partners. As Austria has been an EU member for only a relatively short time, the development of partnerships as a result of participation in EU programmes is only now beginning to have an impact.

The partnership approach to unemployment and social exclusion has been the subject of considerable debate in *Belgium*. Social policy is in a transitional state between the old 'industrial era' in which a social democratic compromise facilitated inter-class solidarity, to a 'tertiary or ultra-market' society where mass unemployment is destabilising this compromise and creating exclusion. In this context, 'the welfare state has admitted that its response to complex social problems such as social exclusion is ineffective.

Its intervention is too compartmentalised, too unwieldy, and too removed from the marginal groups which it is trying to reach. In addition, faced with budget deficits, the state is reducing its investment in social policy and is seeking to find additional funds from "partners"' (Carton, Delogne, Nicaise and Stengele 1996).

The municipalities and public services in Belgium are responsible for social welfare and are under considerable pressure to develop a partnership approach. The Public Centres for Social Welfare (CPAS) have a mandate for job creation and labour market reintegration and are being urged to develop greater co-ordination at the local level to develop stronger networks of co-operation with training organisations, the voluntary sector and industry. This has led to numerous and varied local initiatives that are currently proving a key testing ground for a decentralised local approach. The role of local authorities has been greatly enhanced by new supra-local policies. In 1990 the Flemish government established the Flemish Fund for the Integration of the Underprivileged (VFIK), under which 15 municipalities developed multidimensional local anti-poverty strategies. The VFIK has now been strengthened and extended as the Fund to Stimulate Social Action (SIF).

The social partners' traditional importance in Belgium is reflected in the institutionalisation of consultation on labour relations. During the more recent period this has led to the development of a new concern with groups at risk in the labour market. In 1989 representatives of employers and employees at national level launched an interesting initiative, in which a special levy of 0.18 per cent of the overall wage bill of companies would be used to provide employment training initiatives for members of groups at risk. The agreement was renewed in 1991 and the current levy is 0.15 per cent. There is also increasing trade union involvement in local development initiatives and social enterprises, such as the Initiative Locale pour l'Emploi (ILE), but the association of this development with a shift from public initiative to a more individualised responsibility has led the trade unions to reemphasise the importance of macroeconomic consultation.

In *Denmark* there is a long history of partnership at the national level between the traditional social partners (employers and trade unions) and the nation state: it may be said that a national contract between the organisations of the employers and the employees laid the basis of the Danish welfare state. But Denmark also has strong traditions of local organisation and of decentralisation, and these have been important factors in the establishment of local partnership-type initiatives, many of which include grass roots organisations. Since the late 1980s there has been rising concern among policy-makers about the problem of social exclusion, and national policies and programmes have been introduced to promote local partnerships. The EU Poverty 3 programme has also been an important influence.

In post-war *Greece*, under the dictatorial regime, the state controlled every aspect of life, and did not allow the development of independent social organisations such as trade unions, co-operatives and other associations. The economy depended heavily on state intervention and assistance. Consequently, prior to the establishment of parliamentary democracy in 1974, none of the conditions for the development of a partnership approach to social exclusion existed (Robolis, Papadogamvros, Dimoulas and Sidira 1996). After 1974, free expression was allowed together with the basic rights of assembly and association. By the 1980s, the paternalistic character of state politics began to diminish and a rudimentary form of state corporatism emerged, with a gradual movement towards a pluralistic process for articulating interests, support for local government and dialogue with the voluntary sector. However, the development of social welfare policies has tended to be piecemeal and unco-ordinated, and based not on associative principles but on a traditional model of state support.

At just under half the average of all EU countries, per capita GNP in Greece is lower than that of any other member state. However, the improvements in living standards and welfare provision mean that social exclusion was not recognised as a problem until the last decade, when there has been a protracted economic crisis, restrictive income and financial policies and a downturn in the employment market. At the same time, Greece has been transformed from a country of emigration to one of immigration, resulting in new problems of social exclusion.

The centralised nature of the Greek state and the very limited tradition of independent action on the part of local government and the voluntary sector means that partnerships at the local level for combating problems associated with social exclusion are not at all well developed. Those which do exist have usually been set up under EU programmes such as the Poverty 3 programme and the NOW (New Opportunities for Women) Community Initiative, but the development of partnerships associated with these programmes has met with great difficulties. Those partnerships that were instituted were seen as foreign and imposed from the top down. Nonetheless, the philosophy of these programmes has had a definite influence, especially perhaps in local government, leading to proposals to create partnerships to implement a number of sub-programmes of the Operational Programme on Social Exclusion under the second Community Support Framework.

The *Italian* context for local partnerships is complex because of the fact that the welfare system is markedly fragmented on a regional basis. However, a consistent trend is one of pressure on state welfare provision, driven by fiscal constraints, which threatens the search for a more adequate response to problems of exclusion. As a consequence, while formal local partnerships are not a major feature, there are a variety of partnership relationships between the public sector and other actors (e.g. the private sector, charities, trade unions, co-operatives, associations).

Luxembourg, with its high standard of living and small population, does not face problems of social exclusion on the same scale as other European countries. Moreover, because of the small size of the country, social policies operate primarily at the national level, and not on an area basis. Nonetheless, a number of urban renewal initiatives have been developed on partnership principles.

In the *Netherlands*, the primary policy framework concerned with social exclusion has been the national Social Renewal policy, implemented through a system of global contracts with the municipalities. Recently, steps have been taken to introduce greater co-ordination in tackling social exclusion within national government. The intention was to provide a basis for a more integrated local approach to social exclusion, and for co-operation between public services, welfare and voluntary organisations and local employers. However, there are relatively few formal local partnerships on the lines of the definition adopted in this research.

Swedish policies to combat social exclusion are closely tied to the Swedish welfare state, which is based on principles of universalism, solidarity and the provision of income-related, non-means tested benefits. The constitution establishes that public authorities, at central and local level, have the overall responsibility for welfare. However, during the 1980s the welfare state came under pressure for two main reasons: slower economic growth and increasing demands on public services. The 1990s recession intensified these problems and brought a major increase in unemployment and marginalisation. In this context, new forms of welfare provision involving private and voluntary providers have been investigated. This has led to increased collaboration at local level between agencies, which may be a precursor of more formal partnerships.

Making sense of national specificity and cross-national similarities

What wider conclusions can we draw from a review of trends in each of the member states of the EU? One is that of national specificity. The picture that emerges when we are able to survey national experience right across the EU is clearly one of great and continuing diversity, reinforcing the evidence that suggests that distinctive socio-economic patterns, practices and cultures formed and maintained within national boundaries, and the considerable differences in the nature, structure and impact of national state policy, remain central to any explanation of the development of local partnership across the EU. This is not to say that all national welfare regimes are completely frozen, but that they are changing to different degrees and to some extent even in different directions. A particular determinant of national trajectories is the role of national (and/or regional) government programmes that encourage (or in some cases require) and fund different types of local partnerships which are present in some countries but not in others. There are several kinds of policies and programmes that play this role:

- National programmes to support *integrated local development and regeneration*, in both *urban and rural* contexts, have been a driving force in the establishment of local partnerships in a number of countries, including the United Kingdom, Ireland, France and the Netherlands. In some countries, programmes of this type are the responsibility of the regional authorities, as in the case of the Flemish Funds for the Integration of the Underprivileged, and the Funds to Combat Social Exclusion in the Walloon region of Belgium. However, not all of these programmes embody a specific commitment to a formal local partnership approach. There are also considerable differences in the priority that policy objectives concerning poverty and social exclusion are given within such programmes.
- National programmes supporting *social development or local community development*, as in the Community Development Programme in Ireland and the Social Development Programme in Denmark, can be particularly important in supporting local partnerships that are specifically focused on deprived communities and problems of poverty and social exclusion.
- Programmes promoting *local economic development and local labour market* initiatives, such as the Local Enterprise Programme in Ireland and the Labour Foundations in Austria are a third type of programme that supports local partnerships.
- In some member states, including Ireland, the Netherlands and Portugal, recent policy initiatives have been taken to develop stronger and more integrated policy responses to poverty and exclusion at the national level.

It is clear from the research that the presence or absence of such national (or nationally determined) policies is one of the crucial factors influencing the extent to which local partnerships have emerged, and the orientation of such programmes has a similar influence on the directions in which local partnerships in different countries focus their activities – on problems of unemployment, on the social dimensions of exclusion, or on a more integrated approach to local regeneration.

Alongside the role of government programmes supporting local partnerships, the relative effectiveness with which different welfare systems have coped with problems of poverty and social exclusion appears to be one important factor in the extent to which a local partnership approach has been adopted in different member states. The pressures on the welfare state are both perceived and real. They involve both the 'scissors effect' of being caught between growing demands on state welfare and a fiscal or tax crisis, and criticisms of the effectiveness of the state in addressing complex social and economic questions, such as social exclusion. These pressures have been felt as both a need for new and complementary sources of funding for social and welfare policies, and a receptiveness to alternative forms of provision, by both the for-profit and the not-for-profit sectors. However, the degree of pressure on, and change to, the welfare state does not correlate in a simple fashion with the prominence of local partnership. A 'mixed market' of providers may develop through collaboration between providers on a primarily non-local basis, and at local level inter-agency working, public-private collaboration, and involvement of users and consumers need not take a formal partnership shape.

The analytical categories of state, market and civil society are useful in making sense of both national specificity and cross-national similarities, but only if carefully specified. As state apparatuses themselves have become increasingly differentiated, we find many types of state organisations in local partnerships: representatives of national ministries, national agencies, local agencies, semi-public organisations, civil servants and elected members, local and regional representatives from the national state, in addition to representatives from local and regional authorities and agencies. In major cities for instance, even the local state can be highly differentiated, fragmented and not always co-ordinated. No wonder then that the French for instance, and also the Finnish to some extent, have understood partnership first and foremost in terms of joint working within the public sector, because in these countries most organisations involved in combating poverty are still more or less related to the public sector. In such countries, the state remains very dominant within the public sphere.

In terms of the market, there are obviously major differences between the type and scale of firms involved in local partnerships. In general though, our case studies show that the social partners, business organisations and often trade unions are likely to be seriously involved in local partnerships of this type only relatively infrequently and under specific conditions.

Traditional social partners have difficulty in committing themselves to a serious investment in the territorial dimension of combating social exclusion even if there are interesting exceptions to the rule, as for instance in small-scale partnerships such as those in Wulkow and Wedding in Germany where small local employers share local community perspectives, or in LEADER partnerships where the emphasis on the promotion of entrepreneurship is attractive.

Finally, civil society is also a complex and changing category, encompassing a wide range of different kinds of organisations, interests and actors.[1] Voluntary sector organisations are the first type of organisation to be present in many partnerships. Among them, one should stress the Catholic church and its organisations (in particular in Spain and Portugal), although again there are important local differences from city to city. But the voluntary sector now includes many organisations that are best described as semi-public in that they are structurally dependent upon public funding. As local service delivery is increasingly contracted to such organisations, they are becoming increasingly important in partnerships. Community groups and

1 These include the familial networks that are often essential features of localities and communities, although our research did not generally reach down to this level.

associations are more active in some countries than others – not much in Finland, Austria or France, but more in the United Kingdom, Ireland, Spain and Portugal.

The picture is therefore one of great diversity. Nonetheless, on the basis of the evidence that has been presented in this book, it may be suggested that the local partnerships across the EU fall into four main groups in terms of the involvement of different actors from the public, private, voluntary and community sectors:

1   Broad, multi-partner partnerships, including representation of public, private, voluntary and community interests. This is, for example, the dominant model in local partnerships in the United Kingdom and Ireland and in many local partnerships supported by EU programmes. Of course, there is considerable variety as to how and to what extent these main partner categories are represented.
2   Partnerships in which the main partners are the public, voluntary and community sectors. This category includes both partnerships between the public sector and substantial not-for-profit agencies (e.g. in Spain and Portugal), and others in which the core of partnership is between local voluntary and community organisations and public agencies (e.g. the grass roots partnerships in Germany).
3   Partnerships wholly or very largely among public sector authorities and agencies (examples range from formal partnerships in France to more informal partnership working in Finland).
4   Partnerships in which the main partners are the social partners and state agencies. These local partnerships (e.g. in Austria) replicate a number of features of national corporatist practices at the local or regional level.

Local partnerships, social exclusion and welfare regimes in the European Union

If the above typology starts to identify similarities and differences within a framework defined by national practices, it is also useful to consider how the evolution of local partnership relates both to different conditions of poverty and social exclusion in the EU (referring back to some of the debates reviewed in Chapter 1), and to the well-known theorisations of 'welfare regimes' that have emerged in different parts of what is now the EU (Leibfried 1993; Abrahamson and Hansen 1996) and beyond (Therborn 1987; Esping-Andersen 1990; Pinch 1997). While the debate on welfare regimes is longstanding, it is only relatively recently that there has been much interest in the local dimensions of policy which may be associated with different regimes (but see Madanipour, Cars and Allen 1998). While it must be acknowledged that the attempt to fit national experiences into a 'regimes' framework poses problems, and there is continuing evidence of the difficulties of doing so (Cousins 1997; Gough, Bradshaw, Ditch, Eardley and

Whiteford 1997), nonetheless the concept of welfare regimes potentially offers important insights, not only into what unites as well as divides experience within groups of countries, but also about the nature of change and the forces behind either fragmentation and differentiation, or convergence, within the EU and indeed more widely.

Four main European welfare systems are identified in the literature (although Esping-Andersen uses a three-fold categorisation):

- Comprehensive welfare systems are associated with the *Scandinavian welfare states*. These systems are the product of societies in which strong and progressive labour movements have been instrumental in achieving a welfare system based on principles of equality (although this has been strongly contested in terms of gender equality). Welfare policy has been centred on the right to work, as well as on compulsory income transfer strategies. The universalist principle is applied not only through income redistribution outside the sphere of work, but also by the state acting as employer (especially for women). The state underpins a concept of social citizenship by subsidising or providing entry to, or non-exit from, the labour market. Both national and local state agencies play an important role. The model is seen to apply to Sweden par excellence and to Denmark and Finland with significant modifications.

  As the chapter on Finland has suggested, local partnerships have not been a major feature in these countries, which are also among the more recent EU member states, and until recently have been among those where poverty and social exclusion has been a marginal feature (to use one of Paugam's categories). While a local dimension is recognised as an important part of a comprehensive welfare state, which can ensure local responsiveness of provision, a partnership model is inconsistent with the dominant role of the state, and the clear separation of the roles of the state and the market. Partnership-type relationships tend therefore to be restricted to more informal collaboration between public agencies, or between public and not-for-profit providers of social services. However, while there is continuing popular support in these countries for the universalist welfare state, there are also growing pressures upon it, especially (as in Finland) with a substantial rise in unemployment, threatening to produce 'disabling poverty'. This may now be creating more fertile ground for local partnership. In addition, EU accession in the case of Denmark and now Sweden and Finland is creating new pressures to recognise the partnership approach in order to access resources from EU programmes (Heikkilä and Kautto 1996).

- Corporatist welfare regimes are associated with so-called *conservative* welfare systems, in which major vested interests, especially the employers and trade unions, are concerted by a strong central state to generate a segmented welfare system in which benefits are distributed according to the relative power of the parties involved. Here (e.g. Germany and

Austria) the state acts not as employer but as the compensator of first resort, subsidising exit from/non-entry to the labour market. Social exclusion has predominantly been marginal, although the integration of the former East Germany has introduced a new problem of disabling poverty and exclusion.

Here the principle of partnership (state and social partners) is found at national level, but not locally because effective corporatism is seen to require the organisation of interests and their concertation by the state nationally. Moreover, this model of corporatist partnership is based on the separation of the roles of the private sector (economic growth) and the state (social policy), and not the mingling of economic and social that partnership suggests. In Germany, consequently, local partnership is identified either with external influence (EU programmes) or grass roots organisation among excluded local communities marginalised in an 'organicist' social order (Silver 1995) and corporatist welfare regime (Birkhölzer and Lorenz 1996). Some recent trends in Austria suggest, however, that tendencies towards decentralisation within the federal state and towards a 'mixed market' in welfare, as well as growing EU influence, may now be promoting new partnership relationships to address economic and social policy issues at the regional and local levels (Kain and Rosian 1996).

- Neo-liberal welfare regimes with *residual* welfare systems. Here the welfare system is the product of weaker middle class mobilisation behind the welfare state, so that their interests are partly and increasingly met by the market but a reduced welfare state is preserved for the working class. How big this is will be determined by how much of the middle class it also continues to serve. The welfare state is a selective, work-enforcing mechanism and a compensator of last resort. The context is one of market-based 'civil' citizenship, and not the social citizenship of a comprehensive welfare state. The development of a local partnership approach seems to be particularly consistent with welfare regimes tending towards the residual in a context of disabling poverty (as in the United Kingdom). It appears to offer a cost-effective means of targeting specific areas of working-class welfare need, through local regeneration programmes with a 'workfare', 'enterprise' agenda, which hope that poverty and exclusion will be ameliorated, and local regeneration achieved, by improving local economic competitiveness. It is consistent with the emphasis on private provision of public services and competitive mechanisms for the allocation of resources.
- Unevenly developed or rudimentary welfare systems in the *Latin/Catholic rim* countries. These are characterised by a more partially developed and fragmented welfare state, such as the neo-liberal model stressing residualism and forced entry to the labour market, but in the context of an enduring domestic/community tradition of welfare. Paugam (1998) associates such countries with 'integrated poverty', where large sections

of the population may be poor but there is less stigmatisation of poverty. The rural economy remains important, providing a basis of subsistence. There is no full employment tradition, especially for women. In many of these countries, however, the constitution now promises a modern welfare state. Spain, Greece, Portugal and southern Italy are normally included in this category.

This model suggests certain factors consistent with local partnership (e.g. the need for collaboration between the state and the not-for-profit sector) but not others (weak welfare state, lack of involvement of social partners). The legacy of 'authoritarian statism' and clientelism in the economy and society are important reasons why local partnership may be difficult to establish (Rodrigues and Stoer 1996; Estivill and Nartinez 1996). However, as modernisation erodes the traditional, organicist social order, and poverty and social exclusion tend to become of a disabling character, partnership is increasingly becoming a way of managing the consequent tensions. Moreover, the political importance attached to EU membership and the importance in these countries of the resources offered by EU programmes and policies as a contribution to fulfilling the 'welfare promise' appear to be leading to growing internalisation of the partnership model.

The development of local partnership within the EU itself appears to be an amalgam between elements of different regimes: a (French) discourse of solidarity, and a corporatist conception of social partnership (even if, as we showed in Chapter 2, that conception has been widened to include other interests), within an overall policy context in which economic neo-liberalism is dominant. Recent contributions to the debate on welfare regimes have stressed the role of the EU in promoting 'regime competition', by eroding nation-state sovereignty and capacity in social policy without a compensating development of a substantial and active European welfare policy (Leibfried and Pierson 1995). Current European social policy, it is argued, is fragmented, constituting a weak European 'centre' in which the business interest is dominant. Such a fragmented social policy environment permits competitive deregulation and undercutting to the potential detriment of the more comprehensive welfare regimes. Dominant EU economic integration and deregulation objectives also promote the trend towards a 'mixed market' in welfare provision involving collaboration between public, private and third sector providers. Thus, the EU encourages a local partnership approach as much or more by the environment of regime competition that has been created, and the encouragement of a mixed market of provision, as by the establishment of specific programmes and policy initiatives constructed on a partnership basis.

However, while it is thus possible to suggest certain associations between different welfare regimes and the emergence of local partnership in a number of countries, other cases fall less easily within such a framework.

Ireland is a case in point, and is a country that is seldom discussed in the welfare regimes literature (but see Adshead and Quinn 1998). Ireland could be seen as a rudimentary welfare regime until EU programmes and funding began, with other factors, to promote change. Local partnerships now play perhaps a more important role in Ireland than in any other EU member state. Corporatist arrangements for national policy formulation are strongly developed and have not been significantly eroded in the recent period. The quasi-clientelist nature of Irish politics which downplays left-right political ideologies, and the strong influence of nationalism, both provide a receptive context for corporatism. However, Irish corporatism reflects a weaker commitment to a strong welfare system than the 'classical' corporatist model, and the balance of forces within it may be as close to the public-private partnership of the United Kingdom as to other 'traditional' corporatist countries. EU funding and membership are also extremely important in the Irish polity, and the weakness of Irish local government leaves a void at local level which local partnership has partially filled. It is to this local level of governance that we now turn.

Towards local social governance?

The rise of local partnership seems to demonstrate that neither the market, nor the state, nor civil society alone, are capable of dealing with the complex problems of both economic growth and the accompanying social dislocations which cross-cut the boundaries and responsibilities of institutional structures. The articulation of a number of elements from each 'sphere' into a dynamic structure is increasingly widespread, although this cannot be taken for granted and the constraints are always important. Such combinations may vary from one place to another, suggesting that there is no one dominant social order but various possible modes of governance, in which resources can be reassembled and mobilised within a collective project.

In this process, territory should not be conceived as a passive space. Thus, if we relate the emergence of local partnership to combat social exclusion to changes in welfare regimes, what we may be seeing is an indication of a limited territorialisation or local/regional decentralisation of European welfare systems. This point requires further development however. Esping-Andersen (1996) underlines the major challenges for welfare states but he and his colleagues typically underestimate a number of 'silent changes' taking place in many countries. Because they are concerned with the national institutional arrangements and the trade-off between employment and equity, and also because they are keen to demonstrate that despite external pressures, national welfare states are not simply privatised and in decline, they do not address the issue of the internal reorganisation of welfare states. This is not really surprising: after all the nationalisation of welfare has been a constitutive element of nation states and a condition for universalism in provision (De Swaan 1988).

Today, however, most national states and their elites are more aware of their limits and their interests in limiting public expenditure. There is always an inherent ambiguity associated with the territorialisation of social policies: its tendency to association with public expenditure constraints. It is a powerful tool for national states to deal with difficult social issues, but also to limit the growth of expenditure, and, with it, of redistribution. That logic has been behind the development of local and regional health agencies (e.g. in France, Sweden and the United Kingdom). It is driven by logics of rationalisation and efficiency, which, at times, may make sense even without the threat of neo-liberal restructuring.

In contrast to what is often said in the United Kingdom, Esping-Andersen is right to underline the fact that: 'in most countries, what we see is not radical change, but rather a "frozen" welfare landscape. Resistance to change is to be expected: long established policies become institutionalised, and cultivate vested interest in their perpetuation....Thus social security systems that are backed by powerful interest aggregations are less amenable to radical reform and, when reform is undertaken, it tends to be negotiated and consensual. Continental Europe is the clearest case of impasse, while Australia and Scandinavia represent change via negotiation' (Esping-Andersen 1996: 24).

Like glaciers, however, these frozen welfare landscapes are not actually static. Several developments point to this. First, the long rise of meso-government in Western Europe (Keating and Loughlin 1996; Le Galès and Lequesne 1998; Jouve and Négrier 1998), although not mainly associated with welfare and social policy issues, is also leading to a different kind of restructuring – deconcentration, decentralisation reforms, federalism or quasi-federalism, even recentralisation sometimes – in which local and regional governments play an increasing role. EU policies that, as Geddes and Benington show in Chapter 2, have actively promoted partnership as a policy norm, were also associated with the attempt at the 'moment Delors' to associate regions and different territories more actively with the reconstruction of Europe (Ross 1995).

This rise of meso-level government brings with it a bottom-up logic. If nation states have an interest in decentralising social policies, various groups of elites in cities and regions are playing an increasing role in politics and policies in most European countries and are increasingly willing to do so. One should not forget that local elected elites are often in direct contact with social exclusion, poverty and other social problems and they have some incentives to act, or at the very least to be seen to act. As a result of the particular nature of urban politics (though it varies from country to country), local elites tend to be increasingly active in dealing not only with economic, but also with social issues.

Although one must be sure not to generalise, there are, at least, many cases where strong mobilisations are taking place locally to combat poverty. The case studies of our research bear witness to that phenomenon. In other words, as far as social policies are concerned (social security is a different kind of world), territorial differences associated with forms of decentralisation may constitute one way forward for changing some elements of the welfare state, without necessarily going along the lines of welfare to work or retrenchment. As Hassenteufel (1998) puts it 'think social, act local' seems to be, in some countries in Western Europe, one of the ways forward for the welfare state. The rise of local partnership that we document in this book constitutes one element of this trend whatever its role (essential in the United Kingdom and Ireland, marginal but innovative in Portugal, Finland or France, for example).

A degree of territorial autonomy in the implementation of social policies within a centralised logic is not wholly new. Except in Scandinavian countries, considerable variations always took place from city to city, locality to locality. Policies were rooted and implemented in different local societies. As our case studies have shown, significant differences exist between industrial cities such as Porto, Tyneside or Lille, and between rural areas from western Scotland and Ireland to Brandenburg. What seems to be taking place, however, is a gradual shift in the degree and extent of local autonomy. This increasing variation within each country is even a policy objective for many central states as part of 'new social policies', and partnerships are indicators of these.

Our conclusions are nevertheless rather ambiguous. On the one hand, some of the partnerships we have studied seem to point, if not quite to local welfare systems in the making, at least towards a strategic restructuring of urban welfare (e.g. in Lille, Limerick or Porto). Beyond the cases of partnerships in the formal sense, there are signs of the wider institutionalisation of collective action between various types of partners. This may take different forms – very articulated towards the national public sector in Finland, or more balanced between the Catholic church, the local authorities and community groups in Italy, Spain and Portugal. This hypothesis about the development of local welfare systems is consistent with other recent comparative research on 14 European cities, which also demonstrates the limits of national analysis of social polices and the importance of local regulation of poverty (Oberti 2000).

On the other hand, and recognising the critique of a 'new localism' (Lovering 1995) and French sceptics such as Palier (1998), local partnership may also hasten fragmentation within social policies, with some limited territorialisation providing weak elements of local integration while expenditure and control is recentralised. The national chapters in this book indicate some elements of such recentralisation, for instance the centralisation of social expenditure in Finland (see also Letho 1999) and the enhanced central regulation of urban policy in France and the United Kingdom.

Thus, the partnerships analysed in our research suggest that 'welfare states in transition' are at the same time, in some respects and some places, more and less territorialised. Variations among and within countries are on the increase and variations between strands of social policy remain very strong, for instance between combating poverty, health and social security. Unless one adopts the pessimistic and slightly deterministic view of the Schumpeterian workfare state, there are still a large number of contradictory trends at work within European welfare states, at European, national, regional and local levels. Hierarchical models have been challenged in numerous ways, even in centralised countries, for good and sometimes not so good reasons. Over the last two decades and more, in many countries public policies have been characterised by various mixes of uncertainty, interference between various policy domains, multiplication of actors and objectives, and contradictory constraints (Lascoumes 1996; Wildavsky 1979). Contemporary problems raise questions that cross horizontally over bureaucracies and sectors, and vertically over different levels of government. Programmes and networks of actors are characterised by deep heterogeneity, not only in emerging policy domains (e.g. the environment, AIDS), but also increasingly in mainstream policy areas such as welfare, education or economic policy. Our research supports this view of public policies as differentiated, based upon various types of communities and networks where actors are brought together in collective actions which are at the opposite end of the spectrum to a 'ballistic' model of public policy 'fired from the centre'. That does, hopefully, leave some room for manoeuvre for local initiative.

Our comparative research provides evidence of the ambiguities and dynamism of public policies: the negotiating processes around partnerships reveal attempts to redefine public policy in a flexible way in order to face ill-defined problems and goals. If combating poverty and social exclusion initially seems a straightforward goal, in practice it embodies a degree of generality that provides considerable room for manoeuvre to define, design, 'bricoler' (Lascoumes 1996), or 'trancoder' (Callon 1984) various types of intervention. Our case studies confirm that in all countries, public policies against poverty and social exclusion are not 'given'. A grounded approach shows how, locally, the problem is defined in a cognitive frame that can be adopted by local actors. The dynamic of partnership offers some remarkable insights into these processes. What is illuminating is the fact that these adjustment processes are continuing and ubiquitous. Both failures or successes – for example, problems in getting support from major actors (see for instance the German tensions with the traditional social partners), or success in securing finance – lead to constant negotiation between local, and between national and local, interests.

In this process, organisational changes within partnerships often reveal such adjustments between the interests and representation of actors. While a significant literature on these issues tends to emphasise the cognitive dimension (Sabatier and Jenkins-Smith 1993; Muller and Surel 1998; Smith 1996), our research tends to emphasise the dynamics of organisational change and collective action. Once a general goal has been established, there is no need for a clear cut and shared cognitive frame of reference. By contrast, the broad goal of combating social exclusion gives room for manoeuvre for all types of representation.

There are important implications here for the kind of further research needed to understand the restructuring of public policies across various European countries. The processes that are underlined in the different partnerships are fine-grained and unlikely to be captured by quantitative analysis. It is comparative case studies, researched through a common methodology, which are likely to give us some key insights into the processes at stake.

By using such methods, we have thus tried to avoid common myths about local public policy. In much research in public policy, the 'local' – a city, a locality, a region – tends to be presented as an integrating factor. Thanks to local roots, it is often claimed, new social policies may be more democratic, more transparent, more effective, more long-term, and more coherent. In social policy in particular, territories appear as a potential arena for a new generation of renovated public policies. Unfortunately, even if there is a mobilising myth and some important potential, our evidence on this is contradictory and points to the need for caution. On the one hand, the rise of local partnerships and their actions are interesting signs of attempts to territorialise (through an integrated approach to combat poverty) public policies. On the other hand, such partnerships may merely incorporate local actors into national and European programmes and policies, of which the logic and the legal and financial constraints are centrally determined and limited.

Conclusions

It is frequently argued today that local social policies have been subordinated to, or eroded by, economic imperatives. However, our research shows that local actors and agencies do not only organise in order to protect or enhance their economic position in the face of economic competition between cities and regions. This book bears witness to the fact that the maintenance of social cohesion and the fight against increasing social exclusion has also become a priority in many areas, not only for elected elites but also for a good number of groups that are able to put pressure on local authorities, and hence the rise of a number of partnerships oriented not only to prestigious, flagship regeneration projects, but also to combating poverty and developing and implementing social policies.

This double meaning of governance (social and economic) contains echoes of what Stoer and Rodrigues (Chapter 7) identify as the difference between 'partenariado': 'a formal partnership that takes advantage of outside resources, adopts a vertical approach, and is concerned to guarantee the effectiveness of investments' and 'parceria': 'sensitive to local needs, making the most of and giving value to local resources, more relational and less contractual towards the development of the community'.

This analysis, and the evidence presented throughout this chapter and book, demonstrate that the development of partnership is part of a dynamic process of change in the evolution of welfare systems and of local governance. This dynamic is driven from a number of directions: by local actors; by nation states; but also by the actions and policies of the EU. The local partnerships that we have discussed in this book thus represent an *emergent model of local social governance* (Perkmann 1997). This is a model that is being strongly promoted by the EU, but one that is still contested and open to capture by different interests, within the EU itself, within different nation states, and at the local and grass roots levels. In this context, a major danger lies in the association of local partnership with the erosion of national and European social commitments, as has been the case in the United Kingdom, for example, and appears to be dominant within the EU. To what extent, in the next 10 or 20 years, European states will still be able to resist or adapt neo-liberal pressures (e.g. ideologies, policy instruments, financial frame-work) that are building within and beyond each country, remains to be seen. The question is whether alternative, more socially progressive models of local partnership might emerge from a number of possible directions: from the introduction of local partnership principles within the Scandinavian welfare states; as a dimension of still-developing welfare systems in southern Europe perhaps; or even in countries including France, Germany and the United Kingdom under centre-left governments. This book suggests that there is, at any rate, some worthwhile room for manoeuvre for political mobilisation and positive outcomes.

In this book, partnership to combat social exclusion was our point of departure. We have examined a wide range of case studies demonstrating some of the possibilities and limits of local mobilisation to combat poverty. The rise of partnership experiences, once we succeed in putting aside naive and normative assumptions about their effects, may be interpreted as an attempt to create new local capacity for governance (capacity to legitimate, to incorporate, but also to experiment and innovate?), involving new alliances and conflicts within changing local societies. However, we have tried to remain aware of the fact that changing scales of social policies are anything but neutral and the ever-present possibility that one face of the territorialisation of welfare arrangements may be the retreat of the state from universal commitments. If the impact of the new local partnerships that are emerging across the EU is to be a positive one, then there needs to be a multi-level debate, spanning and linking local, regional, national and European interests and questions. We hope this book makes a contri-bution to such a debate.

References

Abrahamson P and Hansen F K (1996) *Poverty in the European Union*, Strasbourg: European Parliament.

Adshead M and Quinn B (1998) The move from government to governance: Irish development policy's paradigm shift. *Policy and Politics* 26, 2, 209–25.

Bagnasco A and Le Galès P (1999) Cities as local societies and collective actors, in *Cities in Contemporary Europe*, Cambridge: Cambridge University Press.

Birkhölzer K and Lorenz G (1996) *The Role of Partnerships in Promoting Social Cohesion: Research Report for Germany*. European Foundation for the Improvement of Living and Working Conditions, Dublin, WP/96/33/EN.

Callon M (1984) Eléments pour une sociologie de la traduction, *Année Sociologique*, 36.

Carton B, Delogne R, Nicaise I and Stengele A (1996) *The Role of Partnerships in Promoting Social Cohesion: Research Report for Belgium*. European Foundation for the Improvement of Living and Working Conditions, Dublin, WP/96/32/EN.

Cousins C (1997) Social exclusion in Europe: Paradigms of social disadvantage in Germany, Spain, Sweden and the United Kingdom. *Policy and Politics* 26, 2, 127–46.

De Swaan A (1988) *In the Care of the State*, Cambridge: Polity Press.

Esping-Andersen G (1990) *The Three Worlds of Welfare Capitalism*, Cambridge: Polity Press.

Esping-Andersen G (1996) *Welfare States in Transition: National Adaptations in Global Economies*, London: Sage.

Estivill J and Nartinez R (1996) *The Role of Partnerships in Promoting Social Cohesion: Research Report for Spain*. European Foundation for the Improvement of Living and Working Conditions, Dublin, WP/96/34/EN.

Gough I, Bradshaw J, Ditch J, Eardley T and Whiteford P (1997) Social assistance in OECD countries, *Journal of European Social Policy*, 7, 1, 17–43.

Harding A (1997) Urban regimes in a Europe of the cities? *European Urban and Regional Studies*, 4, 4, 291–314.

Hassenteufel P (1998) Think social, act local – la territorialisation comme réponse à la crise de l'Etat-providence, *Politiques et Amenagement Publique*, 16, 3.

Heikkilä M and Kautto M (1996) *The Role of Partnerships in Promoting Social Cohesion: Research Report for Finland*. European Foundation for the Improvement of Living and Working Conditions, Dublin, WP/96/36/EN.

Heinelt H and Smith R (eds.) (1997) *Policy Networks and European Structural Funds*, Aldershot: Avebury.

Hooghe L (ed.) (1996) *Cohesion Policy and European Integration*, Oxford: Oxford University Press.

Jessop B (1993) Towards a Schumpeterian workfare state? Preliminary remarks on postfordist political economy, *Studies in Political Economy* 40, 7–39.

Jouve B and Négrier E (eds.) (1998) *Qui gouvernent les régions en Europe*, Paris: L'Harmattan.

Kain E and Rosian I (1996) *The Role of Partnerships in Promoting Social Cohesion: Research Report for Austria*. European Foundation for the Improvement of Living and Working Conditions, Dublin, WP/96/31/EN.

Keating M (1991) *Comparative Urban Politics*, Aldershot: Edward Elgar.

Keating M and Loughlin J (eds.) (1996) *The Political Economy of Regionalism*, London: Frank Cass.

Lascoumes P (1996) Rendre gouvernable: de la traduction au transcodage, in CURAPP, *La gouvernabilité*, Amiens.

Le Galès P and Loncle P (1996) *The Role of Partnerships in Promoting Social Cohesion: Research Report for France*. European Foundation for the Improvement of Living and Working Conditions, Dublin, WP/96/37/EN.

Le Galès P and Lequesne C (eds.) (1998) *Regions in Europe, the Paradox of Power*, London: Routledge.

Leibfried S (1993) Towards a European welfare state? On integrating poverty regimes into the European Community, in Jones C (ed.) *New Perspectives on the Welfare State in Europe*, London: Routledge.

Leibfried S and Pierson P (1995) *European Social Policy: Between Fragmentation and Integration*, Washington DC: Brookings Institute.

Letho J (1999) Different cities, different welfares, in Bagnasco A and Le Galès P (eds.) *Cities in Contemporary Europe*, Cambridge: Cambridge University Press.

Lovering J (1995) Creating discourse rather than jobs: the crisis in the cities and the transition fantasies of intellectuals and policy-makers, in Healey P, Cameron S, Davoudi s, Graham S and Madanipour A (eds.), *Managing Cities, the New Urban Context*, London: John Wiley.

Madanipour A, Cars G and Allen J (1998) *Social Exclusion in European Cities*, London: Jessica Kingsley.

Muller P and Surel Y (1998) *L'analyse des politiques publiques*, Paris: Montchrestien.

Musterd S and Ostendorf W (eds.) (1998) *Urban Segregation and the Welfare State*, London: Routledge.

Oberti M (2000) Diversity and complexity in local forms of urban anti-poverty strategies in Europe, *International Journal of Urban and Regional Research* 24, 3, 536–53.

Palier B (1998) La référence au territoire dans les nouvelles politiques sociales, in *Politiques et Amenagement Publique*, 16, 3.

Paugam S (1998) Poverty and social exclusion: a sociological view, in Rhodes M and Meny Y (eds.) *The Future of European Welfare – A New Social Contract?* London: Macmillan, 41–62.

Peck J (1998) Geographies of governance: TECs and the neo-liberalisation of 'local interests', *Space and Policy* 2, 5–31.

Perkmann M (1997) *The Politics of Regional Co-operation: New Regional Geo-economic Strategies and the Building of Transnational Pseudo-Territories*, EURRN Regional Frontiers conference, Frankfurt/Oder.

Pinch S (1997) *Worlds of Welfare*, London: Routledge.

Rhodes M and Meny Y (1998) *The Future of European Welfare: A New Social Contract?* London: Macmillan.

Robolis S, Papadogamvros V, Dimoulas K and Sidira V (1996) *The Role of Partnerships in Promoting Social Cohesion: Research Report for Greece*, Dublin, European Foundation for the Improvement of Living and Working Conditions, WP/96/30/EN.

Rodrigues F and Stoer S (1996) *The role of partnerships in promoting social cohesion: Research report for Portugal*, Dublin: European Foundation for the Improvement of Living and Working Conditions, WP/96/35/EN.

Ross G (1995) *Jacques Delors and European Integration*, Oxford: Oxford University Press.

Sabatier P, Jenkins-Smith H (eds.) (1993) *Policy Change and Learning*, Boulder: Westview Press.

Silver H (1995) Reconceptualising social disadvantage: Three paradigms of social exclusion, in Rodgers G, Gore C and Figueredo J B (1995) *Social Exclusion: Rhetoric, Reality, Responses*, Geneva: ILO, 57–80.

Smith A (1996) *L'Europe au miroir du local*, Paris: L'Harmattan.

Stoker G (ed.) (1999) *The New Management of British Local Governance*, London: Macmillan.

Therborn G (1987) Welfare state and capitalist markets, *Acta Sociologica* 30, 237–54.

Walsh J, Craig S and McCafferty D (1997) *The Role of Partnerships in Promoting Social Cohesion: Research Report for Ireland*, Dublin: European Foundation for the Improvement of Living and Working Conditions, WP/96/38/EN.

Wildavsky A (1979) *Speaking Truth to Power. The Art and Craft of Policy Process*, Boston: Little Brown.

Index

Craig, S. 37, 105, 111, 123, 152
credit unions 116
crime 15–16, 114, 161, 201, 208–9

de-industrialisation 18, 101
decentralisation 30, 200, 204–5, 223,
    234; of administration 59, 63; Austria
    231; Belgium 152; decision-making
    and 62; Denmark and 224;
    privatisation and 223; territorial
    differences and 235; welfare regimes
    and 235; *see also* individual countries
Délégation interministérielle à la Ville
    84
delinquency 15, 37, 85
Delogne, R. 37, 224
Delors, Jacques 32–4
'Delors moment' 221, 234
democratic accountability 209–10
democratic associationalism 208
democratisation of government 204–5
Denmark 18–19, 35, 53, 224, 230
Department of the Environment (N.I)
    183
Department of the Environment (UK)
    176n.5, 186
Department of Social Welfare (Ireland)
    114, 116, 124, 129
Department of Taoiseach 112, 117, 119,
    152
Department of Tourism, Sport and
    Recreation 119
deregulation 134, 175
Direction Départementale de l'Action
    Sanitaire et Sociale (Department
    offices for Health and Social
    Provision) 72
Directions Départementales et
    Régionales de l'Action Sociale
    (Departmental and Regional Social
    Services) 73
Directorate-General of Social Action
    (Direcçao-Geral de Acção Social) 141
disabled people 72, 129, 157, 162
'disaffiliated' population (France) 75
discrimination within civil society 21
downsizing 62
drug addiction 37, 85, 113–14, 161–2,
    208
Drumchapel Opportunities 178

e-mail 201
EAPN 29

Easterhouse 178
Eastern Länder 94
economic imperatives, social policies
    and 237
Economic and Social Committee *see*
    ECOSOC
Economic and Social Research Institute
    115
ECOSOC 26–7
education 36, 79, 140
El Ribeiro county (Galicia) 161n.4;
    partnership 164–5, 210
elderly people 18, 54, 72, 162, 190
Employment Pacts 33
Enterprise Zones 176
Entwicklungszentrum (EWZ
    Dortmund) 93, 99, 104–6, 107n.9
environment, the 213, 236
Ervasti, H. 49, 66
Esping-Anderson, G. 53, 229, 233–4
Essen Council 33
'Estado Novo' (New State) 139, 146
Estivill, J. 12, 32, 39, 152, 155–7, 209,
    232
ethnic minorities 18, 162, 172–3
ETUC 27–9
EU 12 19
EU 14 19
EU, democratic deficit 204; distinctive
    European model 202; employers and
    partnerships 35–6; enlargement 1–2,
    34; financing rules of programmes 63;
    governance 5; implications of
    political restructuring 202–3; local
    initiatives 24; local partnerships in
    35–8; local partnerships, social
    exclusion and welfare regimes
    229–33; new role for 33; partnership
    11, 13, 26, 32, 34, 221; poverty and
    social exclusion 15, 18–19; regional
    unemployment 18; research on
    partnership 7–9; role in Ireland 34–5,
    37, 111, 117, 233; social exclusion
    1–2, 22, 24; social restructuring and
    198; Territorial Employment Pacts
    154; unemployment 17;
    unemployment and poverty 19;
    unemployment and regeneration 37
EU Poverty 3 programme (1989–94)
    30–1, 215; Denmark and 224;
    Friedrichshain and 100, 106–7;
    Greece and 225; Montes de Oca